Uncontrollable Bodies

Testimonies of Identity and Culture

**Edited by Rodney Sappington
and Tyler Stallings**

Bay Press

Seattle

Printed in the United States of America.

Bay Press
115 West Denny Way
Seattle, Washington 98119-4205

Project editor: Patricia Draher
Manuscript editor: Sally Anderson
Designed by Philip Kovacevich

Cover design: Philip Kovacevich
Cover image: Rodney Sappington and Tyler Stallings

Library of Congress Cataloging-in-Publication Data

Uncontrollable bodies : testimonies of identity and culture / edited by Rodney Sappington
and Tyler Stallings.
p.   cm.
Includes bibliographical references.
ISBN 0-941920-27-5
1. Popular culture—United States. 2. Gender identity—United States. 3. Mind and
body—United States. I. Sappington, Rodney. II. Stallings, Tyler.
E169.04.U53 1994   94-17123
306' .0973--dc20   CIP

Photo credits:
Pages 19–23, Robert Flynt, courtesy of the artist and Witkin Gallery, New York; pages 49, 59, © 1950
Turner Entertainment Co. All rights reserved; page 54, copyright © by Universal City Studios, Inc.,
courtesy of MCA Publishing Rights, a Division of MCA Inc.; pages 198, 203, 208, 213, S. Chapman and
C. Kirkwood; pages 242, 248, May Lin; page 255 top left, right, and bottom left, Jan Weaver, bottom
right, Tracy Mostovoy; pages 262, 264, 266, 268, 270, 271, 272–75, Alan Sondheim.

Artwork accompanying "X-Bodies (the torment of the mutant superhero)" courtesy of the following:
Pages 92, 97, 118, X-Men, X-Factor, and all Marvel characters: TM & © 1994 Marvel Entertainment
Group, Inc.
Pages 102, 107, 113, courtesy of Image Comics.
Pages 109, 124, courtesy of DC Comics.
Artwork on page 111 is from Daniel Clowes's *Eightball* no. 12, a comic book series published by
Fantagraphics Books; copyright © 1994 Daniel Clowes.

Contents

9 **Acknowledgments**

11 **Introduction**   RODNEY SAPPINGTON

15 **Introduction**   TYLER STALLINGS

19 **Heroic Measures**   ROBERT FLYNT

25 **Dense Moments**   GREGG BORDOWITZ

45 **An Impossible Man**   LYNNE TILLMAN

63 **With Curse, or Love**   TRINH T. MINH-HA

79 **Revenge of *The Leech Woman***
On the Dread of Aging in a Low-Budget Horror Film
VIVIAN SOBCHACK

93 **X-Bodies**
(the torment of the mutant superhero)
SCOTT BUKATMAN

131 **Cracked Open by the Senses**
RODNEY SAPPINGTON

145 **Born of Normal Parents**
LOUISE DIEDRICH

155 **Love Poems Produced by Staring Too Hard at *Thomas*, a Photograph by Sharon Lockhart**
DENNIS COOPER

167 **On Splitting: A Symptomatology**
or, The Los Angeles Maternal Position
LESLIE DICK
with
Audrey's Bunnies
ELIZABETH PULSINELLI

193 **A Strangely Haunting Love**
TYLER STALLINGS

199 **Laying Me Down** CARLA KIRKWOOD

217 ***Cuerpo Politizado*** LUIS ALFARO

243 **Thanks, Ma** CAROL LEIGH (SCARLOT HARLOT)

263 **Hole** ALAN SONDHEIM

277 **Contributors**

Acknowledgments

We are grateful for the enthusiasm, energy, and thoughtfulness of all the contributors. Our gratitude also goes to Sally Brunsman and Kim Barnett for providing the opportunity to do this book, and to Phil Kovacevich, Patricia Draher, and Sally Anderson for seeing it through production. We are also indebted to the following people for their encouragement, for their introductions to some of the contributors, and for their conversations: John Bermudes, Colleen Crosby, Leslie Salant, Andrea Rosen, William S. Bartman, Robert Atkins, Hans Jurgen Schacht, Thatcher Bailey, Susan Foley Johannsen, Tom Zummer, Randy Sommer, David Deitcher, Benjamin Weissman, and Unna Lassiter. A very special thanks is extended to Leslie Ernst and Ryan Hill, whose thoughts and editorial insights have assisted this project.

—R.S.
—T.S.

Rodney Sappington

Introduction

When Tyler Stallings and I began the editorial process for *Uncontrollable Bodies,* we discussed the body as phenomenon, as a site of physical and psychological trauma, institutional control, and enforced sexual norms and practices. We also had to define how the body was a site of vulnerability and how to encourage writings that would highlight this. We felt one crucial way was to ask writers to locate themselves within their existing commentary on the body. By doing so we could not predict how each contributor would respond, which left room for unpredictable results— for openings, not closures. What appear at first as texts that incorporate autobiography and theoretical critiques on the body are in essence works produced at the juncture between the act of writing and political agency— closing the gap between social critique and everyday life. The politics of such a book dwell on the specific—on the power and urgency of social struggle found in the gestures of daily living. Intimacy is sacred—packed with boundaries, limits, assumptions, privatization, silences, isolation— and an area in which seemingly innocent decisions are made in danger.

In the contributors' explorations on the body, we found inroads to an analysis of *their* body and the cultural forces acting to define it. For all of us who have taken part in this project, the methods for including the personal became clear only bit by bit, in ways no one had anticipated. The efforts of each contributor and our editorial process have been truly organic and rewarding. We feel that these writings extend contemporary thought on the body—particularly in directions that ensure a more interdisciplinary and poetic approach—and cross over into areas that recently have been the domain of theoretical discussion and scholarship. An anthology of this kind would not be possible without a rich history of feminist thought and writing, queer theory, and the reevaluation of the role of autobiography in contemporary culture. We also owe a great debt to recent debates surrounding masculinity.

After months of discussion, contributors have produced works that collectively challenge commonly held definitions of the body. Their complicity in their writings provokes questions on the constitution of subjectivity through a wide range of strategies. Luis Alfaro in "*Cuerpo Politizado*" dismantles and affirms ideas of gay Latino life, and conjures images of his *abuelita*, loss, Hollywood Boulevard, the Virgin of Guadalupe, and drag. Gregg Bordowitz in "Dense Moments" writes himself out of the categories he has helped to create, addressing AIDS activism, sexuality, and the disturbing links between disease and gay male identity.

Contributors have complicated the use of first person through multiple personas and voices, inhabiting different bodies, and at moments feeling "other" to the one body they own. They have also blended fictional and theoretical approaches that address subjectivity across categories of sex, class, gender, and ethnicity. Scott Bukatman in "X-Bodies (the torment of the mutant superhero)" builds an analysis of superhero comics and hypermasculinity, utilizing historical texts and images from popular culture that address bodybuilding and the fascist male body. Dennis Cooper in "Love Poems Produced by Staring Too Hard at *Thomas*, A Photograph by Sharon Lockhart," provides riveting glimpses into abject teen life and desire. Leslie Dick constructs a compelling work based on overlooked notions of the maternal in "On Splitting: A Symptomatology or, The Los Angeles Maternal Position"—including elegant and uncanny photographic works by Elizabeth Pulsinelli that depict infancy and longing. Louise Diedrich has produced a group of drawings entitled "Born of Normal Parents" that explode the body into the space of fantasy, technology, and pathos. Robert Flynt presents "Heroic Measures," a collection of rich photographic images in which the physical and psychological territories of "interior" and "exterior" are blurred. Carla Kirkwood offers readers "Laying Me Down," a journey of the female subject coming to terms with mortality and political struggle.

Contributors make no apologies for challenging notions of personal experience—thus calling into question self and fantasy in relationship to the body. The use of first person is not self-congratulatory, nor a lament for a lost or post-self, nor a site of an "essential" self. Nor will readers find "self" depicted as a storehouse of accumulated knowledge. Writers celebrate pleasures as well as struggles, and invite multiple selves. At times they drift through memory, speaking to the complex task of mining the site of subjectivity. The stages of identity formation are sensual, commonplace, and often close to home—standing in the mirror, stiffening at the hands of a knife, discerning the pleasant scent or fear of a hand caressing the shoulders. Carol Leigh, writing as Scarlot Harlot in "Thanks, Ma," charts a series of stories that highlight questions concerning the rights of sex workers and the perceived "dangers" of female sexuality. Trinh T. Minh-ha in "With Curse, or Love" assembles a compelling series of poetic reflections on the gaze, desire, and mourning. In a revealing work entitled "Revenge of *The Leech Woman*: On the Dread of Aging in a Low-Budget Horror Film," Vivian Sobchack talks about her own dread of aging and analyzes the social fears surrounding aging female bodies. Alan Sondheim in "Hole" explores the hysterical heterosexual male body as a site of projection, fantasy, and masochism. Lynne Tillman in "An Impossible Man" takes readers through images of her father, his vulnerabilities, and his body as seen in other bodies. Tyler Stallings, in "A Strangely Haunting Love," incorporates reflections on the annihilation of the ego, cyberspace, asexual reproduction, and Jean-Luc Picard of "Star Trek: The Next Generation."

Writers have woven their experiences throughout these stories—establishing narratives that speak of violence, childhood, disease, disappointment, love, depression, self-loathing, and transformation, recasting gods, and severing social conventions. Who has the authority to speak? Whose identity is sanctioned? Whose experience is universalized? Contributors address moments when language and "self" suffer categorical rupture. Their work is rigorous and inventive, and at times lies in the realm of the fantastic. How do we implicate ourselves in framing our desires, and acknowledge this implication in our writings? Acts of witness are often expressed through confession and testimony, outrage and analysis. The "uncontrollable" turns out after all to be a point of collapse, discarded and overlooked discourses on the body.

Though discussion on the body may fall in and out of fashion, and academic debates may shift, my personal hope is that the struggle to think intelligently about the body and its place in culture will not diminish, and that artists will be unafraid to embarrass themselves when questions need to be raised and experiences affirmed that challenge closely held attitudes and beliefs. Language remains a vital tool for navigating through contested ideological terrain, giving course to action, and constantly reframing one's experience. Writing is a means of excavation, made visible by discovering that *loss* is a point of departure.

I grew up believing in this loss. I was certain that uncovering my desires would be accomplished only through excruciating effort, earning it—a fallout from training as a Southern Baptist and a "good boy." As a good boy I was atoning for my sins and for those I would never commit—for the sins of others. It was a masochistic contract, the original rupture in the garden, resulting in fiery images, rage, drugs—and later impenetrability. The central myth of this life was an ever-awaiting afterlife. It presented itself before me and tempted my family like a sure evacuation plan. I have inherited parts of this body and left parts behind—adopted sections of the western pulp novels that my mother read—carving out a self that still clings to its armor and defenses with all its force. This "it" is me, no separation, no closure—not yet. Though I inherited this dual desire to be impenetrable and permeable—sealed and expanding into a cosmology of endless desert space (the heavenly space of Cinemascope westerns)—I have continued to dance with these contradictory phantoms.

Maybe I am overstating my point. My father taught me that "common sense" and sexuality were rewards I would someday receive if I was "good" enough—an eventuality I would surely regulate and monitor. Even today, my identity is in a state of flux, my senses always on alert, awkwardly poised, and exposed. Perhaps years ago, as I imagined myself a robot-warrior taking in sci-fi movies, and as social workers and police poured through my family's doors on "domestic calls," I would have asked our voyeuristic neighbors, clutching their children, locking the front doors to their houses and trailer homes, which one of us was uncontrollable? What were they trying to bring into careful scrutiny? Did they care? Were their shadows bound up in us? In me?

In memories of childhood, I see that the effort of asking critical questions is at times frightening or nearly impossible—and may not always produce the desired results. Yet those questions need to be asked, if not at the moment, later—not lost to social mandates that eclipse experience in strict ideology or dominant notions of self. What are the socially inscribed controls on the body? How are these boundaries personally negotiated, and most important, how do we play a role in their enforcement and redefinition? These sixteen essays and visual works are *passages*, moments cracked open by the senses. They are sensuous and analytical, acts of memory and imagination.

Tyler Stallings

Introduction

Uncontrollable Bodies presents theorists, fiction writers, filmmakers, activists, poets, performance artists, visual artists, and sex workers whose previous works have described intense bouts with the symbolic world but who now turn their probes upon themselves. They admit to recognizing something when looking in a mirror. If another mirror is set opposite this mirror, it creates an infinite vision, as reflections reflect one another. The mirrors are set perhaps by their hands or by someone else's. The contributors ask how we function when so many mirror handlers and so many reflections are simultaneously apparent. This question also highlights the significant use of images in this anthology.

The contributors' answers in part are a view of themselves as bodies separate from their reflections, but also acknowledge that these reflections inform the creation of their identity. This conundrum suggests that an in-depth perception of one's world may occur only when a point of observation is chosen, at least momentarily—not a point from which to transcend, but one upon which to stand so that one's world can envelop, split, and multiply oneself. The contributors suggest that "experience" is constructed through immersion in the confusion between who produces meaning and who consumes meaning.

Through an immersion in the co-editorship with Rodney Sappington, I find notions of myself have been multiplied, ruptured, enveloped, expanded, and lost. The co-editorship's outward effects have been disturbing sometimes to the people who wanted a hierarchy, desiring that *one* of us be in charge. And often we have been considered lovers because of the collaboration's intensity. These projections have surprised but also delighted us, as they pose questions regarding the future portrayal of ourselves to one another and to the world at large.

Our state of immersion is an example of how one's image is created, by oneself and others, through perception/projection and mirroring/ portrayal. This formula of complicity in making one's image produces a vulnerable state. The contributors create a similar state of vulnerability not only in their subject matter but through their use of imagery, thereby extending the dialogue about how they perceive themselves.

Much of the inspiration behind my and Rodney's desire for an image-laden book originated with a mutual interest in underground 'zines. Through a creative use of image and text, 'zines are perhaps the best cultural example of an intense interaction between projection and portrayal. Producing a 'zine is a search for a voice in response to feeling jettisoned and unrep-resented in the mainstream press. 'Zines inject the personal into the public: stacks can be found in record stores, clubs, and coffee shops. Some are created in one night and disappear after the first issue; sense of purpose and spontaneity are the driving forces. Like the creators of 'zines, the contributors in *Uncontrollable Bodies* are enveloped by the perceptions of others, yet through an awareness of this process, navigate a course that challenges and expands their identities. There is a mutual understanding about the merging of the real and the represented in today's world. The shifting nature of one's identity and the act of switching between observer and participant are acknowledged as normal events.

This *shifting* and *switching* define in part how the visual is approached in *Uncontrollable Bodies*. Literally taken, "visual" implies use of the eyes and the sense of sight. Western tradition has depended largely on sight to determine the meaning of things. However, a definition based solely on sight cannot account for the nuances and details noticed by the other senses. For example, we can never say we know what a hamburger *is* just by looking, because one swift smell can reveal spices, grease, and memories associated with eating this particular food. In this sense, the contributors use images to create unaccountable narratives and dialogues within the *real* of their texts and to maintain a level of ambiguity within their logic. Thinking of their works in terms of the visual points to an emphasis on details resulting from an awareness of the shifting nature of meaning around something real. The visual is used to resist their and others' desires for clear identities. The closest the contributors can ever come to a *real* of themselves, within the context of this collection's exploration of subjectivity, is to view the reflections of their bodies as the primary *images* for use in reconsideration of their symbolic worlds.

These distinctions between the use of images and the visual point to a larger discussion, only intimated in this collection, about developing a physical relationship with images. Perhaps I am describing only a fantasy by suggesting that vital physiological functions in humans could become dependent on linkages to images, in which an emphasis on the visual is about embracing ambiguous identities. This explanation of the relationship between language and body also describes the interaction between desire and biology. It is a discussion about the coagulation of disparate parts into one body, or the process of monster making. This is a fantasy about the joy found in making oneself into spectacle.

Robert Flynt

Heroic Measures

Untitled, 1992, Cibachrome print, 40 x 30 in.

Untitled, 1993, chromogenic print, 30 x 24 in.

Untitled, 1993, chromogenic print, 30 x 24 in.

Untitled, 1993, chromogenic print, 30 x 24 in.

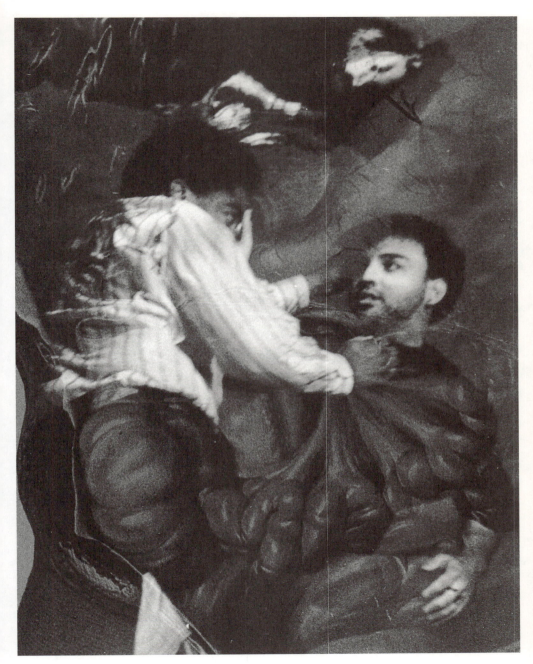

Untitled, 1990, chromogenic print, 30 x 24 in.

Gregg Bordowitz

Dense Moments

I'm sick and I don't want a cure. I like my illness. It's just as much a part of me as any of my other characteristics. I identify as my illness. Today, I feel relatively fine. Probably won't see thirty. Living with infection, me and thousands of other people worldwide. I have a disease, an infection that horrifies the uninfected for two reasons. First, because the cure is unknown. Second, because the routes of transmission are well known. Sex. Intravenous drugs. Pregnancy, mother to child. Pleasurable, life-affirming things. The kinds of things people have guilt about regardless of their association with this disease. The knowledge of my infection coupled with the careful monitoring of the state of my immune system forces me to face a simple fact: I will die. Of course, I may not. Like everyone else, I could get hit by a car, be murdered, kill myself. Barring these contingencies, it is almost certain that I will die of this disease. I don't know when. Perhaps there will be a cure. Perhaps I can successfully fight the infections my failing immune system will be increasingly unable to fight. More contingencies. Fact is that I don't know when, but I'll die of it.

I've led these twenty-eight years motivated by a strong desire to change the world, occasionally disrupted by bouts of indolence. This is one of those periods marked by hopelessness. The only activity I can perform without disgust is storytelling. That makes me kind of religious. I don't believe in god, but I have great faith in the power of testimony. Not confession. There are differences, very significant to me, between the confession and the testimony. Through testimony one bears witness to one's own experiences to one's self. Through confession one relinquishes responsibility for bearing witness to and for one's self with the hope that some force greater than one's self will bear away the responsibilities for one's actions. The testimony is the story of a survivor. The confession is the story of a sinner. Both are motivated by guilt. If the survivor does not bear witness to his experience, he may blame himself for the pain he feels despite the fact that the pain was caused by another person's actions. If the sinner does not reveal the nature of his sins, he will suffer the consequences of his actions through punishment inflicted by god. The testimony is secular. The confession is religious. Each can involve the other. The testimony is offered to an other, who listens. The confession is posed to an other, who has the power to punish or forgive. They are two distinctly different acts because the precondition for the testimony is a historical cause and the precondition for the confession is a subjective cause. Psychoanalysis engenders both confession and testimony by making subjectivity historical and history subjective. Confession presupposes guilt. Testimony presupposes innocence. Coming out is a form of testimony. Recovery is a form of testimony. Disclosing one's HIV status is a form of testimony. All of these can take the form of confession. Testimony is a means of gaining sovereignty of the self. Confession subjugates the self to a sovereign force. A testimony that leads to confession recapitulates repression. A testimony, performed successfully, can lead toward liberation. (An idealization.) A testimony once started cannot cease. The telling must continue. A confession implies an end, but it is an endless repetition. I want to assume the largest measure of responsibility for myself possible. This can be earned only through a greater understanding of my limits: the limits of my thinking, my actions, my expressions. This is a testimony.

For an entire year I woke up at precisely 9:20 a.m.—the exact time Ray died—without fail. I watched Ray die. One night I went by the hospital to see him. He hadn't been recognizing anyone for about two weeks. When I came into the room, I knew he was going to die that night. I kept saying to his mother that I would leave, but I remained. I wanted to see him die. Shit. I'd given so much energy and time to his survival, he owed me this. I'd never seen anyone die and this was my opportunity. Later, I realized that I had to witness his death. I wouldn't believe it if I wasn't there. I'd watched Ray give up life at an infinitesimal pace. If I didn't see this to the end I'd feel an inconclusiveness, a suspension of belief, an absence, not a loss—forever. When he was gone, his lack of presence was total. I said to myself, There's nothing. There's nothing. I kissed the forehead that for months had been oily with sweat. It was cool and dry. I didn't make the connection between the exact time of my witnessing Ray's death and the particularity of my sleep disorder until I woke up on November 9, 1991, at 9:20 in the morning, the one-year anniversary of Ray's death. I haven't woken up from sleep at that time of day since. Watching Ray's death corrupted my innocence. Ended my unquestioning faith that every next breath will come.

I spent all night watching him die. Every few minutes asking the nurse to increase the morphine drip. A few days earlier, the decision had been made to take him off all medication except pain killers. At some point in the early morning, the nurse had increased the morphine to the legal limit. When asked to continue, he looked at us angrily and said, "This is pain control, not euthanasia!" and abruptly walked out. I thought that I'd get up off the fucking chair and just increase the dose myself. I'd seen the nurse do it often enough. The liquid dripped through the tube attached to his arm like sand through an hourglass. Die. Just die. He'd been alive but gone for an immeasurable period of time. I'd sit bedside watching, waiting for him to make some noise, some articulation, a string of sounds I could recognize as Ray's speech, not satisfied for days and now I wanted done with it.

Ray gave me a present two weeks before he died. He asked his sister to buy me a copy of Artaud's *To Have Done with the Judgment of God*. He requested that she inscribe the inside cover of the book: *Dear Gregg, To our future shared transgressions. Love always, Ray.* He had an enormous ego. Its size was completely justified by the immensity of his brilliance. Our friendship was based on our arguments. We loved to best each other by quoting theory to support our own frail positions. Ray was California—a handsome Chicano fag with brown skin, long black hair, beard, pronounced cheekbones. He posed in costume as Christ on more than one occasion with great realness.

I must remind myself constantly that murderous feelings toward the sick and dying are common. When he died I wailed. Stuff came up I didn't think I contained. And relief. I finally had permission to grieve. Standing over Ray's barely living dying body, I wouldn't allow myself to acknowledge his coming death. It felt like betrayal. Aware that he would die, hopeless, I remained a present witness to his survival until the end.

Do you believe in the possibility of witness? Is it still possible to bear witness to another person's struggle? In *Survival in Auschwitz*, Primo Levi called the camps a laboratory. He described them as an arena of experimentation where modern forms of suffering and misery were patented. The Nazis produced a new type of alienation. Levi, the survivor, described a situation so miserable, in which living conditions were so degraded, that it was impossible to turn to another person in the same situation and together acknowledge the level of misery. The oppression was total, commiseration was impossible. The possibilities of witness were foreclosed and some people drowned, lost in a vast abyss, alone. This situation defines fascism for me. This is hell. This is not my reality, it's my worst nightmare. Those hardest hit by AIDS have struggled to prevent such foreclosures. We've organized ourselves into groups and institutions, formed communities against a horrible violence.

Been in a support group of the infected for over a year. Six white gay men meeting every two weeks, each taking his turn talking while the others listen. Sometimes when I'm speaking in my support group, the familiarity, the repetitiveness, of my monologue frustrates me. The others in the group have heard it all before. I'm fairly articulate about my situation: I'm lonely. Very lonely. Safer sex can be good once you get the hang of it. Intimacy, that's where the real trouble is. Who wants a lover who could die? Who wants a lover who is constantly being reminded of his mortality? I don't trust people who want to be in a relationship with me. I don't get it. Why would they? I don't want to fall in love with someone infected, sick, whatever. I guess it's not a matter of choice. You fall in love with whomever you fall in love with. Of course, I could always run. Bolt. Head for the hills. I have in the past. Being HIV-positive, I'm not supposed to feel this way, right? The correct position: People with HIV/AIDS are capable of everything healthy people are—sex, love. Well, that's a nice bit of denial. I'm not living a normal life, am I? Does everyone think about their death all the time? Consciously? A friend, HIV-negative, straight, told me, "Look, everyone's gonna die. I could go out in the street and get hit by a bus." "I wish you would," was the first thought to come to mind. I didn't say it. She was just trying to be a friend. Probably saying it for her benefit more than mine. Why can't I fight for myself? I hear other people with HIV complain about the HIV-negative world. "They won't have sex with us." "They won't love us." Some positives limit all their sexual and amorous relations to other positives. Is that possible? Isn't that like arbitrarily limiting your desire to only people with hazel eyes? I could understand that, actually.

Representing ourselves, to each other, we defy the representational limits we are forced to adopt. The ways they imagine us on TV have changed over the years. At first, in the early '80s, we were presented as darkly lit or scrambled faces, sometimes sitting behind potted palms. Pictured as criminals, terrorists, and prostitutes. In the mid-'80s, we began to appear without disguises seated next to talk show hosts. We were allowed to speak of our experiences, but only to the host, like we were reporting on some faraway event, another culture. We were still a phenomenon to be observed by a general public. Of course, this setup functioned to reaffirm the boundaries between us and the general public, to assure the audience that there was no threat to them. We haven't seen a person with the disease looking out beyond the TV screen into the television audience and addressing other people with it, forcing the realization that there are infected people watching television, part of the audience, part of the public. He's handsome. White. Well-groomed, but casual. Gap clothes. HIV-positive.

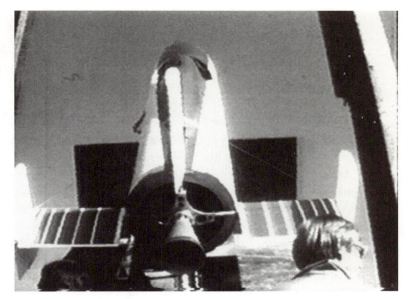

Still from *Fast Trip, Long Drop*, a motion picture by Gregg Bordowitz, 1993

Close-up. Talking to you in your living room. I am a criminal, a terrorist, a prostitute. The media makers were right about that. I'm a threat. I was fucking him, not something I do often because I prefer to get fucked. I wanted to infect him. The whole purpose of bringing myself to orgasm was to infect him with the virus. The idea of infecting him excited me as I jerked myself off. I shot my semen, dripping coolly drawn lines down the side of my right tit, not seeking out the far reaches of my partner's insides as I had wanted and imagined moments before.

How would you feel if I was your lover? What questions would you have for me? The other is presumed to pose an impossible demand on the subject, who never knows what it is the other wants. What will satisfy the other? People with AIDS and HIV are often pictured as a burden on society imposing impossible demands—on the health care system, the infrastructure, the moral order, the family. How would you feel if I was your lover?

It was the first time I asked a guy to fuck me. 1985. I wanted it bad and I was very scared. We were both very drunk. His cock was immense. I thought it would tear me apart and I wanted that. "Fuck me," I demanded, "just fuck me." He was having trouble getting it up because of the liquor. I got mad. "Fuck me! Can't you fuck me?" I was lying on my stomach in a delirious, semiconscious state. He crammed his half-hard cock into my tense hole. I was near dead drunk, but not relaxed. I was in pain as I felt his cock, finally filled with a credible amount of blood, slowly take up space, filling my ass. He went in and out, progressively going deeper as I tried to mentally stretch my shrinking anus. He suddenly stopped, quietly gasped the word "shit" as I felt his cock going limp. I don't know if he came or not. In the morning, it occurred to me that he should have worn a condom. He died a few years after and I have often thought that this was the instance of my infection. I don't know, he wasn't the last, nor certainly the first, to have my ass. He was just the first person I begged to fuck me. That's something.

I wanted him to fuck me without a condom. I received his cum as a gift. I wished for a legacy that I could receive in the form of a gift—the love and approval of a father. I wanted to achieve his stature. His greatness could be passed to me through his semen. A condom would thwart this transference. Was this the instance of my infection? The trauma always happens after the fact. We know it happened, because of its effects. I know I was infected, because a test shows that I have antibodies to the virus. More tests show that my immune system is compromised. I take experimental medications that produce side effects. All of this adds up to the fact of my infection, an event I can never locate in time with any certainty. It's like the time my father left us. This is a primary event in my life, an event that is interpreted and made more significant by events that happened to me later. In many ways, all the significant events in my life confer new meaning on the primary event—the loss of my father.

I was twenty-three years old when I thought I had found what I'd been looking for all my life—a feeling of belonging. I joined ACT UP—the AIDS Coalition To Unleash Power, a diverse nonpartisan group united in anger and committed to direct action to end the AIDS crisis. A cause. What brought me to this group was my increasing awareness of the epidemic and its implications for my future. Guilty and scared, I knew that the sex I was having, particularly anal-receptive sex, had possibly exposed me to a newly identified virus. That the meetings of the activist group were held at the Lesbian and Gay Community Center taught me something. The gay community was the only place to go to get information about this disease. More than just information—support. I had never wanted a sexual identity. I liked sex with men and women and I was successful at both. The possibility of exposure, my concerns and fears about it, centered around the fact that I enjoyed and often practiced what was listed as the most high risk activity. A homosexual act. I don't know when exactly, but sometime shortly after entering the community center I decided that I had better become a part of this community if I was going to get the information and support I needed to think about this illness.

I tested positive on the same day an ACT UP meeting was scheduled. That night I had to speak at the meeting about a demonstration I had been organizing. It was a protest at City Hall concerning the lack of availability of drug-addiction treatment and the lack of a clean needle exchange program in New York City. I decided that I would admit publicly at the meeting that I had just tested HIV-positive. I was so pissed off that I had to deal with this awful shit that I was going to make everyone deal with it. I wasn't going to own this alone. It would be easier to tell everyone this way. Then I wouldn't have to face any one person to tell him or her the news. Turn the public into the private.

The room was packed with about four hundred people. I stood nervously rocking back and forth on my heels, staring directly down into my notes scribbled on a yellow pad. I started slowly in a low quivering voice: "Next week, on Tuesday, we are going to have a demonstration that addresses issues we as a group have not addressed before. We are going to deal with AIDS and substance abuse. A lot of people have said that this is not an issue for our group . . . and uh . . . a lot of people think this isn't an issue for us . . . and um, uh . . . I just tested HIV-antibody-positive."

There was silence in the room. I heard a couple of gasps.

"I got infected because I have a drinking and drug problem that has prevented me from being able to negotiate and insist on having safe sex. I'm not telling you this to talk about myself. I'm telling you this because I think a lot of other people in this room have had the same experience. Issues of drug use and AIDS are our issues. The connection between drug abuse and safe sex must not be left out of any discussion about AIDS and substance abuse. It's important to recognize this connection because too often the issues are reduced to a single issue of needle use. This reduction legitimates misconceptions about drug use and users. It reinforces the view that IV drug users are alien and criminal. Substance abuse is not an issue of criminal law. The focus should be on treatment and services.

"We've got to ask ourselves who are the gays and who are the drug users? Who are the fags and who are the junkies? We have got to seriously question the names and categories used to separate the groups of people hardest hit by this epidemic. We have to take responsibility for these issues. We're demanding a clean needle exchange program to help IV drug users remain uninfected by HIV until they can get clean. We're demanding free drug-addiction treatment upon demand to anyone who wants it. So be there next Tuesday at noon."

I ended with my voice strong, but my hands were shaking. There was silence and then scattered applause. Some people came up to me afterward and thanked me. A couple of people approached me and confided that they, too, had had trouble practicing safe sex when they were drunk. It was a fairly cogent speech, considering the events of the day. I thought I was facing the news head-on. Doing the only thing I could do. Act. I was running. What I did was crazy. Created a storm around me so I wouldn't have to be emotionally responsible to anyone. Sure, everyone I'd had sex with, whose name I could remember, would find out they'd had sex with someone now infected. Either I'd tell them or, more than likely, they'd hear by word of mouth. I'd taken care of that. But I couldn't, wouldn't, deal with the fallout, the real possibility that I had unknowingly infected people. They might be mad at me. Even if I didn't do it purposefully, they still might be mad. Their anger would be justifiable. I didn't want to take responsibility for their anger. I didn't know that I didn't have to. Just because someone's angry at you doesn't necessarily mean that you're guilty.

But wasn't I guilty? I'd broken up my parents' marriage. A very powerful four-year-old, I was. Capable of mass destruction. I drove my father out of the house. Ruined my mother's life. Seven years old, playing outside with a friend, I point to the man on the porch, my stepfather: "That's not my real dad. My real dad's gone." My mom, sitting next to my stepdad, pulls me by the arm. She is pissed. Tells me never to tell anyone outside the family that he isn't my father. Never. I'd revealed a secret. It was all my fault.

I accept the blame. The guilt I feel greatly affects my actions. After the speech to ACT UP I took on a persona—Gregg Bordowitz, HIV-Antibody-Positive Gay Man. I came out all over the place. Every time I put myself forward as an HIV-Positive Gay Man I was flattening out the terms of my identity to further the cause of an agenda: the enfranchisement of people with HIV and AIDS. I disclosed an aspect of my sexuality, my homosexuality, because it was a factor in my infection. Each time I came out about my HIV status and my sexuality I felt authenticated, legitimated. I felt that my concerns mattered. More than that, my disease and my sexuality, viewed as indistinct by many, became terms around which others identified. Disclosing my status, coming out, I didn't feel alone. I didn't feel sick, perverse. I felt that I was on the side of right and justice. I was enabled to overcome my shame. That's important. A matter of survival. The disclosure would vanquish my guilt temporarily. I had to repeatedly and insistently assert my new identity, fighting against an internal conclusion that my pleasure had led to my death. Through a kind of exhibitionism, I was trying to exorcise the discourse of blame that would judgmentally bring sentence down upon me for getting fucked up the ass, liking it, and getting a fatal disease from it. Where did this discourse exist? Among the homophobes. Among the right

wing. In my own mind. Sometimes, I believe that my homosexuality is a disease and that I deserve to get sick from it. This thought can overtake me at any time. I think it in my dreams. I hear it in the voices of kind friends and see it in the faces of my relatives. It's always present. I am not resigned to it. I fight it. I won't grant it sovereignty. I refuse to be ruled by it. Now, I no longer feel compelled to present myself publicly as HIV-positive. I am not my disease. It's a shallow identity. It doesn't have the history, the significance, of other identities I have, like being gay or Jewish. I was taught as a child that there are two kinds of people in the world—Jews and non-Jews. I thought that my Jewish identity was the aspect of my character that made me different from everyone else. I always felt different, apart, alone. When I was fifteen I realized I was of the "working class." That's what made me different. Went around telling everyone, I'm a socialist. At eighteen, I moved into Manhattan, lived with my first boyfriend. Realized I was queer. Thought this was what made me different. There was a finality in this realization. I thought that I'd finally figured out why I'd always felt different. Now, I realize that my class identity didn't displace my religious identity, and my sexual identity didn't displace my class identity. I am all these things, and their interrelatedness somehow constitutes my identity. HIV is a disease. That infection has taken on the status of an identity that reveals the immense sense of shame we're all operating with in this puritanical culture of ours. Living with HIV is awful. It's terrifying. It's tedious. I don't want to spend the rest of my life being identified as a disease. I am much more than that. Don't reduce me to that. I can no longer reduce myself to that. The shameful feelings behind my status as an infected person still exist, but I no longer need to subordinate my identity to the level of my status to ward off evil, uncertainty, and death. A kind of alchemy, turning shit into gold, stigma into pride.

I often imagine that I am acting in the interests of the public good. I picture this entity as a jury presiding over my pleasure. It's a guilt-ridden fantasy. Who am I acting good for? And who will punish me for evil thoughts? Will Daddy spank me? I hope so. I hope he sticks a big stick up my ass while Mommy watches. Further, she says. Deeper. The conviction with which I act comes from deep-seated rage. I know I have it in me. I have fantasies of murder. As I noted before, I've imagined myself infecting others and I enjoy that fantasy. I don't know what to do with this information. I recognize myself as the subject of these sentences and I'm scared. I'm frightened of death and the fear overtakes my desire.

In a dream, I'm in a Lower East Side apartment lying on a couch in the center of the room. Ray, sick with lesions covering his body, is sitting in the corner, silent. A woman is lying on top of me. We're fucking and just as I'm about to shoot I remember that Ray is in the corner. Then, the woman turns into a man. The dream starts again. We're having sex and just before I climax I see Ray sitting in the corner and the guy on top of me turns into a girl.

I lost my virginity to a girl two years older. She was fast. Gave me a blow job in a duck blind in the woods behind her house on our first date. As she fellated, I tried to reach down her pants to finger her. Told me I didn't have to. This being my first blow job, it never occurred to me that you could get pleasure from someone without giving it back immediately. I felt guilty. Couldn't believe that I was supposed to sit back and enjoy this. Wasn't I the one responsible for the good feelings here?

The times and places of my sexual encounters as a teenager were organized around when and where parents worked. Whose house was empty during the day, at night. Our encounters paralleled the shifts of our parents' jobs. That I had sex with girls and yearned for sex with guys reveals the repressive context of my teenage years. It also reveals the formation of my desires shaped earlier in my life partly by my parents' divorce. I wanted my absent father's love and I depended on my mother's. She depended on my love and approval. I didn't know that then. I grew up thinking it was the duty of every boy to take care of his mother's emotional needs. This duty was a temporary position until my father returned. My stepfather never filled the position. Not through any fault of his own. When my father left he became an entity larger than any human. He became a category.

I would have drunk gasoline and lit my ass on fire if that had been the only way to get out of Long Island. Moved to the city in 1982, the summer I turned eighteen. Started drinking every day. Used to drink with bums on the street. Thought maybe I'd become one. Woke up in a doorway on 34th Street once. Scared me. Tried to go on the wagon. Didn't last long. Managed to keep the habit without going on the street. Don't know how. Wouldn't allow myself to. Learned how to manage the use. First time I did coke was in the YMCA that I lived in with some other art students. School of Visual Arts. Buncha young fags and dykes lying all over each other on a single bed. None of us were self-identified as lesbian or gay. Don't remember much about the actual experience of doing coke for the first time. Moved in with my first boyfriend. First guy to fuck me. When I met him he was wearing a green mod mac with a huge pink triangle sewn onto the back. He had his social security number tattooed onto his forearm like a camp survivor. A punk gesture which greatly contradicted the lyrical color-field paintings he made in the front room of our studio in Cobble Hill, Brooklyn.

Somewhere along the way my values changed. I once held a romantic, devout belief in beauty. I was a painter when I moved to Manhattan. I've always wanted to be an artist. All my life. My paintings were often shown in the cafeteria of P.S. 186. Later, in high school, I spent most of my time in the art rooms making abstract expressionist paintings. I wanted to be Jackson Pollock. When I attended art school I started making monochromatic paintings. Ad Reinhardt. All black. Painting became a task. I realized that I didn't enjoy the act of painting. I loved the act of making meaning. I started painting myself out of my pictures, applying the paint on the canvas with a roller, executing the task as fast as I could. I became more interested in how the object hung on the walls. Then I became fascinated with the walls. First as surface, later as architecture. I went from viewing the gallery as a structure to questioning it as an institution. Who determined what hung on the walls and why? Who attended galleries and why? Whose interests were being served and what did I desire? I began making video because I needed to work in a time-based medium to answer all these questions. The first work was about my sexuality in the context of AIDS. I became interested in AIDS as a political crisis. Protest groups were forming. Video making became a means of documenting the emerging movement. Started working collectively to make documentaries. Began writing and publishing critical

analyses of my own work. I adopted a set of aesthetic principles to which I was, until recently, committed: reduce the category of beauty to efficacy, the category of form to function, the category of audience to community. Today I'm sitting here writing myself out of the categories I reduced myself to.

I stopped drinking and doing drugs for pleasure, substituting an entirely different pharmacopoeia: Bactrim, AZT, Zovirax, DDC, DDI. I've been living with HIV for four years and I've remained relatively asymptomatic for AIDS. Lots of colds, a few minor skin rashes, warts, but no opportunistic infections. I initially took AZT—an antiviral drug that slows the progress of HIV replication—for over a year, every four hours. I'm part of the beeper generation. Carried my AZT in a box with a timer that beeped every four hours to remind me to take the pills. I was always waiting for the beeper to sound in public places, anticipating the embarrassment it would cause me. Eventually, I stopped using the beeper. Removed the batteries. What the fuck, they don't know if this works, who cares if I take it late, early, whatever.

I take Bactrim to prevent pneumocystis carinii pneumonia. I added Zovirax to my regimen because theoretically it prevents infections that could threaten my eyesight, or cause severe fatigue. It's also a herpes treatment. At this point I can no longer take AZT because the cumulative effect of its toxicity adversely affected my liver. So, I started to take DDC—an experimental antiviral that I got through my doctor as part of a study to measure the drug's efficacy. Label on the bottle: *Dideoxycytidine has been associated with contact sensitivity. Persons handling this drug should take measures to avoid prolonged contact with tablets or tablet dust.* How do you take a drug you're not supposed to touch? These drugs yield no pleasurable effects. Side effects: AZT: nausea, growling stomach-empty-speediness. DDC: loss of feeling in the feet and hands, signs of neuropathy. I can't take DDC anymore. Dead hands are not compatible with the purchase of a laptop. My hands fell asleep, a long nap. I went off the drug and all the feeling came back.

I feel discouraged but I don't think I'm going to die. It's not because I'm brave, I just can't wrap my mind around death. It's still in the abstract to me. Like my T-cell counts are on paper but I'm feeling fine. The blood tests I get every three months count the number of T cells I have. They're lymphocytes, the cells that HIV attacks. So, it's important to know your number because if it's a low number you may be in trouble: it means your immune system can't respond. Anyway, my T cells are low on paper but I'm feeling fine, so it's all in the abstract.

I have a range of emotions that goes from anger to rage. I'm proud of my anger. I want to work with it, develop it, make it more powerful. Sometimes, it's all I have. I hate some of the spiritual crap people try to hand me to calm me down—like everything happens for a reason. There's no reason, no reason at all for why I'm HIV-positive, why some people get sick, why some people die. No reason.

In the spring of 1988. March and April. I tested HIV-antibody-positive. Stopped drinking and doing drugs. And I told my parents I am gay. I went out to their house on Long Island to talk to them. They live in what is called a "development"—rows of houses attached to one another within a maze of cul-de-sacs. Strathmore Court. At the time, my stepfather was working any fix-it job he could get and my mother was working as a salesperson in a department store. My sister was in high school. Strange, that I would wait to talk to them about my sexuality until after having tested HIV-antibody-positive. I knew that I wasn't going to let them know about my HIV test. First, I would tell them proudly that I was gay. Once they accepted that, if they accepted it, I would, sometime in the near future, talk to them about AIDS. (I didn't tell them about being HIV-infected until over a year later.) I didn't want them to associate my homosexuality with illness. Actually, it was I who didn't want to associate my homosexuality with illness. Fantasies of telling my family about my life on my deathbed had become a preoccupation. I would avoid this scenario regardless of how painful it would be to confront my parents.

The day I came out, I was sitting with my parents at the kitchen table. My sister was upstairs watching TV. My parents must have sensed that I was going to broach some serious topic, because if I weren't I would have been upstairs watching TV too. Throughout my life, members of my family always occupied the same seats at the kitchen table. I sat on the same side as my mother, facing my stepfather. On this day, I occupied the seat my sister usually sat in, facing my mother, my stepfather to the left of me. I told them. I said that there was something they should know and accept about me if they expected me to include them in my life. I am gay. My mother burst into tears. My stepfather got up to pace. My mother couldn't stop crying for about two hours. My stepfather surprised me with his response. It was OK as far as he was concerned. Attempting to quiet my mother, he appealed to her to look at the bright side: "Linda, Linda, look. Come on, stop crying. Look, he didn't kill anybody, and he's not a drug addict," he said emphatically looking at me for assurance. At least I hadn't killed anybody. At some point my sister came downstairs to see what was happening. Looking at my mother, who was trying to contain her sobs, she asked what was wrong. I looked at her and said that I had just told our parents that I am gay. She started crying, too, like she'd been cued. I thought to myself, the whole thing feels scripted. My sister must have felt implicated. Maybe this meant she was queer. Maybe she thought she'd have to tell people at school. I still don't know, we haven't talked about it since. Through time my parents have come to deal with it. They're now aware that I have this infection, although their response to learning this was much less emotional than my coming out. I thought it should have been more painful. I don't think they realized the implications, and I gave them a very optimistic picture. I didn't admit to them that I fear my own death in the next few years. I lied to them. Told them it was like diabetes. I can keep it under control. I fed them the bullshit I'd love to hear someone else tell me, and the things I knew they were capable of hearing. I'm tired of representing the situation in ways that take care of the needs of the listener. Fuck you. I know it's not my fault, but I'm angry at you. Testimony. Confession. Why should I have to explain it all to you. I need you. LISTEN TO ME. Don't go. Don't . . . When Ray was dying, he became extremely religious. He hadn't been religious, was even somewhat anti-religious, and I found myself in a predicament: I wanted to be supportive because I loved my friend, but I don't believe in god. At his bedside, we would talk about god often. After a long silence, with tears in his eyes, in a child's voice begging permission, he asked me, "Can I believe in god after I've read Nietzsche?" Pause. *God is dead. He remains dead. And we have killed him.*

We both had to laugh at the high level of pretension behind that question. We weren't prepared for this. The critical theory we valued so much had failed us. Not because of its inadequacy, because of its limits. We, Ray talking, I listening, had come up against the contingencies we had until then disavowed. And why not? He was twenty-six then, so was I, and our heads were crowned with the twisted branches of our own ambitious weaving. You can have only a very inadequate knowledge of the duration of other bodies.

I was bar mitzvahed in an orthodox temple. It was the cheapest, my grandfather wanted to pay, therefore he sent me to an orthodox temple. The musty smell of old books and the company of men. It was a formative experience. I was such a good student that for my bar mitzvah I performed, in addition to my haftorah, the entire Shabbat service. I professed a deeply felt belief in god that suffered and failed many tests after my bar mitzvah. Still, the entire framework of my thinking presupposes the category of god. Retain the category of god in one's thinking as a category of the unknown, as an arena of forces that lie outside, or on the periphery of comprehension. Something more than mere random variables and chance. Forces motivated without intention. No will. Forces not motivated by a human mind, but motivated, nonetheless. Arbitrary and motivated. God is a structural necessity. Spinoza: *God is the immanent, not the transitive, cause of things.* God has neither intention nor will. The category of god can be retained, but its human image must vanish. It's a category of mystery composed of forces beyond understanding. Amoral. Nonjudgmental. Causal. Can one pray to it? No. What can one do? Resign to it. There are some things beyond our control, beyond our understanding.

In the spring of 1988. March and April. I tested positive. Stopped drinking and doing drugs. And I told my parents I am gay. This was the densest moment of my life. The moment when I first realized that what matters is the meaning I make of my life. The moment when I began to write my own story. Yes, I am the subject of these sentences. My story began and now it ends with a single explanatory event in mind. The death of my father. It is for his eyes this is written. For his ears this is told. His imagined interest. That it can only be imagined causes me great pain. Probably always will. I can live with that pain. I don't have to suffer for it. Before the spring of 1988, I was very far away from believing this.

I was eight or nine when my mother tried to run away with my step-father's best friend. One morning I was awakened by the sounds of yelling and shuffling coming from the kitchen in our Queens apartment. I walked into the kitchen to see my stepfather in his pajamas holding a steak knife to his chest and crying, "Take it out. Go ahead, take my heart, too. Go ahead." My mom was shrieking for him to put the knife down. John, my step-father's best friend, was standing there. He said something too, like, "Be cool man. Be cool." All three of them stopped dead looking at me. I'm not clear on what happened next. I remember holding on to my stepfather and wailing, "I don't want to go." I didn't want to lose him. We left with suit-cases and some of my toys. GI Joe. My sister was just an infant then. That night at John's house I asked my mom if this was going to happen again, implying that this father-changing thing was becoming a routine. She laughed and started to cry. Don't remember how long we stayed with John. Driving in the car, John asked me if I was angry. He told me it was OK if I was mad at him, it was OK even if I was mad at my mom. I mumbled that I was OK. One night my stepfather showed up with my grandfather and my uncle. The men. After a long talk among everyone concerned—my mom, John, and the men—I was packed up along with my sister into my grand-father's blue Granada. We returned to Queens. I never saw John again. For months, my mother and stepfather held closed-door conversations. For months, maybe years, I misrecognized every strange man who walked down the block toward our building for John. I thought he was coming back to take us away. I had mixed feelings about that. I feared it and I longed for it.

I expected either one of my parents to leave at any moment. I was torn between a strong desire for the love of my father and the love of my mother.

I conceived of them as mutually exclusive categories and I tried to demonstrate my love for each without allowing the other to see my efforts. I've spent my adult life bouncing back and forth between relationships with women and relationships with men. Caught between the love of a man and the love of a woman. I've been in that situation many times. Not until very recently have I recognized the logic behind this pattern. These instances exemplify the ways I've developed for coping with the possibilities of loss. If I am torn between two love objects, I always have somewhere to go, and if one decides to withdraw his or her love, I will always have the other. My efforts are calculated to prevent the pain of loss. I expect it like I anticipated my father's death.

Dad, I'm glad you're dead. You're more interesting that way. The only photos I have of my father are a publicity shot when he was twenty, toothful smile, strumming a guitar, and bar mitzvah pictures of thirteen-year-old Les wearing tallis. I spent my childhood waiting for my father to return and set things right. I mistook every strange man walking toward me on the street for my father. The Jew lives in an anticipatory present. Always waiting for the Messiah. I've been waiting for my father to return ever since he left. He's dead. And I'm an adult now. I've struggled all my life to be able to write this. It's absurd. So simple. He's not coming back.

My father died when he was thirty. I just turned twenty-nine. All my life I've thought that I am inescapably like my father. In many ways I've acted as I have imagined him to be. I was given a folder of material concerning my father from my paternal grandfather. It contains hundreds of pieces of paper having some relation to my father. Newspaper ads for a guitar school he owned. Invitations to recitals. Some pictures. Canceled checks. The accident report concerning my father's death and a photostat of a newspaper report on the accident that killed my father.

Due to a misprint in the *Times News*, Idaho's Largest Evening Newspaper, Twin Falls, Idaho, Monday, September 9, 1974, two paragraphs of an article concerning my father's death were misplaced inside the lead article, concerning Evel Knievel's unsuccessful stunt. The headline of the lead story read:

FAST TRIP, LONG DROP

Evel Knievel tried—but failed—to conquer the Snake River Canyon with his steam rocket in the dust and wind late Sunday afternoon.

But, Knievel said later, "to lose a beautiful canyon and river is not to me a real loss."

The rocket fired at 3:44 p.m., about 20 minutes later than scheduled, in front of a jump-site crowd estimated at one-fifth the size expected—about 10,000 people. Perhaps another 10,000 watched from Shoshone Falls, along the rim and from rooftops....

A California man, walking from Shoshone Falls along Falls Avenue late Saturday night, was struck and killed in a car-pedestrian accident. Sheriff's officers said Leslie Hugh Harstein, 30, North Hollywood, a producer of special shows, was killed as he and his wife were walking toward their automobile, which had been left on Desert View Drive.

Hospital officials said Mr. Harsten was apparently killed instantly about 10 p.m. Saturday. Cloyce Edwards, county coroner, said the man died of head injuries and was dead at the scene. He was struck by a pickup truck and camper also traveling west.

. . . Knievel's wife, his three children and numerous relatives watched the launch from the canyon rim. Linda remained silent, according to an observer, during the takeoff, as relatives shouted, "Oh, my god." When the skycycle disappeared behind the rocks, she ran to the edge crying, "Where is it?"

Informed by a reporter her husband was alive, "she just grinned," the reporter said.

Another strange coincidence—Knievel's wife is named Linda, my mother's name, my father's first wife. I'm his only kid.

SOME FANS FELT CHEATED

Sunday night a near riot erupted after a group of campers at the jump site, believed to be unhappy over the failure of Evel Knievel to provide free beer, began burning and tearing up concession stands, fences and automobiles.

Still from
*Fast Trip,
Long Drop*

A disappointed fan, I am my father's absence. Can we be the subjects of the following sentence? I am the author of this story. Now the author faces his own death. He says, I am the beginning of something, the end of another.

GREGG BORDOWITZ

A vehicle. A failed rocket. There's a void to be leapt. An impossible void. How can I make it? He's gone. Am I here? The author of this story is already dead. I will tell his story. I am a witness. I will make it my own. Telling it, I survive. Concluding, I will die. Deliverance?

I make plans for my inevitable illness. After Ray died, I moved into an apartment building with an elevator. Ray lived in a walk-up five flights up. I carried him up and down the stairs when it became impossible for him to make the trip. I don't want anyone to have to carry me and I will not be trapped in my apartment on a sunny day for fear of asking friends to carry me out. Some say my pragmatic approach is morbid but I'm proud of it. I feel like I'm taking care of myself by preparing for the worst. Ray wasn't tested for HIV until he became ill. He found out after the TB when he had about eighty T cells. I was tested well in advance of illness. I'm relatively healthy at the moment but I live with constant anxiety and an acute awareness of my mortality. I think about my funeral sometimes. I like to think that people will miss me. They'll say, "He was brilliant," or, "He was fucked-up, but I loved him anyway."

I don't want to die. I've come head up against the actual limiting dimensions of my body. I now realize that though my actions once seemed to extend far out along chains of causality, they never actually got any farther than the surface of my skin. I am scared to die. I am living with this infection. I live in spite of it. I fuck. I love. I'm loved. Eat. Sleep. Shit. Laugh. Living is so much more than biological function, life can be nothing less. I have a life. It's hard-won. But sometimes, I'm miserable and ashamed, deeply ashamed. Have I fit all of this within the frame of the picture? Did all of this come to rest within a single composition? I can feel some force inside me struggling to reach a degree zero. I don't know what constitutes that level of knowledge. I can't tell whether it is a yearning for something, or an urge to cover something up. I'll never reach it. The zero. I can't be nothing. I have a past. I have substance. To nullify it would be suicide, and that is not my intention. I want to live unfettered by the enormous weight of my substantiality. To sublate. Abandon the old self—the one with the quirky ways that are no longer sufficient in and of themselves to answer life's quirks. 9 fucking 20 a.m. and I have to change. I'm too many things. Too many contradictions. Too many people. I'm writing and I'm reading. I'm gay and I'm straight. Working-class and bourgeois. Jewish and American. Faithful and hopeless. Ethical and evil. Reasonable and irrational. Testifying and confessing. Living and dying. Unresolved, irreconcilable, inconclusive. Contingent. Mortal. Ambivalent. And not resigned.

An Impossible Man

Daddy's lying on the floor, on his back. I'm sitting on his chest—I'm two or younger. I sit very close to his face. I kiss his face all over. I love him before reason.

There's a sense, it's longing, probably, that I could join, if there was enough time, all the time of the world, that tiny moment with the present— if something like that would occur in infinity—and feel his skin, his face, the face I touched then.

He touched me and left unquestioned and questionable marks on me. I couldn't control my strangest, happiest, darkest, wildest, and most unsettled responses to him, with him. He was almost a response in me; he occupied not just a part of me, not just a place in my life, but life, in the beginning. At the very least he was there at the beginning.

"In the beginning" signals the start of unresolved and unresolvable stories. In the beginning is fantasy, Freud's "protective fiction," and the fantastic is beautiful and horrible. Fantasy is one of the tenacious claims of childhood.

(I have a memory of him, but it's not him. It's my will-him-into-being. He's a lost and a found object.)

My father died ten years ago. I didn't believe he would, I just mouthed the words. Then he did. It seems simpler, easier to write about dead people. They can't object, or complain, and as far as stories go, there's a "natural" and "appropriate" ending to appropriate for one's own ends. But it's harder, really, because of one's compulsion, need to, which is inhibited and chastened by the lack of the object who could object. There isn't a yearning to write about the living as if they were alive; they are. Even friends or enemies who have merely fallen away are still alive and have the potential for presence again. Bad things can be undone, maybe. There's no potential from death. Except, a common wisdom goes, for the living to expect freedom, a kind of deserved liberation. It's reassuring and handy, as if "freedom" were death's dowry. When really it's incommensurability.

My father was one of three boys, sons. He was the middle son, his mother's favorite. He became the father to three girls, daughters. (I'm the youngest.) He was, I thought as a child, sometimes uncomfortable, or awkward, in our family: he was the only man at the dinner table, the only man on our trips, the only man at our table in a restaurant. We shared him, unequally, it would turn out. Each daughter had a different father, her own father, and the mother/wife, a husband who was different from the father. (I didn't realize that, then.)

My father was special especially in his difference from us. His singularity was a kind of burden to him, I think. An insecure man, he was uncertain about how to be with girls and vulnerable because of his uncertainty. At least he seemed to me, when I was little, vulnerable because of it. I grew up believing that he was—and consequently men were—as sensitive as we were. Maybe more.

I can remember thinking that my father's having his penis on the outside of his body was another sign of his vulnerability, his fragility. We girls were so much more compact and lucky, I thought. Our sex was protected.

One afternoon my father was about to sit down on a couch in the den.

Lynne (age eight or nine): Aren't you afraid you're going to break it?

Daddy: What?

Lynne: Your penis.

Daddy: Why?

Lynne: Don't you have bones in it?

Daddy: In my penis? No. Who told you that?

Lynne: I learned the word "boner" at school. You don't have bones in it?

Daddy collapses on the couch, laughing.

But Daddy's penis was no laughing matter. It was never mentioned. He had to "cover himself," to guard us from his nakedness when we reached a certain age, but since I was the youngest, while he and my sisters were already covering themselves in front of each other, I could still be uncovered and so could he. I went to the toilet with him and watched him piss. I took my first shower with him because, at the age of five, I was afraid of showers. He said he'd take me in with him, and he'd bring an umbrella. We got in and he slid the glass doors shut. He opened the umbrella and turned the water on. We stood there, not getting wet. Then, when I wasn't anxious anymore, he closed the umbrella. I don't remember talking about it again. Maybe it was our secret. More likely he and my mother laughed about it later, privately.

He loved to laugh, but he often appeared surprised to find something funny. His eyebrows—maybe one more than the other—would jump up onto his forehead, as if he were puzzled or curious that something could make him laugh, and then, having thought it over, he'd laugh. But my father was given as much—more—to depression. He careened from high to low, where he stayed longer, all his fortunate and unfortunate life. He could be petulant, childish, and demanding; he had his way more often than not. He seemed to need to be taken care of.

("In human beings," Freud wrote, "pure masculinity or femininity is not to be found either in a psychological or a biological sense." Early on I saw my father as vulnerable and my mother as tough, very tough, tougher than she really was, especially in relation to him, I learned later.)

He seemed to need to be taken care of, though he was physically strong. Until my father had his first heart attack, I had never seen him sick. Sometimes he stuck pieces of Dr. Scholl's rubber pads between two of his toes, which crossed. Maybe I was aware that he slept badly. But that, to me, wasn't being sick, then. His illness was intangible, irrational—anxiety, depression, guilt. Neurosis. It was the valley I entered when I walked downstairs to the basement to sit next to him, to try to make him feel better.

November 1990
Dream that my sister B. tells me—she wakes me up in my dream to tell me—that Daddy's had another heart attack, and part of his heart, a greater part of his heart, is atrophied. He's not dead? I ask. No, she says. And then Daddy and Uncle J. walk into her former apartment. Maybe—I'm not sure—there's a hallway. Daddy's kind of sheepish, almost embarrassed at being alive. It's an expression I remember him having when he felt I loved him too much. I throw my arms around him and say, I'm so glad you're not dead.

His beginnings were meager, poor. He was a first-generation American, with an immigrant Russian Jewish mother and father; his father was a shirt maker. I don't know what my father felt about his father. His father didn't live with them but visited weekly; it's a story I never learned enough about. My mother says his family was never hungry. None of his brothers is alive to ask about the early days. I have no idea what their apartment looked like. If I were a visitor in my father's house—maybe I am—it would be strange to me. I don't know how I found out he was his mother's favorite. Maybe my mother told me, or his brother, or he did, long ago.

One night, when he was married, in his own apartment and already a father, he was eating a delicious steak. Excited, he woke my sisters—I wasn't born yet—because he wanted them to have a taste. I can imagine the scene: Daddy sitting close to his little daughters on their beds, their eyes half shut with sleep. He is eagerly, happily, feeding them pieces of what money can buy.

He loved to eat. He used to exclaim that I was so delicious he was going to put me in the oven, cook me, and eat me. I was confused about that, because he loved food, so it was a compliment, to be wanted like that. But I didn't want to be cooked in the oven, that was terrifying. But just as now I can't separate his psychical body from his physical body, as a child— and maybe for children generally—there was no way to make a distinction, to divorce absolutely the pleasure of his wanting to eat me from not wanting to be put in the oven. Everything was possible, impossibly real, and make-believe.

(If my father had been a writer, perhaps he would've concocted a fairy tale about a father who loves his children so much he wants to eat them. I probably am.)

Writing, I catch traces of his hands in mine, they sneak up through my fingers as particles, the short, light hairs above my knuckles, part of my inheritance from him. I have short hands, too, or small hands. Actually, my hands are more like my mother's.

My father's hands are gripping the steering wheel and he's driving me into the city, New York, and he and I are alone.

Lynne (nine): Manhattan is an island?

Daddy: Yes.

We are crossing the 59th Street Bridge, and I look ahead at the huge buildings on the island.

Lynne: Why doesn't it just sink?

He glanced at me, bemused or dubious, I'll never know. I wanted to interest him. He explained what an island was, that Manhattan wouldn't sink just like that, fast. I believed, maybe mistakenly, that he enjoyed the ridiculous idea, the absurdity, that it might sink, just like that.

(Maybe he fought all his life against seeing himself as ridiculous and was at home with the absurd and could play ridiculously with me.)

I wasn't satisfied with his island answer, whatever it actually was. I didn't have a strong sense of the physical world. I wanted it to be there and

Father of the Bride (1950)

not to be a problem. I wanted it to be a stable foundation, but it wasn't a foundation for me, really.

(Is the body a foundation, and for what?)

My father liked driving, to jump behind the wheel and go. Let's go to Coney Island. Let's go to town and pick up a pint of coffee ice cream. Let's go to the docks and look at the boats. Except there were terrible fights in the car, and my mother would scream that he pull over because otherwise we'd have an accident. He could turn, in an instant, from a charming Dr. Jekyll into a snarling Mr. Hyde.

June 1992

Dream I am in a strange house, with D., who's not there, and P., who tells an advertising exec, an old man, to call and see me. I give him directions to the house, but can't remember the street I'm on, a cross-section with some French names or phrases, familiar ones I can't remember now. The earlier part of the dream was horrific—a man stuffed himself inside a large, bearlike dog and then committed suicide; the last shot of him was with a maniacal but dead grin on his face, his eyes wide open. I think P. gives me and the old man a ride, or just me, to go visit the old man. P. drives like a maniac.

Daddy could become a monster on purpose. When my friends came to the house, he played this game—Want me to scare you? We'd sit in the dark den, happy fear building as minutes passed, waiting for my father to throw open a door—we never knew which one or when—and charge in, like the creature from the Black Lagoon. He'd creep slowly toward us, all misshapen and bent over, then stand over us, waving his arms like a lunatic, and leap up and down, making weird noises, being the bogeyman. Sometimes he did that when I was alone in my bed upstairs. It was, definitionally, thrilling. He was my prohibited, purloined father/lover, a monstrous desire, appropriately in gothic drag.

(But for him? What did it serve? Did it relieve him of the burden of being a monster the times when it wasn't on purpose, when he couldn't control himself?)

The longer he's dead, the harder it is for me to remember in any detail or with any vividness how he forced me, bodily, out the front door of the house; how he chased me around the house with a strap; how I hid from him in the bathroom and locked the door. When I try to call up scenes like these, to set them on the stage of memory, or to stage them as memory, a dull curtain descends. The scene meets interference, is somehow obliterated or forced off. And the memory withers, frays, as if it can't hold up to scrutiny or can't be contained, not the thought of it. Then I—who am I then?—fumble to replace the bad lost moment with a less terrible but no less lost moment. And it's then that I'm most aware of picking and choosing a past, a father.

Probably the people who are most afraid make and become the best monsters; it must be a counterphobic truism. My father was preyed upon by his fears. He often quoted "the only thing we have to fear is fear itself," and he feared it, the unnameable. As a child he was terrified by the rats in the basement where he was sent to collect coal. Maybe he was afraid of the older, tougher neighborhood boys, the loss of his mother's love, his older brother's anger. The alien world outside his immigrant mother's apartment.

There were two stories he told about job hunting. One time he was advised that the way to find a job was: Go to a very tall office building, to the top, and then walk down every floor, and knock on every door, asking if anyone needs help. He followed that advice. The other story was about the first job he actually applied for, when he was twelve. He wanted to be a busboy. He thought busboys worked on buses and he'd spend his summer vacation seeing America. Instead he carried trays.

He was comforting about my fears: of the shower, of dying when I was six, of not being able to "do the work" in first grade. After watching an educational movie at school, when I was seven, that showed how kids playing on the Long Island Railroad's third rail were electrocuted and how a little girl was blinded because bad boys threw stones at the windows of the train, I feared the Long Island Railroad. I didn't want to go anywhere on a train ever again. One day my father took me to the city by train. When the train crossed over a trestle, where bad boys could've waited as they did in the educational movie, I dropped to the floor. If my father tried to reassure me, which I don't remember, he didn't insist I sit in my seat immediately or pressure me to get off the floor. He acknowledged my terror, took it to heart, or at least respected my anxiety, or knew how improbable it was that he could change my mind about fear.

If he feared the loss of his mother's love, he never hated her. If he feared the loss of her love, then all his life he took care of her, generously, without complaint. I thought, as a child, he was even proud of her, though she was strange, different, difficult—foreign. He provided her with her own comfortable apartment, with a nurse or housekeeper when she needed it. He dressed her in fur coats when, my mother still remarks, she herself wore a cloth coat.

August 1990
Dream that Daddy is dying again. I see him alive, with his face very full, like his mother's. But then he turns into my mother, and she is dying. Then I am given a copy of Ronald Fraser's *In Search of the Past*, a book which I had already bought for myself.

Actually, I keep forgetting his face, it's blurred as if my glasses were permanently lost. Going away, gone now, there now, *fort/da*. He's transparent, an empty illusion. His nails—I don't see them. They were wide, stubby maybe, hard, not easily broken. I can vaguely visualize his arms—they were well-formed. So were his legs. And though his chest had almost no hair on it, his forearms were covered with dark-brown hair. Descriptive words come easily, but not him; words for loss, too, though there aren't enough of them, and they're inadequate, because none is sufficient for how nothing it all is. None is as absent as absence. Already in his ephemeral image is death, and he's never a solid body anymore.

(If I write "I hold an image of him," the image dissipates faster than those words can be read. But you can return to the words.)

When my father wrote letters, he usually wrote over some of his words, to correct his penmanship, to make each letter clearer. The result was a sloppiness I interpreted as playfulness, impatience, or frustration—some kind of inventiveness. Trying to find his hand, I sometimes imitate his handwriting. I trace over the letters of words though they can be read. I could stop myself, but I don't want to. There's a second of indecision, and I know if I do it, the letter will become sloppy, but I do it anyway, as if to say, it's out of my control, can't be helped, I'm my father's daughter. It's feeble—this attempt to exhume him, to find him in me as if I were the ground or surface and he were a deeper layer. I feel something when I do it, but it's false, too deliberate.

When he was a kid, my father played a lot of handball (he saved the leather glove that he used to wear on his right hand), and he could play much later in life. He wasn't as good at tennis as my mother, he was strong and wild; but on the handball court, he was fast and accurate. And he was short—my father used to joke that he would be a star basketball player in a midget league—but he was proud of his well-developed body, and aware that he was handsome. He liked to stay fit and, way before jogging was fashionable, he would take us girls for runs with him on the beach, in the winter, to develop our leg muscles. He would always insist that we hold ourselves erect, backs straight—Stomachs In!—and one exercise he had us do was: Stand against a wall and descend into a squatting position, then sit there, to strengthen thigh and stomach muscles, then shimmy up, keeping spines flat against the wall. (To this day posture is important to me. Backbone?)

He didn't have sons, he was athletic. (Not surprisingly, as the last, late child, I was supposed to be the boy.) He conducted exercises with us as if we were in the army—he was the sergeant. It was always a little funny; he thought it was funny too, I think, or maybe ridiculous and ironic. Here we were being his sons in a kind of masquerade of "masculinity."

(Could I have learned to appreciate "masculinity as masquerade"? Do I now?)

He was a textile converter, a designer of fabrics, and an innovator of synthetic threads. Though he was one of the bosses, he chose for his office a very small room, a large closet; his beloved baby brother (by fifteen months), Al, his partner, took the grand "executive" room. My father thought Al was "the creative one." He deferred to his baby brother, who died much earlier than he.

Uncle Al's was the first dead body I ever saw, lying in a coffin, in a plain room of bereavement. My father and his uncle, for whom Al was named, stood at the casket. My great-uncle was at Al's foot, crying, my father near Al's head, staring at his face. He was waiting for Al to come alive. Hopelessness, anguish, despair, a longing I'd never known, drew his face into a portrait of intolerable sadness. I had never seen him look that way before (or ever again, it would turn out). Where he could not forgive himself, or us, anything, Daddy could always forgive Al.

December 1990
Dream Daddy's alive, but then he dies. I say to my mother, At least I got to hear his voice again.

I couldn't believe Pop—that's how he signed his letters and how he was addressed by us sometimes—would die. He was supposed to have died four years before he did. The doctors called his being alive "a miracle." They didn't explain what that meant until he did die. Then we were told that my

Cape Fear (1991)

father had only 18 percent of his heart muscle working; the rest was atrophied. The miracle was that people are not supposed to be able to survive with less than 33 percent of their heart functioning.

He read everything about the heart and had his own theories. One was to exercise, no matter what. The other was to have a teaspoon of cider vinegar every day, "to cut the grease." He had low cholesterol, so he told us that the hardening of his arteries was genetic, not environmental, and cholesterol didn't always matter. He kept up his strength. He used to go for fast walks, with weights around his ankles. He wanted to build up his heart. In part, the doctors attributed the miracle to the fact that all his other organs were in good condition. He was strong. There was nothing wrong with him except his bum heart, we all said.

January 1992
Dream that, after visiting W.'s house, whose wine glasses are sparkling clean, spotless, I'm in a small kitchen. There is a bottle of dishwashing liquid. It's pink. It's called Miracle.

The night he nearly died, my two sisters, my mother, and I waited in the hospital waiting room, all night. Four women, all for him. Pop was never easy in his harem; he was embarrassed, perhaps, at his largesse, the excessiveness, the display of females around him. But he was also vain. Probably we fed his pride while simultaneously humiliating him. He was easily humiliated and wanted to be liked. The only man in our family, he was privileged to be unique in our midst. And to be depressed, generous, moody, inquisitive (he read late at night, books scattered all over the floor around his side of the bed), surly, playful, violent, angry, weak, handsome, smart, harebrained. All these things. A man, the only one. He was allowed a wide range, a wide berth, by me.

(My father must have represented to me a mix of "feminine" and "masculine" attributes, a balance, unbalanced, in one body. I see how I align him with his "active" body, the physical house for a sometimes "passive" man. But what is "active" and what is "passive"? Aren't these terms as unfixed and unstable as sexuality itself?)

Death destabilizes and unfixes. I look at photographs of Pop. He's different in each. Death deconstructs. Daddy's unstable and unfixed. A picture is always a picture. Inevitably, each one disappoints, it's a flimsy post-factum. Just a picture I like or don't. I keep mental images.

His upper lip was fuller than his bottom one, which I can't recall at all, and one side of his upper lip was raised more than the other, but I can't remember which side. Facing him, I think it would be his left side. His eyes were large and hazel, sometimes nearly green. To me he looked like Gene Kelly and the aged Henry Fonda of *On Golden Pond* and the top of John Garfield's head, from the eyes up, and the bottom of the older James Mason's face, the line of his mouth especially. And an elderly Chinese man I once passed on Mott Street. The Chinese man had deep creases in his face, which my father didn't ever have, but he looked uncannily like my father. I catch flashes of him in countless other men and women, and infants— he's a shake of the head, an innocuous movement, a flared nostril. I'll see him for a second in mental pictures as various and inconclusive as photographs. He's buried in many places.

His mother told him he was born on the Fourth of July, so he was an American baby. His birthday was a minor family mystery. He found out he was born on June 28, and for a while that's when we celebrated it. Then, he discovered, but I don't know how, maybe he finally dug out his birth certificate, that he was born on June 29. Right now I remember that for years he thought my birthday was the day after it is. He was never sure. I thought it was funny.

July 1992
Dream that my father has lost a tooth in the back of his mouth. There's a gaping hole in his gum, and it's bleeding. He is indifferent and seems not at all to care. In fact, he is buoyant and energetic, even happy and excited. He is not dead, as he usually is in my dreams. I'm living in a dismal, shabby apartment. A light fixture is damaged; I ask the landlady to repair it. But she says it's not her job. I say, I thought furnished apartments had to be taken care of by the owners. She says no. I walk around the apartment and discover a room that would be perfect for me to write in, and I feel happier about the place. But it's part of someone else's apartment, which I just enter. They're eating dinner, a big family sitting around a large table. They're not unfriendly, but they are surprised.

I accept some of the picture my father had of himself. Even if it's unclear or out of focus, in it he's in the body he liked. He's never just an idea, a thing, an abstraction, though he is by now the most absolute and resolute of abstractions, horribly abstract, in pieces, and undeniably and palpably only symbolic.

(Part of loving, maybe, is to love someone as he or she wants to be loved. I don't know. I can't make a decision about how to love him.)

When I was ten, I knew my father was aware of my body. My mother, father, and I had just been to my father's office, and we were crossing 42nd Street. I was walking ahead of my parents. A man bumped or knocked into me. I kept walking. But my father grabbed the man. He looked as if he was about to hit him, and shouted: I saw what you did. I could call the cops. I saw you. My father's rage, so often directed at us, turned on the stranger, a man. I'm not sure what happened next. I think my father glared at the man as he rushed away. My father stood there. (Should I write "impotently"? He may have experienced a lack in the language that defines and constructs lack for men, a diminution of "manly" power.) He wanted to murder the man who had felt up his pubescent daughter. And he must have known how incapable he was of stopping assaults on me by other men. I think I was aware of that then. My mother and I waited on the sidewalk and watched him as he continued to stand there. He was in the valley again. Then we walked on in silence. What had occurred was unspeakable. Though I was supposed to be the injured party, I wasn't taken care of. My narcissistic father, in a sense, suffered the greater blow, which I witnessed. It troubled me more than the man hitting against me. I was ignorant of what he was doing. If my father hadn't erupted, I wouldn't have known. I knew my father was hurt.

My father's most pungent advice about men was: "Don't be the omnipotent female and think you can change a man. You can't." My mother was always trying to change him, he thought. She couldn't, of course. He didn't hand out much advice about men. I don't think he really knew what to say to us about them, was too self-conscious, being one himself. (Dirty jokes bothered him, and he never told them. Was it because he had daughters or a strange, prohibiting, beloved mother?) I didn't talk to him about my boyfriends, anyway. But one time, when I was grown up, I received a letter from a man I was involved with, a poet. Paying attention to form, the poet wrote the sentences in circles, and to read the letter, I had to turn the paper around and around. My father watched as I read it. Finally, when I had finished, he said, almost indifferently: I'm glad I don't know people like that.

Even so, I prevailed upon him to give me something, a present, to offer to the poet, my erstwhile lover. Sheepishly, my father gave me a Cuban cigar. I could tell it was another ironic gesture.

(Is my father a delusion I shared with him? Was it shared?)

I suppose, though, the ironic gesture I remember most was more sustained, a trope of "masculinity" rather than a single gesture. It was my father's being the sole financial support of the family until his business began to do poorly, and my mother took a part-time job (by then I was fifteen or sixteen). If there was something about the traditional expectations set for men, about what men were supposed to do, that made them— my father—most vulnerable in my eyes, it was this: supporting the family. I studied my anxious father. He worried constantly, putting money in the stock market one day, taking it out the next. He wasn't much of a capitalist. (I think it's why I appreciate *Death of a Salesman*. It can be read as much for "the problems men face" as for "the problems men face under capitalism.")

January 1994
Dream my father dies, and I start to cry. My mother says: But you sat on his lap for two hours before he died.

I write and sit on his lap. I have my father, at least for two hours. Writing about him, I play with him, his body. Since he's dead, he can't object as I know he would if he were alive. But then I wouldn't write this if he were alive. He would hate it. Or he wouldn't countenance it. He'd turn his face away. My unabashed love for him was weird to him, but he acknowledged it. Two years before he died, he and my mother presented me with a framed photograph of him when he was five years old, taken by a photographer who traveled around on horseback. It's hand-tinted.

(What if he didn't love me? What if every interpretation I make is wrong? Is his love for me my necessary illusion? Questions and doubts propose their own resonant and inadequate "answers." When he was alive, his devastating tantrums and violence were a kind of natural disaster. We had a tempestuous relationship. We got along better on the telephone. But I can't relinquish a mostly flattering picture of him. Should I?)

Daddy dead is as unwieldy and vague and unpredictable and resilient and unsure as he was alive.

He loved the ocean.
He dived under big waves, swam far out, and did laps.
He liked to watch the owls in the baseball stadium in Florida, so he went
    to night games.
He was a graceful dancer.
He fed fish in the artificial pond behind his apartment.
He cooked leftovers with soy sauce, but most of it was inedible.

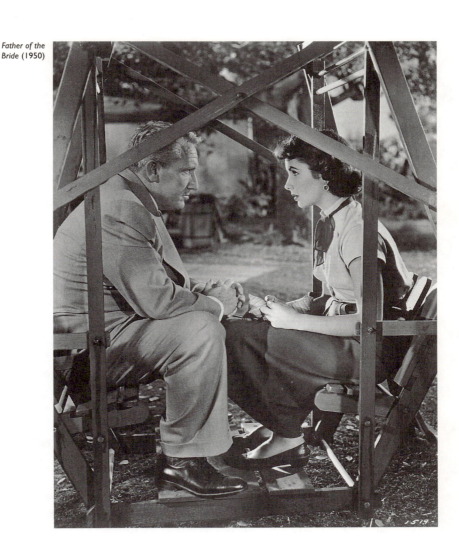

Father of the Bride (1950)

He clipped articles from the newspaper, showed them to me or mailed
them to me.
He always had a lot of change, which he placed on top of his chest of
drawers.
His drawers were messy.
He made faces.
He liked to pull out crabgrass from the lawn.
He had good eyesight and only late in life did he need reading glasses,
which he wore at the end of his nose.
He liked to nap after he ate.
He played gin every Tuesday night with four men who called him
"The Pelican," because he'd finish their food.
He became violently seasick on boats.
He fell asleep at the opera, when he and my mother had season tickets.
He hated sex scenes in movies and didn't like most movies, especially
toward the end of his life.
He loved salty food.
He liked to lecture.
He smoked cigars and pipes.
He was proud that his business had a good rating from Dun and Bradstreet.
He hated Mick Jagger.
He read books to find answers.
He prepared his taxes by himself.
He knew the words to one song only, his high school's: "We are the Boys of
Boys High," which he sang flat.

(My mother has a good singing voice. And she loves movies. She sees
everything, usually by herself. She even saw *The Silence of the Lambs*
alone. When I was a kid, I watched movies on TV with her a lot, and when
she dies, though it's impossible and I don't believe it, I'll go to the movies
without her. Movies could become my imaginary mother. And that will
be another story. Then I'll remember how my not-so-very-tough mother
looked when she asked, probably rhetorically, at the end of a movie on
TV: Lynne, what are you crying about? She says my father was not an
unhappy man.)

I could go on. It's futile. Writing emerges from it and records it, I think,
and the desire to set it down, get it out, get it down, put it out, him, his
stuff and mine, makes any writerly desire comic, converts a page turner

into a stomach turner. It turns my stomach. But then it is also absolutely what I want to do.

Without my consent and with it, totally, I'm driven to mark things out of a life that will end against its will. It's a death I can't write. Uncontrollable death is at the center, central to meaning, central to meaninglessness. Texts will be read in different ways at different times, to mean different things, if they're read at all. They're lively, living bodies. Or dead bodies. Like Daddy who's gone.

Nathan Tillman   June 29, 1908–August 7, 1984

Trinh T. Minh-ha

With Curse, or Love

Photo and text design by Trinh T. Minh-ha
and Jean-Paul Bourdier

Ecstasied

touching
living
the ecstasy
of an in-
finite moment
when riveted
lost bemused
in-timately
looking at
listening to
radiates
like a sweet madness

Drunk in the motions of the look
while the world tiptoes nearby

A Rainy Day

stepping in line
at the airport
ready for departure
alone instantly
I started blinking
wetting my shirt
sensing
with laughter outside
how long inside
it had been raining
how long
I had been carrying
the steam
the heat
the moisture
dew of night
glistening   amiss
the look
the pose
the voice
choking on lines
flooded with
                    sadness

the sob
welled up during the night
finally broke in
                    to tears

that night
by the shriek of pleasure
in the room down the hall
I was
literally moved
to dizziness
for eyes sealed
I lay awake
still
yet restless
my heart racing
till light broke through
                    the night

blaming you I
can't
but feeling it I do
so intensely I . . .   (can't finish the silly poem)

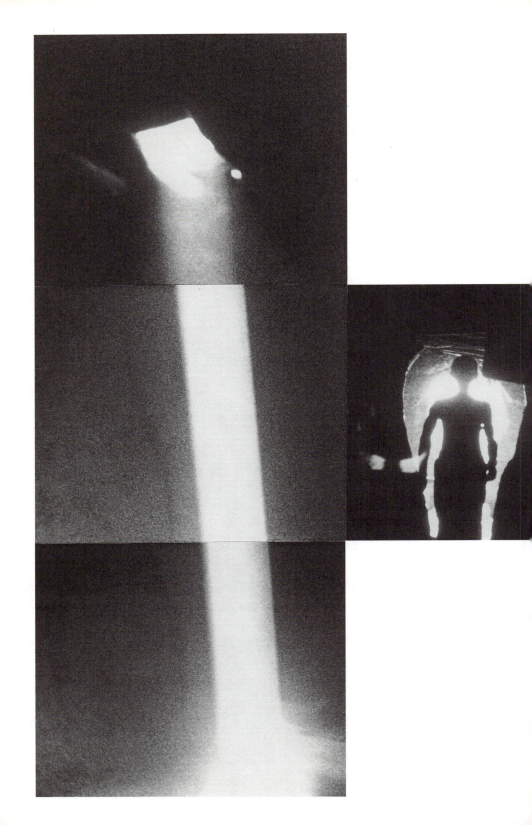

Looking at the Dream Screen

savoring
inhaling your presence purblind
enraptured by the closeness
our bodies hardly body
unable to hear taste see
while other lives unfold on the screen
a dream within dream after dream
that suspends bends
every minute spent side by side
mesmerized as if by the same
images

> *sapid*
> *sa-a-ppy*
> *sit and see*
> *but save the tongue*
> *after all*
> *can I how can I reach out*
> *with words*
> *when touching I can't never*
> *can feel all*
> *I ever feel is the dumb*
> *sleeve of your shirt*

violent forceful obstinate
so it seems with desire
whose power and excess
never fail thoughtless
to mistake wander for wonder
so when a dream in the dark
awakens our moonless bodies
life makes its demands
hitting where it hurts
engulfing all emotions
pretending it knows
how love through bondage
can be lodged in language

the worst thing
I'll have to recite this
twice a day
the worst thing
is to give
meaning to
something that
hasn't got
any

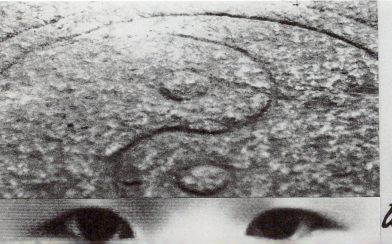

with time
I often wonder
how she fares

today
every nuance
in That voice
crazes her
like the unbearable
(impossible to love)
lustily persistent
(impossible to forget)
scent of musk
every time I hear it
I want to hit that door open
cross that senseless wall
with the savage passion of . . .

a wounded animal
knowing only
how to fling itself
straight at the man
who gives it pain

today
That absence
sets the landscape
afire
with melancholia
and her insides
burn down to ashes
then
sometimes I stop

Scent of Musk

breathing
as I walk down a street
feeling the sun
flowering on my face
so fiery hot
so blinding clear
it hurts

the short stay left its mark
as I now stare out
so strangely
at the familiar horizon
the sea down the hill
framing neatly
the distant cityscape

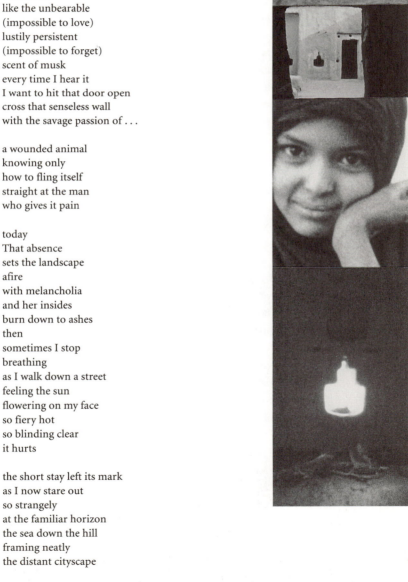

Casual Letter

Sometimes I'd rather see your look than your eyes. If I were to tell the story I would remember only this. In the aftermath of the collision they were, for a second, wordlessly exchanging looks. Caressing . . . no, fleetingly making love with their . . . eyes. There the story would stop. The rest becomes so blurred in my mind that if I continue I will have to divagate again into the open field of the mind's eye. The incident was unreal. I was unreal, light. Trying to prevent both confusion and lucidity to kill desire. Responses in words wavered pathetically between saying too much and saying nothing. In its demands for sensual attentiveness passion turns words into toads, making it impossible to venture into speaking without withdrawing speech. The splinters of a casual accident shattered the play of our dreaming bodies, leading me back to the open field of the mind's eye. . . . It may not be deliberate, but it often turned out to be sillily effective. The way you sometimes smashed the intense feeling of quiet festivity raised by your . . . patiently giving taking presence. Even in the very tenuous contact of the voice. Or in the interstices of it, where I caught in between two sentences a glimpse of a body accessed down to its guts. A sigh, a wordless exclamation, a sound comma, an onomatopoeia of the heart . . . The way you hardly reciprocate with the same, sorry, sickness. The lonely experience of disappointment and senseless anguish you succeed in generating always without your knowing it. Your casualness and apparent disengagement from all obsessive, excessive feelings. "Suffering a bit," as you would say, I am to remain at once monstrous in my demands and defenseless to the slightest injuries. A strange kind of suffering when no one is physically hurt. Constantly led to question the way I am, and I can't bear what I am in this twilight zone of reflection and emotion, I find myself measuring every giving gesture. Mine. Stop reacting with the skin. Mine. In my faulty moves I can blame only myself. Me. Imagination is held captive and ordered to come to an abrupt stop in its wild activities. Now when you affirm, I remain silent. Falling twice over, foolishly. For how could I fix my eyes on yours while searching for their look? Today I find myself puzzling instead, over the degree of their . . . intensity. How true? How far? What's in? You'll never give up yourself entirely, so you casually said. How true. The story goes that a beggar man thus spoke to a beggar woman: Why do you ask for so much? To which the woman answered, Why not, why not ask for more? I thought I'd never known her before, but here I am loving she who can, even when she can no longer

百花齊放

Let a hundred flowers bloom

Ma

To Myself I Say

every time
to myself I say the same
I can never imagine
the day I will write
on ending without end
sadly
someone said it too
the end always there
is in the beginning
I saw it forgot knew
now remember
too well ever to forget
so I must say to myself

This Body

babble away adore
I am not this fragile body
laughing as I mourn
mourning as I love

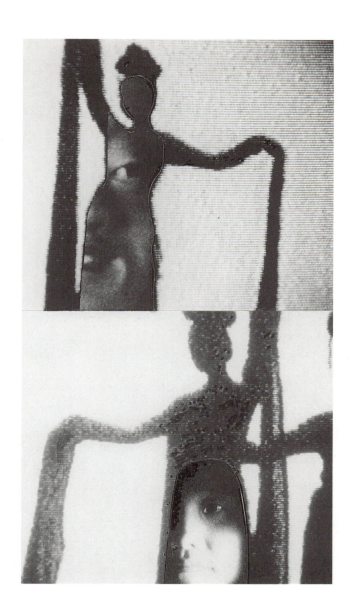

Vivian Sobchack

Revenge of *The Leech Woman*
On the Dread of Aging in a Low-Budget Horror Film

On Saturdays in Brooklyn, when I was a child, my younger sister and I used to go to the movies, where we'd sit all day watching the cartoons, coming attractions, and double feature loop themselves several times over until it was almost dark outside and we knew our mother was just starting to get anxious. I loved science fiction films, tolerated westerns, was indifferent to musicals and melodramas, and—like all the kids around me—squirmed whenever a couple kissed on screen. Both my sister and I loved horror films especially—at that time, before Psycho, *often set in the Carpathians, or at least not in Brooklyn, and remote from our quotidian life. Nonetheless, they still seemed close enough to fire our imaginations and make the walk home in the darkening twilight titillating and perilous. Insofar as my mother confirms my recollection, the wolf men, the Frankenstein monster and his bride, Dracula and his daughters, never invaded my dreams, but my more susceptible sister almost always had nightmares on Saturday nights. In contrast, I never found those early horror films all that horrible or really scary, although I did find them incredibly poetic, and I almost always identified with the monsters, whatever their gender (assuming they had one). Now, a grown woman and film scholar, I am surrounded by the intellectual discourse on horror, a discourse that is thoughtful but never quite gets to a description of my experiences—either then when I was very young and gloried in a sense of my own difference and its power, or now when I am middle-aged and often surprised by moments of fear and horror—both at the movies and in my life.*

The horror film has been seen by many contemporary, psychoanalytically oriented, feminist scholars as a misogynist scenario elaborated within a patriarchal and heterosexual social formation and based on the male fear of female sexuality. To put it simply and reductively, on the one hand, male fear is generated by male desire—and the power women have over its satisfaction. On the other hand, male fear is generated by female desire—the desire of the Other, which provokes the specter of male "lack" in the face of sexual difference and manifests itself in castration anxiety (an anxiety justified recently by Lorena Bobbitt's castration of her husband and revealed in his testimony that she was angry not because he repeatedly abused and raped her, but because he hadn't been able to satisfy her sexually). The elaboration of this male dread of women is played out in horror films at both manifest and latent levels, and all of us, whether practiced in psychoanalytic readings of popular culture or not, are certainly familiar with the genre's dual articulation of women as both "scared" and "scary." Generally speaking, these two "female conditions" are intimately and systemically related—not only to each other but also to the regulation of heterosexual desire and biological reproduction in patriarchal Western culture. Indeed, it is nearly impossible to think about the threat of "scary women" in horror films without recognizing that threat as emerging from a woman who, first, was scared. Nonetheless, perhaps because it's more interesting and certainly more empowering, feminist scholarly emphasis has been on the "scary" rather than "scared" women of the horror film and on describing the relation between the psychic dread they cinematographically engender and their sexual and reproductive potency.

Here, however, I want to talk about another sort of "scary woman" in the horror film—one whose scariness, while related to her sexuality, has less to do with power than with powerlessness, and whose scariness to men has less to do with sexual desire and castration anxiety than with abjection and death. Here I want to talk about the middle-aged woman who is both scared and scary—the woman who is neither lover nor mother, the woman who becomes excessive by virtue of her being regarded as excess. This is a woman who can't be dealt with as either the object or the subject of the gaze. Indeed, up until very recently and under the pressure of changing demographics and actuarial tables, in films (whether horror films or not) and in culture, she has been so threatening and disgusting a sight that the gaze slides quickly over her and disavows her visibility. Not yet static and frozen in time as a feisty but safe Jessica Tandy in *Driving Miss Daisy* and *Fried Green Tomatoes,* not yet clearly physically and peacefully "old" (as if there were such stasis, as if it would be sweet), this woman evokes in herself and to others the horror and fear of an inappropriate and transgressive sexual desire that lingers through the very process of aging, physical degradation, and decay.

Myself a fifty-three-year-old woman, this scary woman scares not only men but also me—although I am ashamed to admit it. Much as I attempt to counter my fear of aging with intellectual rationalization, cultural critique, or humor, I find myself unable to laugh off a recurrent image that truly horrifies me even as I joke about it. The image? It's me and yet her, an Other—and, as her subjective object of a face has aged, the blusher I've worn every morning since I was a teenager has migrated and condensed itself into two distinct and ridiculous red circles in the middle of her cheeks. This image—which correspondingly brings a subjective flush of shame and humiliation to my cheeks for the pity and unwilling horror and contempt with which I objectively regard hers—is that of an aging woman who not only deceives herself into thinking she is still young enough to wear makeup and poorly applies it, but who also inscribes upon her face the caricature both of her own desire and of all that was once (at least to some) desirable.

This, to me, is the image of a *really* scary woman—and all my demystified knowledge of the cultural practices that posit her as such do little to demythify or rob her of her negative-affective power to scare me. Subjectively felt, she engenders humiliation and its ancillary horrors. Objectively viewed, she is ludicrous, grotesque. Subjectively felt, she is an *excess woman*—desperately afraid of invisibility, uselessness, lovelessness, sexual and social isolation and abandonment, but also deeply furious at both the double standard of aging in a patriarchal culture and her acquiescence to male heterosexist values and the self-contempt they engender. Objectively viewed, she is sloppy, self-pitying, and abjectly needy or she is angry, vengeful, powerful, and scary. Indeed, she is an *excessive woman*, a woman in masquerade, in whiteface. She is the Leech Woman, the Wasp Woman, the 50 Foot Woman. She is Norma Desmond and whatever happened to Baby Jane.

This quasi-autobiographical confession is meant to point to the doubled nature and complex phenomenological affect of the cinematic figuration I want to address here—namely, the explicit engendering of the cultural fear, loathing, and anger directed at the mortal fact and process of physical aging in the scared and scary women of a number of low-budget horror/science fiction films made in the American context, primarily from the late 1950s through the mid-1960s. In chronological order of release these are *Attack of the 50 Ft. Woman* (1958), *The Wasp Woman* (1959), and *The Leech Woman* (1960), this last providing my primary or "tutor" text for its explicit and sustained focus on the process and horrors of aging. Indeed, in their variations on a theme, all three films are explicit.

Yet explicitness is relative. I first saw these films while still in my teens and yet I must not have seen them at all. I do remember the nameless pleasure I felt when each of the female characters—"transformed" from scared to scary by extraterrestrial contact or special serum—was suddenly empowered to carry out excessive acts of vengeance. I don't recall, however, thinking specifically about the reasons for this vengeance; nor, even though I was female, do

I remember feeling uncomfortable with the way these women were figured in their scared, pre-scary, state. The boys in the audience—in all likelihood simultaneously disgusted, titillated, and scared by the sight of someone the age of their mothers still radiating desire—were intending toward the moment when their fear and desire would take visible shape to prove its monstrousness. However, I, a girl still in my teens, was also directed toward that moment. Not only did I, too, find it disgusting to think that my mother still "did it," but what did such an alien state as middle age have to do with me? Thus, as I watched these women, like the boys, my highly conventionalized disgust and fear was of them, not for them. Nonetheless, unlike the boys, I think I sensed the pleasure of their revenge.

Attack of the 50 Ft. Woman tells the story of Nancy, a wealthy, childless, middle-aged woman unhappily married to a philanderer and prone to sloppy drinking. (We're told she's been in a private sanitarium for treatment.) After a close encounter with a (please don't laugh) "space ball" and the giant alien man within it, she collapses and is taken home to eventually—impossibly—awaken 50 feet tall in a bedroom too small to hold her. Using her bedclothes as a bra and sarong, she strides off to town and the roadhouse where her husband is romancing a younger woman (generically named "Honey"). As one shocked male bystander says to another as she passes: "She'll tear up the whole town till she finds Harry . . . and then she'll tear up Harry." Calling her husband's name, she pulls off the roof of the roadhouse and plucks him out, only to be killed (and to kill him) by electrocution from felled power lines. However hysterical both the 50 Foot Woman and the special effects, there is a sober side to this tale of a woman's humiliation and revenge. Toward the beginning of the film, as Nancy lies in her bedroom after her close encounter but before her transformation, downstairs her doctor speaks to the concerned family butler about her "wild story" and strange behavior and says: "When women reach the age of maturity, Mother Nature sometimes overworks their frustration to a point of irrationalism. Like the middle-aged man of our age who finds himself looking longingly at a girl in her early twenties." If this non-sequitur analysis makes us raise our eyebrows, consider the following from Freud, writing on obsessional neurosis in 1913:

> It is well known, and has been a matter for much complaint, that women often alter strangely in character after they have abandoned their genital functions. They become quarrelsome, peevish, and argumentative, petty and miserly; in fact, they display sadistic and anal-erotic traits which were not theirs in the era of womanliness.[1]

There is a half-truth hidden somewhere here, but it has nothing to do with some inherent postgenital transformation and everything to do with a sense of lovelessness, a sense of being invisible and untouchable. There was a period in my middle age when I felt dried up and experienced an aridity that had nothing to do with a postmenopausal lack of vaginal lubrication. Rather, the phenomenological truth of this sense of desiccation, this "dry spell" in my affective and sexual life, was grounded in what seemed a forced exclusion from the sexual economy, from the sensual, a deprivation of the caresses from another that make one sensitive to one's own skin. Peevish, argumentative, sadistic? You bet. The desire to assert one's bodily and desiring existence knows no bounds, and is indeed 50 feet tall.

The Wasp Woman is a much simpler film; Roger Corman, who made it, went straight to the surface of the matter. The film essentially begins in an executive boardroom with a severely dressed and bespectacled middle-aged woman executive coldly chewing out what appear to be her male subordinates for the company's poor sales. We find out that she is Janet Starlin, a single woman of forty, who heads a now fading cosmetics empire. The reason for its recent failures? A daring male executive tells her, "It's because of you." He explains that people were used to seeing her picture in the advertisements, which read, "Return to Youth with Janet Starlin," but now that she's aged and her picture no longer appears in the ads, the consumer no longer feels any product identification. Fixed on remedying her situation in all ways, Janet speaks to her chemists about the royal bee jelly they've been using and inquires whether wasp jelly might have a more dramatic effect on forestalling the aging process. They're not buying any; as one puts it, "Socially, the queen wasp is on a par with the black widow." Janet, however, looks to her own devices and finds a scientist willing to experiment with wasps. Eventually he finds a serum that not only reduces but also reverses the aging process. Watching the rejuvenation of lab animals, Janet does not want to wait for FDA approval, first offering herself as a human guinea pig and then—after she does begin to look younger—stealing into the lab to administer more and larger injections. She looks twenty-two and gorgeous for her stated forty years, but there are side effects: Overdosed with the royal wasp jelly serum, she regularly turns into a Wasp Woman—that is, a woman in a sheath dress and heels, with the head of a wasp and the urge to kill. Eventually, of course, after the non-gender-specific murders of a number of people, she is killed herself. *The Wasp Woman*, then, is a simple but paradoxical little cautionary tale: "There are some things that woman is not meant to *know*," i.e., the secret of rejuvenation; and yet there are some things she must always *be,* i.e., "young." What is most interesting about the film is that, watching it, one gets the feeling that Janet Starlin's monstrousness has less to do with the fact that she is a single, independent, and powerful corporate executive than it has to do with her age. As one psychotherapist wrote in a revisionist "self-help" book several decades after the film was made: "Ageism is, in fact, the last bastion of sexism. . . . The last mental barrier to equality is the almost visceral disgust for the older woman as a physical being."[2] This same psychotherapist relates that, perhaps unaware of *The Wasp Woman,* a friend told her: "I'm prepared to die, but not to look lousy for the next forty years."[3]

Now, fifty-three, in front of the mirror, I look at my face and contem-plate—with desire and fear—cosmetic, plastic, surgery. My skin is still good for those who never saw it before (when I was young). But my eyelids are wrinkled, and a crease runs downward from the right side of my mouth and makes me look less happy than I am. I pull my facial skin up taut and I do see myself again rather than my mother when she was middle-aged. But I am also afraid that if I do it, if I really do it, they'll go for the broad stroke and I'll emerge with a face I don't recognize as mine. Which is ironic, because right now, looking in the mirror, the face I see is also a face I never quite recognize as mine. I am, of course, appalled more by my desire than by my fear. I'm an intellectual, a feminist, and supposed to know better. But still I care. I, too, am prepared to die but not to look lousy for the next forty years.

The Leech Woman, as I've said, is the most complex of the three films in bringing together the self-abjection and drunken sloppiness of the despised and neglected middle-aged wife with the science fictional rejuve-nation fantasies that will supposedly—and superficially—do away with the need to resolve social problems that are far more than skin deep. The plot deserves a somewhat detailed recounting not only for its explicit and ongo-ing address of the humiliation and abjection suffered by middle-aged women, and the justified rage they feel and often express in excessive acts, but also for its recurrent dramatization of the disgust and dread their physical presence engenders in men.

June Talbot is forty-something and a self-pitying yet self-aware drunk. (Drinking in these films, for middle-aged women, is clearly coded to con-note disgusting and excessive behavior and physical sloppiness.) At the film's beginning, a nasty confrontation with her endocrinologist husband at his office convinces her to give him the divorce he wants. He is visited, however, by a wizened, mysterious African woman named Mala, who proves to him that she has the secret to an age-retarding powder and a rejuvenating serum. She persuades him to finance her journey back to the Nandos tribe from which she was taken over 140 years before by slavers. Greedy for wealth and knowledge, the doctor cancels his divorce plans, professes his need for June (which goes only as far as his need for a human guinea pig), and, guided by a local hunter, they both take off after Mala into the wilds of a stock-footage African jungle. During the trek, June wonders why her husband is so cold toward her, only to be reassured rather easily by a cursory, contemptuous, and momentary display of affection. Soon, however, June realizes his intentions to use her as an experimental subject and runs off into the jungle, to be saved and brought back by the handsome white hunter. Shortly after, the three are captured and brought to the Nandos village, where Mala tells them that they will learn her secret but must die when she dies the next morning.

That night the three outsiders watch a ritual ceremony with Mala at its center. The scene and the speech that prefaces it are extraordinary. In the midst of this low-budget and ridiculously colonial vision of "primitive" African tribal life, the words of old and wizened Mala lose none of their resonance, righteousness, and power. She says to those who watch:

> For a man, old age has rewards. If he is wise, his gray hairs bring dignity and he is treated with honor and respect. But for the aged woman, there is nothing. At best, she's pitied. More often, her lot is of contempt and neglect. What woman lives who has passed the prime of her life who would not give her remaining years to reclaim even a few moments of joy and happiness and know the worship of men. For the end of life should be its moment of triumph. So it is with the aged women of Nandos, a last flowering of love, beauty— before death.

The secret of Mala's rejuvenation is revealed. *Nipe* (the pollen from a rare jungle orchid) is mixed with the pineal hormones of a male victim, who must be stabbed fatally at the base of his neck with a special ring that extracts the fluid. The now youthful (and lighter-skinned) Mala rises beautiful, proud, and imperious and tells them that while they must die with her the next morning, the night is theirs, and she offers June her youth again. Morally horrified by the murder necessary for rejuvenation, June refuses, but her husband urges her to accept as a cover for his and the guide's escape. Cursorily, he tells her that, of course, he will return and rescue her. June now clearly grasps her situation, and she agrees. And when she is told that she may pick any male to supply the pineal hormone, she surveys the village men, then wheels around and chooses her husband. (Mala says, "You have made an excellent choice. You will have beauty and revenge at the same time.")

June is transformed into a gorgeous young woman, and the guide is entranced. He finds a way for them to escape, bringing with them the pouch containing the *nipe* and the lethal ring. They make love in the bush. June, however, starts to age, as the effect of the serum is temporary, and each time it wears off it leaves the user older than before. The amorous guide not only proves fickle but is also horrified and disgusted. He withholds the *nipe* from June and tries to leave her. In the process, he becomes trapped in quicksand, and June—extracting the pouch as the price of his rescue—coolly leaves him to die. She returns to America as her own niece, although she resumes her own persona when she ages and must find a new victim. As her niece, she romances the young family lawyer, whose fiancée, Sally, is determined not to let the intruding sexpot interfere with her marital future. As herself, out to find a source of pineal hormone, June dresses in widow's weeds adorned with expensive, visible jewelry, frequents the seamy side of town, and picks up a man who takes her to a secluded spot, admires her jewels, asks, "You dig young guys, honey?" and if she has any relatives, and then attempts to strangle her. Instead, she murders him. The film's denouement occurs after Sally, brandishing a gun, visits the "niece" (now clad in lamé lounge pajamas, and icing champagne for a tryst) and warns her to stay away from the lawyer. June scuffles with Sally, knocks her out, extracts the girl's pineal hormones for future use, and then begins a romantic evening with the young lawyer. The police arrive—apparently some of June's identification was found near her previous victim's body— and during the questioning, June begins to age. She excuses herself and mixes the *nipe* with Sally's hormones, but the female pineal fluid doesn't work. "I killed Sally for nothing," she says in horror. Downstairs the police hear a crash and a scream and break into June's bedroom. From the open window, they see her body—dead and incredibly decrepit on the ground below.

The Leech Woman and its companions are extraordinary texts—no less for their explicit address of the horrors of female aging in a patriarchal society than for an awe-inspiring obviousness that threatens to strike the film exegete dumb. Indeed, insofar as *The Leech Woman* lets its real cultural fears "all hang out," it thwarts the scholarly elaboration of psychic processes of displacement and condensation, of poetic processes of metaphor and metonymy. The hermeneutic challenge of the film and its earlier companions comes not from their breathtaking literalness, their astonishing demonic prosody, but rather from the complex allegories of reading they suggest. That is, the figuration of such excessive and excess women prompts us, as James Clifford writes of ethnographic allegory, to say of these films "not 'this represents, or symbolizes, that' but rather, 'this is a (morally charged) *story* about that.'"[4] The story here is about aging, desire, and the body, and its moral charge is derived from the double standard of which Mala speaks, a standard that elicits a complex of engendered emotions from both the women and the men who bear it: fear, humiliation, abjection, shame, power, rage, and guilt. Furthermore, this story and its moral and emotional charge have not changed very much since the 1950s and 1960s; it can be read across the history of American film, beginning perhaps with the breakdown of the extended family (an effect of the rise of urban centers), but coming to the foreground in the post–World War II period, which marked the cultural repression of a great many working and independent wartime women back into the patriarchal home, now dislocated to the featureless, cultureless suburbs. This period seems marked by the phenomenological awareness that many middle-class women, barring motherhood, had nothing to do, an awareness that war brides were aging, possibly unfulfilled and "frustrated." Coincidentally, this period also saw the proliferation of high technologies developed during the war throughout the public sphere, where they intersected with, among other institutions, medicine and the biological sciences to create a science fictional milieu that gave rise not only to the generic emergence of science fiction feature films but also to a notion of a technologized and, ultimately, perfectible human body.

Indeed, although it is true that women have "come a long way, baby" since the end of World War II, the increasingly technologized quotidian life of our culture since the war suggests that a phenomenology of contemporary body consciousness would reveal that the "progress" of coming "a long way, *baby*" is intimately tied to fantasies of rejuvenation and agelessness. With "advances" in electronic and medical technologies and new aerobicized forms of Taylorism come the promise of bodily overhauls, replacement parts, and a fulfilled, if rigidly disciplined, existence as an ageless "lean, mean machine." Hence, for heterosexual women, there has been an increasing emphasis on looking—if not staying—young and an increasing contempt for those "undisciplined" bodies unable or unwilling to "pull themselves together," "stay in shape," or regularly avail themselves of cosmetic surgery. *Death Becomes Her* says it all. Hence also, for both heterosexual and homosexual men, the current ideal is the ageless "hard body" of the "cyborg" (whose pecs—Donna Haraway notwithstanding—are certainly not those of a liberated woman).[5] Despite the sacrificial ending of *Terminator 2*, the Terminator is never terminal; what resonates is the immortal promise: "I'll be back."

I, too, am about to become a cyborg, although what I value about the experience has less to do with cheating death than with rejuvenation. My leg having been amputated recently because of recurrent cancer, and a number of operations having forced me into increasing physical inactivity, I now find myself learning to use a prosthesis. I look forward not only to being enabled again but also to wearing high heels. And, after months of extreme and rigorous exercise, all the clothes I never gave away fit me again. In anger at its built-in self-criticism, I gave up dieting years ago and, hardly a glutton, worked on accepting myself "as I was." Nonetheless, slim has always gone with young, and now I'm overjoyed at my weight loss and do feel younger. There is something truly perverse at work here: I feel less the loss of the leg than the loss of weight. I feel more attractive and younger now that there is less of me. And I didn't have to diet. This is the power of the cyborg woman—and, although ironical, hardly the irony out of which liberation is wrested.

Today—even more than in the decades in which films like *The Leech Woman* or *Whatever Happened to Baby Jane?* were made—the visibly aging body represents a challenge to the self-deluding fantasies of immortality that mark the dominant technoculture. Furthermore, in a sexist as well as ageist technoculture, the visibly aging body of a woman has been and still is especially terrifying—not only to the woman who experiences self-revulsion and anger, invisibility and abandonment, but also to the men who find her presence so unbearable that they must—quite literally—"disavow" her and divorce her. As one psychologist dealing with aging relates: "I once heard a man say to his gray-haired wife, without rancor: 'I only feel old when I look at you.'"[6] And another writes:

> There are male archetypes of death—the grim reaper, the skeleton. Perhaps it would be more accurate to say that they are neutral, because of their impersonal quality. They symbolize abstract mortality. But aging with its catalog of fleshly indignities is the human face of death, and it is a woman's face. There is no male counterpart to the witch or hag ... [and here I would add the Wasp Woman and the Leech Woman] or any male figure who rivals the horror and loathing she inspires. She is the scapegoat par excellence for our fear of aging.[7]

Julia Kristeva, in dealing with the phenomenon of abjection and its relation to horror, suggests that abjection has various forms. Particular to the exploration of the issues of female aging I've dealt with here is her distinction between the abject that comes from without and the abject that comes from within. The abject that comes from without includes "excrement and its equivalents (decay, infection, disease, corpse, etc.)," which "stand for the danger to identity that comes from without: the ego threatened by the non-ego, society threatened by its outside, life by death."[8] These excess middle-aged women of low-budget horror films, these visibly decaying bodies that reach out to touch a man who recoils in horror, these "non-egos" who threaten society less by their rage than by their presence, certainly engender this form of the abject.

In contrast, the abject that comes from within is described thus:

> Cells fuse, split, and proliferate; volumes grow, tissues stretch, and body fluids change rhythm, speeding up or slowing down. Within the body, growing as a graft, indomitable, there is an other. And no one is present, within that simultaneously dual and alien space, to signify what is going on.[9]

While Kristeva makes reference to pregnancy and cancer as possible forms of inner abjection, her description also holds for the bodily changes in the 50 Foot Woman, the Wasp Woman, and the Leech Woman. Within the transformed, monstrous, and visible bodies of these women divided against themselves in desperation, anger, and self-loathing, there is indeed an "other." As psychotherapist Elissa Melamed suggests in her book *Mirror, Mirror: The Terror of Not Being Young*: "We often experience the changes of aging as somehow alien to us, as if the 'real self' is frozen in time, imprisoned somewhere within the aging body."[10] Thus, abjection suffered by the women aging in the horror film is doubled. Is it any wonder that they cannot possibly survive?

It is now a commonplace to acknowledge the complicity of ageism and sexism in white heterosexist culture in the United States. Professionals and academics across a range of disciplinary areas have pointed to the social and economic problems consequent to the cultural practice of regarding the growing number of older women in our society "like guests who have tactlessly worn out their welcome," who are seen "not as a resource, but as a 'problem.'"[11] The opening image I presented as "my" scary woman belongs not only to me but also to others. Along with the "bag lady" or the "cat lady," she exists as the abject, excess, excessive figure of a great many women in our culture—including the psychotherapist I just quoted above, who recalls a woman she saw at a hairdresser's: "her skin . . . plastered with a tannish coating, further overlaid with spots of pinkish color. Only her eyeballs and the inside of her mouth were recognizably human tissue."[12] She continues:

> As I look back, I am not proud of what I felt: a mixture of pity, scorn, and above all, denial that [she] could have anything to do with me. . . . Why couldn't she see herself? And I told myself loudly

that this could never happen to me. . . . Yet one day, the memory
. . . came back to haunt me. Somehow or other, I too was now over
forty. I didn't really like it—even worse, I was ashamed to admit
that I really didn't like it. . . .

As a psychotherapist, I realized that I was obviously dealing with
something deeper than some wrinkles and gray hairs. I was feeling
divided . . . against myself: a changeless person trapped inside a
changing body; a centered person at odds with a needy person;
an honest person ashamed of the "me" who wanted to play the
youth game.[13]

The prose here might seem simple, but the phenomenology of the experience of this process of change is complex and alien—however much we
are now intellectually aware of the self-displacing, decentered, constantly
mutable subject. At least in our fantasies, many of us would still rather be
the scary woman that is the beautiful, frozen mask of Catherine Deneuve
in *The Hunger* than the chilling whiteface of the self-deluded Baby Jane.

*And yet, there is a passion that speaks to me in Bette Davis's grotesque
performance as the child star who never grew up but did grow old in* Whatever
Happened to Baby Jane? *(1962). That painted face, expressing glee and spite,
pleases and excites me in its outrageousness and its outrage. Ludicrous, grotesque, overpowdered and rouged, mascara and lipstick bleeding into and
around her wrinkled eyes and mouth, Davis's Jane is a manic proclamation
of an energy that does not want containment, that refuses invisibility and
contempt. I feel her somewhere deep within me even as I want to avert my eyes
and not look upon my possible future.*

*At the post office this week, I—a middle-aged woman in good clothes and
great shape (but for want of a leg)—stood in line in front of an old woman in
mismatched clothes who had padded toward me on flat feet. Acutely aware of
her because of this essay, I wondered how scared and scary she was and why.
I saw no transgressive desire on her face—only a misshapen package in her
arms. And if she had a rage to live, it certainly wasn't evident in her comport-
ment. I could not tell if she was scared, but what scared me was her clothing.
She wasn't in rags, but the colors and patterns clashed, had not been in any
way coordinated, and her clothing seemed merely a bodily covering, put on
as an afterthought. The dread she elicited from me was, on the one hand,
economic. Like the "bag lady" and the more genteel "cat lady," she embodied
my fear of not being able to "take care of myself," and her ragtag clothing
marked the social reality of an increasing number of elderly women living on
impossibly inadequate incomes who are lucky to merely "make do." On the
other hand, however, the dread was existential, if certainly also acculturated.
Not being able to "take care of myself" presaged a slide into "not caring"—*

not caring how I looked, not caring whether or not I "pulled myself together," not even caring about the sensual pleasures I used to get from color or from silk on my skin. This was a not caring that was hardly liberating, merely defeating. I think (although I'm not absolutely sure) I would rather inappropriately, transgressively, gleefully tap dance (prosthesis and all), wear makeup and a bow in my hair, and spite the world around me when I am really old—particularly if it remains the world it is. This would be the real revenge: to insist that I am alive and in the world and ever full of desire.

Notes

1 Sigmund Freud, "The Predisposition to Obsessional Neurosis," in *Collected Papers*, ed. James Strachey (New York: Basic Books, 1959), 2, 130.
2 Elissa Melamed, *Mirror, Mirror: The Terror of Not Being Young* (New York: Linden Press/Simon & Schuster, 1983), 30.
3 Ibid., 42.
4 James Clifford, "On Ethnographic Allegory," in *Writing Culture: The Poetics and Politics of Ethnography*, ed. James Clifford and George E. Marcus (Berkeley: University of California Press, 1986), 100.
5 Donna Haraway, "A Manifesto for Cyborgs," *Socialist Review 80* (1985), 65–107.
6 "On Gray Hair and Oppressed Brains," in *Women, Aging and Ageism,* ed. Evelyn R. Rosenthal (New York: The Haworth Press, 1990), 38.
7 Melamed, 54.
8 Julia Kristeva, *The Powers of Horror: An Essay on Abjection*, trans. Leon S. Roudiez (New York: Columbia University Press, 1982), 71.
9 Julia Kristeva, *Desire in Language* (Oxford: Basil Blackwell, 1980), 11.
10 Melamed, 47.
11 Ibid., 25.
12 Ibid., 9.
13 Ibid., 10–11.

Scott Bukatman

X-Bodies
(the torment of the mutant superhero)

1. Origin Stories

I don't read superhero comics anymore. I'm probably not as worried about
my dick as I used to be. Well, *that* isn't exactly true—but I no longer deal
with it by reading about mutant musclemen and the big-titted women who
love them. I still read comics: several alternative titles (*Hate, Eightball,
Dirty Plotte*) continue to engage, and there've been *Sandman* and *Swamp
Thing* to look forward to, but it's those costumed characters, always fighting
(whether for truth and justice, or because it's what they do—and *they're
the best at what they do*—or because it beats working), that have lost their
charm, their appeal, and their relevance to my life. When I was contacted
by the *Uncontrollable Bodies* folks, I wasn't sure whether they were respond-
ing to my work on electronic identity or my earlier study of Jerry Lewis.[1]
The not-so-hidden moral was that my work was more invested in bodily
control, its lack and loss, and the fragmentation of identity than I'd sus-
pected. Meanwhile, here were these hyperbolic, dual-identified bodies that
I would ignore each week in my search for more "adult" comics. Those
superbodies, it must be said, made me nervous. Clearly it was time to jack
back into superhero culture, to see what was happening, and to whom.

Elsewhere I have argued that narratives constitute adaptive technologies: the metaphorical cyberspaces of William Gibson's *Neuromancer*
allowed a wholly legitimate envisioning of the invisible spaces of information circulation (Bukatman 1993). In its turn, that envisioning permitted a
reconception of human possibility within electronic culture. More than just
a mythological reconciliation, an illusion, fiction yields what Jameson has
called a "cognitive mapping" of a (possibly reconfigured) subject into an
intolerable space (1991, 54). When it's working, narrative can become a
testing ground for the conditions of being. Peter Brooks has written that
"modern narratives appear to produce a semioticization of the body which

is matched by a somatization of story: a claim that the body must be a source and a locus of meanings, and that stories cannot be told without making the body a prime vehicle of narrative significations" (1993, xii). Admittedly, Brooks is writing of Proust and Lawrence, not of Plastic Man or The Thing; still, I would maintain that superhero narratives do present a significant somatization of modernist and postmodernist social concerns. Superhero comics embody social anxiety, especially regarding the adolescent body and its status within adult culture. Superhero bodies are mysterious, invested with magical abilities and a metamorphic pliability; if they are marginal bodies in the body of high literature, this still should not blind us to their importance. "So far from using bodily magic as an escape," the anthropologist Mary Douglas argues, "cultures which frankly develop bodily symbolism may be seen to use it to confront experience with its inevitable pains and losses. By such themes they face the great paradoxes of existence." (1966, 120).

Superhero comics present body narratives, bodily fantasies, that incorporate (incarnate) aggrandizement and anxiety, mastery and trauma. Comics narrate the body in stories and envision the body in drawings. The body is obsessively centered upon. It is contained and delineated, becomes irresistible force and immovable object. The body is enlarged and diminished, turned invisible or made of stone, blown to atoms or reshaped at will. The body defies gravity, space, and time; it divides and conquers; it turns to fire, lives in water, is lighter than air. The body takes on animal attributes; it merges with plant life and melds with metal. The body is asexual and homosexual, heterosexual and hermaphroditic. Even the mind becomes a body, telepathic, telekinetic, transplantable, and controllable. Brainiac's brain sticks out of the top of his head, on display as part of a visible, external body. The body is an accident of birth, or a freak of nature, or a consequence of technology run wild. The superhero body is everything—a *corporeal*, rather than a *cognitive*, mapping of the subject into a cultural system.

Anyone who thinks that the superhero heyday has passed has only to step into a comics store to see rack upon rack of zingy new titles. The X-Men are TV and arcade game stars; Batman is in the movies and on TV; and new publishing ventures are burgeoning.[2] TV and cinema want to appropriate the mass-market merchandising mega-clout of the superhero genre. Even Superman made it back into the papers (though the reports of his death were greatly exaggerated). The superhero, a popular icon since the 1930s, has become newly, and increasingly, ubiquitous.

At the center of the revival are the X-Men, once relatively minor characters in the Marvel Comics pantheon. The original stories from the middle '60s lacked the cosmic grandeur of Stan Lee and Jack Kirby's *Fantastic Four* or *Thor* comics or the nerdy charm of *The Amazing Spiderman* by Lee and Steve Ditko, but there was something of interest in the title's exploration of adolescent alienation. Recruited by the telepathic Professor Xavier, the X-Men are teenaged mutants, powerful but undisciplined. Under the cover of his exclusive School for Gifted Youngsters, Professor X teaches his X-Men to control their powers in order to face the threat posed by "evil mutants" bent (of course) on the domination of humanity. When a re-vamped and more powerful mutant team was launched in the '70s, however, the title caught on with adolescent readers. Replacing the all-white antics of The Beast, Iceman, Angel, Marvel Girl, and Cyclops was a more ethnically and visually diverse bunch. The Beast became more bestial, Cyclops more tormented; Marvel Girl was reborn as Phoenix, and an African woman known as Storm took over the leadership of the team. The mysterious, violent, nearly indestructible Wolverine became one of the most popular characters in comics. Scripts by Chris Claremont emphasized domestic interaction and introspection. *The Uncanny X-Men* spawned numerous offshoots, including *X-Men, X-Force, X-Factor, X-Men 2099*, and limited series with individual characters (especially Wolverine). The mutants provided enough torment and combat to propel the super-hero revival that continues today, a revival fueled by inexhaustible reserves of adolescent angst.

The revival continued, and in the '90s revisionism took a dark turn. Superman died (none-too-poetically—he was *beat up*) and came back with Daniel Day-Lewis's hair, Batman broke his back and returned in a semi-cyborged state, and Marvel unleashed darker versions of its own classic heroes. Most of this was in response to the rise of Image Comics, the fastest-growing company in the history of the medium. Image was formed by some renegade writers and artists from the mainstream houses (mostly Marvel), and its roster includes some of the hotter names in the business. Their titles clog the shelves just as in-house advertisements clog their pages. The Image titles specialize in even more intensely exaggerated visualizations of the (barely) human body; there is a powerful hysteria working beneath the surface of muscles, cleavage, masks, and laser beams.

Superhero comics remain a largely subcultural phenomenon, produced largely by young males for somewhat younger males. The recent boom in comics sales in the United States dates from the early '80s, when specialty stores arose to cater to an obsessively knowledgeable audience. Titles began to be produced for this "direct sales" market—these were readers who knew what they wanted, and the industry was only too happy to oblige. As in *Trek* fandom, the lines between creators and consumers have been very permeable, and today's fanboy reader may be tomorrow's writer, artist, editor, or publisher (copyright control has shifted somewhat from companies to creators). Most recently, there has been an explosion of so-called collectibles, and T-shirts, caps, action figures, trading cards, stamps, pins, watches, and "special" editions with embossed-foil (or even holographic) covers have provided still more opportunities for unrestrained consumption.

The following does not pretend to be an ethnography of superhero comics culture—I haven't done the research. I have relied on a conjunction of theoretical and ethnographic writings: Klaus Theweleit on the soldier-male, Wolfgang Schivelbusch on industrial shock, Alan Klein on the "comic book masculinity" of bodybuilding subculture (1993, 8), and Mary Douglas on bodily rituals as social symbolism.[3] I want to demonstrate that what the superhero embodies are ambivalent and shifting attitudes toward flesh, self, and society. Where once superhero comics whimsically presented bodies armored against the shocks of industrial society, too many current characters now seem to simply incarnate problematic and painfully reductive definitions of masculine power and presence. In the 1970s and '80s, mutant superheroes gained in popularity, and these *X-bodies* encourage an alternative understanding of the superbody hieroglyph (one that coexists with hypermasculine fantasy). The mutant body is explicitly traumatic, armored against the world outside yet racked and torn apart by complex forces within. The mutant body is oxymoronic, rigidly protected but dangerously unstable. In its infinite malleability and overdetermined adolescent iconography, the mutant superhero is a locus of bodily ritual.

There is also an autobiography entrenched in this essay, and I'm forced to realize that the autobiographical subject isn't me, the adolescent dreaming of bodily strength and cosmic consciousness, but me, the adult academic who feels compelled to write about superhero comic books. At 7 a.m. one Sunday, in bed with someone that I'm no longer in bed with, I opened my eyes and had a magic thought: *mutant superheroes*. A fertile field, encapsulating a striking number of body issues, but the topic was perfect in another way—it was true to my reputation, and when people asked what I was working on, I could wear an expression of embarrassed pride and say, *Mutant superheroes!* People could cluck knowingly, laugh

X-Factor no. 92
Scott Lobdell,
writer
Joe Quesada,
writer and
artist

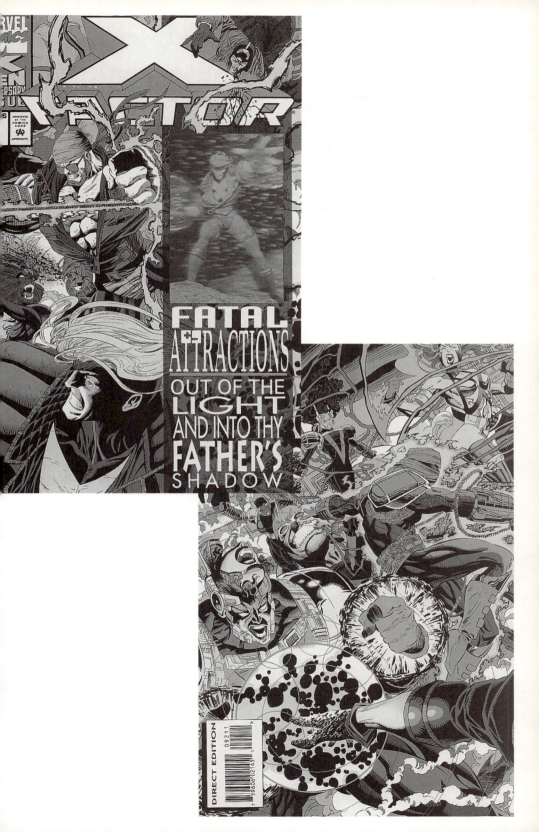

appreciatively, or leave quickly. *Oh, that Scott!* they would say. I tried it out at a couple of parties.

Beyond the not-so-shocking shock value of comics, though, I *do* like the things. In early drafts of this essay I "sutured" the complex pleasures I derive from comics to the reductive discourses of the academy; the very approach I abhor the most. Academia presented me with an imperfect double of my self—*Bizarro Scott*—and now it was clobberin' time. I had to rediscover my fondness for the medium, and for the genre of superhero fantasy, without surrendering my intellectualism. I needed to recapture my own fragmented experience—my trauma, my anxiety, my hurt, my humor, my play, my intelligence, my body, my grace, my clumsiness, my fantasy, and my creativity. This would be my greatest battle.

The writing process has taken its toll. To walk up to the hip chick working the register at St. Marks Comics, a woman who clearly doesn't care whether Wolverine is stronger than Lobo, requires nerves of steel. I had established myself as something of a groove-meister, buying the latest alternatives and Vertigo grunge-horror books, but now I was clutching back issues of *Spawn* and *Cyber Force*. I would ask for separate receipts in a pathetic attempt to separate myself from my "research" purchases, but it was useless. I had clearly lost all hipster credibility. . . .

2. Industrial Strength

I have a picture of myself at about age eight, dressed as Green Lantern. I think (I hope, I *pray*) that it was Halloween. GL was always my favorite of the "classic" superheroes; there was that streamlined costume (no cape!), the power ring, and the secret oath.[4] The ring worked by sheer force of will—thought made physical. In the pages of *Dr. Strange*, Steve Ditko would endow mystical rays and magical incantations with an eerie physicality all their own, but the world of Green Lantern was more familiar in its fancies. Even as a child I was charmed and slightly mystified by the literalness of GL's power ring emanations: huge green hands grabbed falling airplanes and giant ears eavesdropped on crooks. The power ring also cranked out modern machines: an enormous emerald derrick would pick up the criminals and deposit them in jail, or great green springs would cushion a descent (nor were these the only signs of an industrial consciousness—GL's streamlined look suited his secret identity as jet test pilot Hal Jordan). With the ring, the self was no longer bounded by a body, but only by its own self-conception. I doubt that I realized it then, but here was

Freud's omnipotence of thoughts, gelled into an ornament that could compensate for (my) physical weakness.

There are deep uncertainties operating in superhero narratives that mark a symbolic return to a presymbolic space of primal drives and primal fears, as well as later anxieties that are at once psychoanalytical, social, and historical. Wolfgang Schivelbusch reminds us of the disorienting experience of industrialization and its concomitant trauma, the industrial accident. "It must be remembered," he writes, "that railway accidents have this peculiarity, that they come upon the sufferers instantaneously without warning, or with but a few seconds for preparation, and that *the utter helplessness of a human being* in the midst of the great masses in motion renders these accidents peculiarly terrible" (1986, 143, my emphasis). The human body is not designed for the stresses of mechanical operation. As Gustave Claudin observed in 1858 of his rapidly changing world,

> These discoveries . . . bend our senses and our organs in a way that causes us to believe that our physical and moral constitution is no longer in rapport with them. Science, as it were, proposes that we should enter a new world that has not been made for us. We would like to venture into it; but it does not take us long to recognize that it requires a constitution we lack and organs we do not have. (cited in Schivelbusch, 159)

The superhero, who appears on the American industrial landscape in the 1930s, possesses a new kind of body—only the Man of Steel has the constitution, organs, and abilities equal to the rigors of the Machine Age.

Superman makes his initial appearance following the sustained shock of World War I. Schivelbusch notes the newly unleashed terror of sudden death. Where once a soldier could prepare himself for combat, "from the eighteenth century on, such a state of readiness no longer existed. The wound caused by mass fire occurred suddenly, invisibly; it came 'out of nowhere'" (156). By contrast, the superhero body is a body in a permanent state of readiness (*this is a job for . . .*). What's more, if random death now appears from nowhere, the superbody is more than merely resistant; it bears its own mysterious power. Such powers are often technological (well, *pseudo*-technological) in origin: Superman is "a strange visitor from another planet"; Green Lantern was entrusted with his power ring by the Guardians of the Galaxy; Captain America was injected with an experimental supersoldier serum, etc., etc. As embodied by the superhero of the 1930s and '40s, the "utter helplessness of the human being" in the face of industrial stress has been overcome—technological trauma has produced its own antidote.[5]

The first sign that all was not perfect in superhero-land turned up in the postwar era. In the 1950s, American superheroes were saddled with a mysterious and wholly arbitrary "weakness." Superman had Kryptonite (I think it's gone now) as his *bête verte*, and, okay, I could accept that. At least Kryptonite was some *thing*. But Green Lantern's ring failed to work against anything yellow. *Why?* So, like, was his ring only *partly* effective against orange? Where on the spectrum does yellow *end*, officially? The Martian Manhunter was powerless against things made of wood. Hmm . . . did they *have* wood on Mars? When encountering a new hero, you had to know two things—what was his power, and what was his Achilles' heel? They were concomitant, each the inevitable consequence of the other. Thus a writer's convenience took on the force of an ontology.

It was against this background that the Marvel superheroes of the 1960s appeared "realistic." No arbitrary weaknesses for these heroes, but there were self-doubts aplenty. These more psychologized figures quarreled, got depressed, and questioned themselves. The Marvel heroes were rarely gifted by birth or by choice; they were instead transformed in young adulthood by (sort of) varied forces: radioactive spider bites; cosmic ray bombardment in near-Earth orbit; gamma ray bombardment at a military testing ground; a collision with a truck bearing radioactive waste; and a (nonradioactive) stick that, when banged on the ground, made you into Thor, the Norse god of thunder. These comics presented as obvious an allegory of pubescent metamorphosis as one could imagine—The Hulk, for example, got big and hairy and his voice changed. Go figure.

Identity is the obsessional center of superhero comics, as revealed by endless processes of self-transformation and the problematic perceptions of others—Batman hunted by police, Lois hunting for Superman's secret identity. The secret identity is a major issue for the superhero, but if Hal Jordan is the "secret" identity, why does Green Lantern wear the mask? Writing about narratives from the *Odyssey* to the *Prisoner of Zenda* and beyond, Peter Brooks notes:

> It is on the body itself that we look for the mark of identity, as writers of popular literature have so well understood. . . . The bodily marking not only serves to recognize and identify, it also indicates the body's passage into the realm of the letter, into literature: the bodily mark is in some manner a "character," a hieroglyph, a sign that can eventually, at the right moment of the narrative, be read. (21–22)

The superhero body is marked in at least two senses: The secret identity constitutes the body *secretly* marked—this weenie is recognized (by the reader) as the conquering hero—but costume and logo constitute the superhero body as *publicly* marked. Mask, costume, and logo are marks that guarantee the superhero body passage into the field of the symbolic (the *logos*). Like the golem of Jewish mysticism, we might say that the superhero is constructed in the field of writing (the creation of a golem depends upon a mystical word inserted into the clay creature's mouth or ear, but in the 1920 German film version, the inscription is placed in the center of its chest—logo-position). Thus the acquisition of costume, mask, and logo might constitute a "*symbolic* birth," or *rebirth* into the symbolic, which, as Marie-Hélène Huet argues of the golem and other "ex-utero procreations," transfers issues of birth and identity from the field of maternal power to the realm of the patriarchy (1993, 244 and 239).

Alan Klein observes of bodybuilding that "the hypermuscular body" in bodybuilding "is supposed to communicate without an act; its presence is its text" (274). The superhero body is similarly written, but when read it will yield a secret. Hence the fascination with origin stories in the comics: the secret is a secret history, a story embodied by the mark on the surface of the body. In these postmodern times of emphatic surfaces and lost historicities, origin tales are no longer so stressed: the hyperbolically muscular heroes of Image Comics are nothing more or less than what they look like; the marked body has become an underdetermined sign as issues of identity recede into the background.[6] Most of these heroes seem not to have secret identities at all, which is just as well—some have purple skin and are the size of small neighborhoods. But why are they wearing masks?

Clearly the mask serves to protect the self by placing a barrier between subject and world (Klein: "bodybuilders wind up using their bodies as a mask, a male persona with which to ward off insecurities" [276]). The mask, no matter how minuscule, is a sign of the rebirth as what Klaus Theweleit has referred to as the *armored body.* The disturbingly repetitive and consistent memoirs of German *Freikorps* figures reveal a careful deployment of disciplinary and military apparatuses that turn the body into part of a machine, delibidinalized through the imposition of boundaries drawn from outside the subject. The ego is further severed from the weakness and frailty of the flesh through pain: aggressiveness against "outsiders," killing what is not "them," externalizes the fear of ego-dissolution. Hence the masculinist aversion to the liquidity associated with the monstrous feminine—*Freikorps* males exhibited a desire to annihilate the female and reduce her to a "bloody mass." The woman bears libidinal energies that are not beholden to reason; they exemplify the *flow* that threatens to wash away all that is rational (all that is *the subject*) in a cataclysmic flood. Anti-*woman*

becomes a code for anti-*life*.[7] Body and psyche are united as the subject becomes a weapon, an armored figure hiding both the erotic and the mortal truths of its being.

Superhero bodies, despite their plasticity, are armored bodies, rigid against the chaos of surrounding disorder. While permitted the narcissistic luxury of self-doubt, their power and their ultimate triumph are guaranteed; their stories are already written.[8] We are deep within what Theweleit called "the conservative utopia of the mechanized body" (1978, 162). Writing about the investment that Surrealism and Dada also had in the armored body, Hal Foster noted the "tension between binding and shattering tendencies, the play between sadistic and masochistic impulses." Surrealism was defined by the struggle "between the erotic and the destructive, the one never pure of the other" (1991, 94). In cruder form superhero comics replay this struggle unabated, as the display and experience of power become especially hysterical. Erotic energies are sublimated into (other) bodily traumas, emissions, and flows: Battles or the task of controlling the power are acts of self-protection that channel energy flow into focused blasts of multicolored destruction. Self-protection, though, is a blind for self-annihilation; Theweleit writes that in battle, "The man longs for the moment when his body armor will explode, strengthening his rigid body-ego; but a body such as his cannot atomize, as does the mass, by allowing itself to be penetrated, fragmented, and thus destroyed. His body atomizes only if he himself erupts outward. He desires to move beyond himself, bulletlike, towards an object that he penetrates" (179).

The longing for orgasmic battle begins to account for the appeal of the superhero *team* (Fantastic Four, Justice League of America, Avengers, etc.). Schivelbusch, whose notion of a "stimulus-shield" echoes Theweleit's armored body, notes that, from World War I, "warriors no longer did battle individually but as parts of the new combat machine" (152):

> The new military organization concretized the entirely specific sense of the word [shock]: the clash of two bodies of troops, each of which represented a new unified concentration of energy by means of the consolidation of a number of warriors into one deindividualized and mechanized unit. What was new in this military clash was its unheard-of violence (due to the concentration of energy) as well as the degree of attrition of its elements; the latter occurred in direct proportion to the degree of energy concentration. (153)

Brigade no. 6 Ripley, writer Marat Mychaels, artist

Teamups became popular during World War II as a kind of superhero popular front movement against the Axis powers. Thus they were originally a battle formation, an *Überkorps* of reciprocally reinforcing body armors. But their popularity survived the war, and in the 1960s, teams were rampant. One is tempted to turn to Will Wright's study of narrative structures in the cinematic western: he found that such '60s and '70s releases as *The Magnificent Seven*, *The Professionals*, and *Butch Cassidy and the Sundance Kid* were marked by the "organization man" mentality of a newly powerful corporate capitalism. Indeed, the superhero groups not only included frequently fractious[9] members, as did their western counterparts, they also featured jet planes, uniforms, and secret headquarters replete with boardrooms and global communications setups. The Fantastic Four even had their own skyscraper—the Mies van der Rohe–style Baxter Building (all of these headquarters were revealed in panoptic cutaway views detailing the locations of hangars, living quarters, training areas, and missile launchers). It's difficult to imagine corporatist fantasies resonating loudly among ten-year-old readers (*Hey, you got to be the Trilateral Commission last time!*); still, the corporation, the fraternity, the secret clubhouse, and the playground all provide alternative concepts of home and family.[10]

Within the comics' massive pitched battles, obsessively hyperbolized in any number of recent titles from Image Comics such as *Brigade* or *WILDC.A.T.S*, the action is an incoherent jumble of power beams and body parts, and superheroes and supervillains can't be easily distinguished. Although the supervillain may be considered the raison d'être for the superhero, the hero's creation is always precedent, and so the hero summons forth his own nemesis. But these are not battles between individuals, this is *war*: an unprecedented concentration of energy released in an explosion of nearly orgiastic pleasure and hysterical excess. The Image superhero tends toward battlefield (and action film) rhetoric:

> [Wed. 7:02 p.m., Cyberdata Technologies Building, lower Manhattan]
>
> —We've still got to find Velocity, grab Timmie and get out alive. I always knew my S.E.A.L.s training would come in handy someday.
>
> —*Heatwave to all units top to bottom. Rock and roll.*
>
> —*EEEYAA-HEY!*
>
> —You'd think I'd be used to it by now, but Ripclaw's war cry still sends chills up my spine.

The ensuing battle in *Cyber Force* number 3 covers eight densely illustrated pages.[11] Ripclaw leaps into the fray, his clawed hands lunging toward the hapless reader. Where once the heroes respected the classical, clean, six panels per page layout common to American comics, now their pent-up fury overpowers the containing/constraining boundaries of the panel or even the page itself. Theweleit's analysis of the soldier-male is rhetorically tailored to that fantasied soldier-male, the superhero:

> War is a function of the body of these men. . . . In war, the man appears not only naked, but stripped of skin; he seems to lose his body armor, so that everything enters directly into the interior of his body, or flows directly from it. He is out of control and seems permitted to be so. But at the same time, he is all armor, speeding bullet, steel enclosure. He wears a coat of steel that seems to take the place of his missing skin. (192)

In *one* panel, Heatwave stands in the foreground, firing his translucent pink energy beam out the bottom of the frame (*BZZZAK!*), while some armored guy with glasses fires his automatic weapon to the left (*BRAKAKAK!*). An enormous character in the upper left midground is being shot at (*KRAKA BOOM! BOOM! BOOM!*) by about four guys with mobile armor spread out along the right background. The big one is saying: "I got ya covered, Heatwave, but that dude with the cannon's gettin' to be a real pain in the *butt*." The background is a purplish field, pierced by energy beams, explosions, smoke, and debris. The bodies become both armored and flowing in combat, as the seething energies repressed by the elaborate body-armors of the superhero spurt from all directions and every orifice.

3. Androids on Steroids

It seems that every Image Comics character (Maul,™ Heatwave,™ Void,™ Ripclaw,™ Impact,™ Velocity,™ Grifter,™ Spartan,™ and the others) has been, is, or will be part of at least one superhero team (Team Youngblood,™ Brigade,™ WILDC.A.T.S,™ Cyber Force,™ Freak Force,™ Stryke-Force,™ Bloodstrike,™ StormWatch,™ and so it goes). The editor's page in *Doom Force*, a parody scripted by Grant Morrison, perfectly described this kind of title (although the real targets were Marvel's *X-Factor* and *New Mutants*):

> Grant breathlessly painted a vivid word-picture of a colorful band of super-outcasts who bravely battle the world's most powerful menaces on behalf of the very same human race that rejected them. Ironically, these youthful warriors have much more in common with their enemies than with those they fight to protect, but their basic decency leads them to struggle for the cause of justice in a world they barely understand. Their grim, wisecracking demeanor and their good-natured bickering may fool you, but when the chips are down, they're prepared to sacrifice their very lives to protect the innocent—and each other.

(Morrison also copyrighted names for future superhero use, so watch for Gridlock,™ Campfire,™ Eight-Track,™ Rim Shot,™ Mimosa,™ and Spatula.™)

The Image books are a fanboy wet dream.[12] The art is replete with extensive cross-hatching—the tiny lines that have dominated superhero comics since Rob Liefeld introduced the style. In his recent, indispensable formal analysis, *Understanding Comics*, writer/artist Scott McCloud notes that "in the mid-1960s when the average Marvel reader was pre-adolescent, popular inkers used dynamic but friendly lines. . . . But when Marvel's reader base grew into the anxieties of adolescence, the hostile jagged lines of a Rob Liefeld struck a more responsive chord" (1993, 126). Liefeld, once featured in a Levi's commercial by Spike Lee, was a founder of Image Comics, where those "hostile, jagged lines" are deployed in the service of an ever increasingly exaggerated bodily presence.[13]

The Image body is massively muscled, locked into a "dynamic," heroic pose. Despite accouterments such as logos, masks, gauntlets, epaulets, and other superhero accessories, the bodies are essentially presented as nudes (costumes are more coloration than cover-up). The team books feature an assortment of freakish figures either frozen in a group pose or locked in prodigious battle with characters on the other side of the embossed wrap-around cover. Where comics art once emphasized a vigorous flow of line that would lead the eye from panel to panel, recent comics turn each page into a stiffly posed pinup of flexed muscles and dramatic shading. The narrative, not very important to begin with, is further devalued against this fetishism of the superhero's overstated iconographic status; always spectacular in superhero comics, the body is now hyperbolized into pure, hypermasculine spectacle. The superhero body becomes auto-referential and can only be compared to other superheroes' bodies, rather than the common world of flesh, blood, muscle, and sinew.

This spectacle of the body resembles other such spectacles in contemporary culture. The hypermuscled body has moved closer to mainstream culture, whether in the videos of Madonna (remember Madonna?) and "janet" Jackson, the bodily obsessions of academic cultural studies, the movie stardom of Arnold Schwarzenegger, "American Gladiators," the underwear ads of Marky Mark, the increased coverage of bodybuilding events on cable TV—*stop the insanity!* The exaggerated musculature of the Image books suggests the parallel phenomenon of bodybuilding. As Klein and Samuel Fussell have both noted, "One doesn't so much admire bodybuilders for what they can do as far as what they *look* like they can do. The look of power, virility, prowess, counts for more than function, and has

more in common with the world of modeling, beauty contests, or cinema idols than that of sports heroes" (Klein, 215). The *look* is the thing—to emphasize their supersolidity, bodybuilders adopt The Walk: "They burrowed their heads slightly into their shoulders to make their necks appear larger. They looked bowlegged, absurdly stiff, and infinitely menacing" (Fussell 1992, 55). Bodybuilding contests present the body frozen into a set of poses that make the body *appear* powerful, and the final confrontation between contestants is the simultaneous "pose-down," in which each presents his body in as visually compelling a manner as possible. Superheroes present an image of active power, but being imaginary characters their power is also only an illusion.[14] The Image heroes are locked in a permanent pose-down of aggressive appearances and fetishistic display.[15]

It isn't surprising that the bodybuilder's body should emerge most consistently in the arena of superhero comics—comics and bodybuilding have been closely aligned for decades. Arnold came to stardom playing Conan the Barbarian, and Lou Ferrigno was The Hulk for a few years. Bodybuilding articles mentioned by Klein even *sound* like superhero names: "Destroyer Delts"; "Nuke Legs" (Klein, 141). Bodybuilders *like* comics: "Comic-book depictions of masculinity are so obviously exaggerated that they represent fiction twice over, as genre and as gender representation. But for bodybuilders these characters serve as role models" (267). And let's not forget "The Insult that Made a Man Out of Mac": the one-page adventure of a skinny guy with sand in his face who takes a course from Charles Atlas and exacts his revenge. *Oh Mac*, his frighteningly fickle gal coos, *You ARE a real man after all!* Fans will be glad to know that Mac was reborn in Grant Morrison's Techno-Surreal *Doom Patrol* as Flex Mentallo, the most famous superhero of all time (and, truly, who could argue the point?). "I learned how to refine and manipulate the secret vibrational wavelengths of each muscle, each tendon. . . ." A battle against a government conspiracy spelled Mac/Mentallo's doom:

> I thought if I flexed hard enough, I could make it happen. I thought I could turn the Pentagon into a circle. . . . I just flexed. In all the apartments in my building, people began to experience unusual phenomena: spontaneous, uncontrollable orgasms; visions of worlds folded into empty envelopes; astounding new ideas for leisure footware. There were reports of bizarre dreams, all containing the word "obviously." . . . And I kept flexing.

Doom Patrol no. 42 Grant Morrison, writer Mike Dringenberg and Doug Hazlewood, artists

By pitting the spiritual powers of "muscle mystery" against the articulate hierarchies of the military, Morrison exposes the emptiness at the core

MUSCLEBOUND

THE SECRET ORIGIN OF FLEX MENTALLO

Grant Morrison
WRITER
Mike Dringenberg AND
Doug Hazlewood
GUEST ARTISTS
Joliet Jake Workman
LETTERER
Daniel Vozzo
COLORIST
Art Young
EDITOR
WITH SPECIAL THANKS TO
Stevie Bamford AND
James Hamilton

I GUESS IT ALL STARTED THAT DAY IN 1954.

ON THE BEACH.

4

of bodybuilding fantasies—the lack of power that belies its emphatic appearance.

Klein describes something called *roid rage*: aggressive behavioral outbursts that follow sustained steroid use (151). I think of Maul from Image's *WILDC.A.T.S*, my favorite goofy new character—"Maul can increase his body-mass exponentially," the *WILDC.A.T.S Source Book* reports on the purple and green behemoth, "becoming bigger and stronger when necessary. He suffers a corresponding loss in intellect and self-restraint, though, which causes him problems." Maul is a close relative of Bruce Banner, a scientist who, when angered, transforms into that green-skinned, uncontrolled monster from the id known as The Hulk (*Is he man or monster . . . or BOTH?*). We are confronted with an aggressive hypermasculinity, a compensation for psychosexual anxiety that depends upon a ruthless suppression or (in the case of the *Freikorps*) an *obliteration* of the feminine. Thus "the formidable bodies are responses to a shaky psyche. . . . Physique and psyche were different words for overdevelopment and underdevelopment. What bound them was compensation; the bodily fortress protected the vulnerability inside" (Klein, 3). Superman is the hypermasculine version of Clark Kent (Jules Feiffer pointed out that we all know that Superman is *really* Clark, although supposedly Clark is *really* Superman).[16] The hypermasculinity of bodybuilder or superhero-fantasy represents an attempt to *recenter the self* in the body; a reductive conflation of body with subjectivity.

While outsiders see a blatant narcissism in the mirrored gymnasiums and unrestrained body worship of the bodybuilder, Klein finds something else: "Narcissus fell completely in love with his reflection. The bodybuilder would like to, but can't. Inside that body is a mind that harbors a past in which there is some scrawny adolescent or stuttering child that forever says, 'I knew you when . . .' The metamorphosis is doomed to remain incomplete" (41–42). That "scrawny adolescent" is surely a close relative of the one with his arms filled with five copies of the latest Image slugfest. The act of bodybuilding only represents a more activist dedication to the same compensatory, hypermasculine, anxious armored forms that superhero comics present to their similarly insecure readers.

In recent comics, muscular obsession reaches a new pitch. I'm continually struck by the attention to *neck muscles*. In his experience of male gym culture, Samuel Fussell noted that straights and gays preferred to work on different body parts—specifically, hets wanted mega-developed lats (gays preferred a leaner, more classical neck and shoulder line). This is interesting, if true, because the Image heroes have the biggest lats on the *planet.* Indeed, with their thick necks, bulging veins, and protruding tendons tightly swathed in colored skintight hoods, these heroes really become enormous *dicks* sheathed in an array of distinctly baroque (and somewhat painful looking) condoms—an effect both menacing and comical.

The women I know express the same revulsion toward images of bodybuilders' bodies (*thank goodness*), and in fact men find these male bodies to be more "acceptable" than do women (Klein, 216). Superhero readers are also a very male and heterosexist group (with some exceptions for *X-Men* fans), unwilling to directly confront more nuanced definitions of masculine identity. The self-pity that underlies so many superhero titles since the 1960s (the sensitive new age mutant syndrome) indicates an awareness of emotional need, but only within a hypermasculine context. A continuing character in *Eightball*, an alternative comic by Daniel Clowes, is the popular superhero artist (and total geek) Dan Pussey. In "The Origin of Dan Pussey," we visit him in high school as he withdraws ever further into fantasies of muscles and mutants . . .

See, at this point, now that the Ultimate Wars are over, Metallox is starting to feel like the other members of the Vengeance Battalion don't respect him as much because he's a Synthezoid. Okay, so here he is holding his arm with all the wires coming out of it and he says:

Eightball no.12
Daniel
Clowes,
writer and
artist

"You have fought long and hard in your galaxy to see that no man is judged by the color of his skin . . . Is this any different? I, too, have wounds! I, too, feel the stinging loss of our courageous compatriot Heatgirl. My tears may be artificial, but my pain is no less real!"

"Wow," his friend says. "I guess you're right! I never knew comics could be so . . . you know, like a real book!" "It really isn't all just BANG POW ZOOM stuff," Pussey complacently replies.

This tension between hypermasculinity and (a disavowed) emotional complexity finds its most complete figuration in what I like to call "the really, really big guy" in contemporary superhero teams. This phenomenon began with The Thing in the Fantastic Four ("This Man . . . This Monster" was one story), continued through The Hulk in the Avengers and The Beast (later, Colossus) in the X-Men, and has reached a peak in recent titles.[17] Maul, Beast, Coldsnap, Impact, Strong Guy, and Brick are the really big really, really big guys at the moment. These are the most explicitly monstrous bodies in the superhero canon, and are often objects of self-pity—they are the strongest team members, but do they not bleed? Physical strength only *hides* the emotionally complex inner subject; power is not self-aggrandizing, it is rather a cross to be silently borne (fortunately, thought balloons grant expression to this private torment). Morrison's *Doom Force* even managed to parody the "big guy" phenomenon, as Shasta the Living Mountain (*I'm useless . . . everyone hates me because all I can do is turn into a mountain*) sacrifices her life for the team—superhero deaths being another terrific occasion for easy emotionalizing (turns out the team really *didn't* like Shasta, so they just go get something to eat).

Hypermasculine fantasy is also revealed, with unabashed obviousness, in the approach to female superheroes. The spectacle of the female body in these titles is so insistent, and the fetishism of breasts, thighs, and hair so complete, that the comics seem to dare you to say anything about them that isn't just redundant. *Of course* the female form has absurdly exaggerated sexual characteristics; *of course* the costumes are skimpier than one could (or should) imagine; *of course* there's no visible way that these costumes could stay in place; *of course* these women represent simple adolescent masturbatory fantasies (with a healthy taste of the dominatrix).[18] One might note that women participate more fully in battle than they once did. It's worth observing that they're now as powerful as their male counterparts—women no longer have to suffer such wimpy powers as invisibility or telekinesis (*great*—they weren't seen, but they could move stuff around like Samantha on "Bewitched"). They no longer need protection; they are no longer victims or hostages or prizes.

Which isn't to say that all problems have been solved. Zealot, with her swords and razors, for example, "is superhumanly strong and skilled in the arts of killing with her hands and with any and all weapons." The notable lack of castration anxiety here lasts until one reads her origin story: She "was one of the three original founding members of the Coda, an ancient Sisterhood of assassins based in Greece." After centuries of service, "when she grew weary of killing for no reason other than money, she left the Coda and devoted her life to battling its values." Score one for our side—the

Deathmate, September 1993 Brandon Choi and Eric Silvestri, writers Brandon Peterson and Scott Williams, artists

| SCOTT BUKATMAN

demon woman is possessed and contained, killing for *its* (our) values. Then there's Void (with the Invisible Girl, the female superhero as *absence*) with a predictable array of telekinetic and teleportational skills, plus "a certain degree of clairvoyance." She has the liquid-metal sheen of the Silver Surfer and *Terminator 2*'s T-1000, but they never looked quite so damn *naked*.

The rise of women's bodybuilding provides a limited parallel to the new prominence of female superheroes, since the practice has been read by some cultural theorists as resistance to traditional female iconography. Alan Klein, though, adds a valuable corrective to this uncritical embrace by arguing that women's bodybuilding is *still* bodybuilding (191). The overdeveloped body remains a compensation for an underdeveloped ego, a way of hiding inadequacy behind an armored body. Klein may be underestimating the political significance of this gender shift, but his point is nevertheless well taken. Of course, female superheroes *are not* female bodybuilders—they aren't even *real women*, nor are they created by women. There isn't a single Image title starring a female superhero.[19] Female desire is absent—when male creators design women characters, they continue to indulge male fantasies. The new power of the female hero is cosmetic surgery, and the halo of power just adds a further level of exoticism to the spectacle of the female form.

Overall, the trend has been toward masculinized, even phallic, women—armed to the teeth and just one of the boys. Meanwhile (as they say in the comics), Grant Morrison has pointed to the disappearance of "the feminized superhero" (McEnery 1993, 101). The DC comics of the 1950s and '60s often subjected Superman to a dose of *Red* Kryptonite, an unpredictable substance that never worked the same way twice. Inevitably, the effect would be a temporary metamorphosis—Superman would gain the head of a giant ant, or he might be unable to control his powers. The armored body became fluid, shifting in irrational and uncontrollable ways. Comics no longer "feminize" their heroes in this whimsical manner, a further sign of the repression marking the hypermasculine construction.

Hypermasculine trauma reveals itself through the incoherence and hysteria of endless combat: explosions, exposed flesh, and extraterrestrial invasions speak to the terror of the armored body.[20] Klein's evocation of bodybuilding is as applicable to superheroics. "We see men trying too hard to come across as invulnerable and in command," he writes, "because to be less than that is not living up to our advance billing as leaders, dominators, controllers—in short, masters of the universe" (9).

4. The Torment of the Mutant Superhero

When the body engages in the violence of battle, the armor slips. Energies are no longer so thoroughly contained. Similarly, the *mutant superhero* presents itself as a problematic figure. Mutants are genetic accidents; their powers are neither products of radioactive ingestion nor interplanetary travels. They are the aliens among us; to avoid prejudice, mutant superheroes hide their abilities. Mutant powers are stigmata that must be kept hidden from the unreasoning mob of mere normals. Mutant superheroes are not invulnerable; not only are they distinguished by (a frequently maudlin) emotionalism, but their first and most dangerous enemies are their own bodies. Optic blasts shoot from the eyes of the X-Men's Cyclops; he must shield them at all times. Cyclops was the first star of the X-Men; with his ellipsoid yellow and ruby visor covering his deadly eyes he was at once statuesque and sleekly streamlined. But the fashionable mask of Cyclops is more than a mark of his superheroic status: this mask cannot be removed, for to do so would be to unleash death and destruction upon the world. The visor's deadly secret evokes such figures of the monstrous feminine as Medusa and Pandora's Box. But the struggle of Cyclops involves holding back this energy, containing it within himself; to release it would be to destroy his own sense of being (the woman he loves can never see his eyes, he realizes).

These are traumatized, eruptive bodies; the energies that are normally unleashed only in battle now continually threaten to overspill their fragile vessels. The mutant superhero is both armored and flowing. The armored body enforces categories of being by buttressing self against nonself, but mutant heroes are explicitly presented as "categorical mistakes." Theweleit's dissection of the structures that reinforce the subject against the disorder of a chaotic reality echoes Mary Douglas's arguments regarding ritual and somatic meaning. Douglas defines ritual as a metaphorical system for maintaining and communicating ideas of social order: "The magic of primitive ritual creates harmonious worlds with ranked and ordered populations playing their appointed parts. So far from being meaningless, it is primitive magic which gives meaning to existence. This applies as much to the negative as to the positive rites. The prohibitions trace the cosmic outlines and the ideal social order" (1966, 72). Rituals establish and preserve categories and hierarchies; they perform rules of social interaction. Those organized around the familiar space of the body constitute a narrow field of meaning: "The range of situations which use the human body for expression . . . derive essentially from the quality of social relations" (1970, viii). Following Mauss, and rejecting more psychoanalytically based readings, Douglas maintains that the body is always an acculturated body, an always-metaphorical body. Where it figures prominently within cultural rituals, "the human body is always treated as an image of society. . . . There can be no natural way of considering the body that does not involve at the same time a social dimension" (1970, 70).

More specifically, Douglas argues that the body and its boundaries mark a concern with social boundaries and hierarchical order:

> Interest in its apertures depends on the preoccupation with social exits and entrances, escape routes and invasions. . . . The relation of head to feet, of brain and sexual organs, of mouth and anus are commonly treated so that they express the relevant patterns of hierarchy. Consequently I now advance the hypothesis that bodily control is an expression of social control—abandonment of bodily control in ritual responds to the requirements of a social experience which is being expressed. Furthermore, there is little prospect of successfully imposing bodily control without the corresponding social forms. And lastly, the same drive that seeks harmoniously to relate the experience of physical and social, must affect ideology. (1970, 70–71)

Thus the body can serve as a sign of disorder; a categorical mistake: "When a monstrous birth occurs, the defining lines between humans and animals may be threatened. If a monstrous birth can be labeled an event of a peculiar kind the categories can be restored" (1966, 39). While they want to fit in, mutants know their birthright is to exist "outside" the normative. They are categorical mistakes of a specific type; they are, in short, *adolescents*. The first mutant superheroes were the X-Men: "The Most Unusual Teen-Agers of All Time!" Such "marginal beings" (1966, 97) pose a question and a threat to the social body, which must somehow reincorporate this "ambiguous species" (1966, 73) or brand it (*with an X?*) as taboo.

The audience for mutant superhero comics is clearly targeted: an issue of *X-Factor* featured a comics-style ad for Stridex, an acne medication—it seems that Cyclops isn't the only one who suffers the trauma of red facial eruptions (Stridex even *sounds* like a mutant superhero). Where once Cyclops lamented his impossible desire for normalcy in one brief panel per issue (*I've no right to try to date Jean* [Marvel Girl]—*not while my eyes make me a potential danger to anyone near me!*), later Claremont issues might feature a *five-page* conversation between young ex-lovers, culminating in a panel of the girl crying herself to sleep (*Shut up, Peter, please! Don't say any more! It hurts too much!*). It must be said that this infusion of romance comics discourse did, in fact, extend the appeal of the X-Men beyond the confines of the superhero subculture.

The appeal to adolescents immediately connects to Douglas's hypotheses regarding power hierarchies and structures of authority within cultures. In her studies of religious ritual, Douglas has located a correlation between the control of spiritual powers and the position within the social hierarchy. She distinguishes between internal powers that reside within the subject and external forces subject to mastery. "This distinction between internal and external sources of power is often correlated with another distinction, between uncontrolled and controlled power. According to widespread beliefs, the internal psychic powers are not necessarily triggered off by the intention of the agent" (1966, 98). Like the eruptive body of the mutant superhero (Havok, Storm, Random), internal powers are uncontrolled; where once superheroes guaranteed social stability they now threaten to disrupt it. Douglas further correlates controlled power and social authority:

> Where the social system explicitly recognizes positions of authority, those holding such positions are endowed with explicit spiritual power, controlled, conscious, external and approved—powers to bless and curse. Where the social system requires people to hold dangerously ambiguous roles, these persons are credited with uncontrolled, unconscious, dangerous, disapproved powers—such as witchcraft and evil eye. In other words, where the social system is well-articulated, I look for articulate powers vested in the points of authority; where the social system is ill-articulated, I look for inarticulate powers vested in those who are a source of disorder. (1966, 99)

At issue is not whether our social system is well- or ill-articulated; at issue is the mapping of the adolescent subject onto a social order that is *perceived by that subject* as arbitrary, exclusionary, and incomprehensible. "What supreme irony!" Professor X muses in a couple of thought balloons. "The Sentinels had been created to destroy the X-Men—and yet, it was necessary for *us* to smash *them* in order to save humanity—the humanity that *hated* us!"[21]

Douglas suggests "that the contrast between form and surrounding non-form accounts for the distribution of symbolic and psychic powers: external symbolism upholds the explicit power structure and internal, unformed psychic powers threaten it from the non-structure" (1966, 99). The mutant superhero, like the adolescent, is inarticulate within the social system—a categorical mistake that upsets notions of order and hierarchy

through an investment with dangerous, disapproved, and uncontrollable powers. The body of the mutant superhero is, in fact, a ritualized body, "a symbolic system, based on the image of the body, whose primary concern is the ordering of a social hierarchy" (1966, 125). Under the tutelage of Professor X, the mutants are sited both inside and outside society; their powers move from uncontrolled and eruptive to controlled and articulate. By constructing such an alternative social order, the categorical mistake is resituated as a fundamental force of social cohesion. "The rituals," Douglas notes, "work upon the body politic through the symbolic medium of the physical body" (1966, 128).

A recent series called *Marvels* retells the history of the Marvel universe by shifting attention to the citizens of New York who can catch only brief glimpses of Thor as he rockets by a D train stalled on the Manhattan Bridge. Superheroes are the stuff of legend, and Captain America is sublime: "Just to catch a glimpse of him—always in motion. Always moving forward—like a force of nature in chain mail. Never a hesitation or a backward glance. We were in awe of him. Of *all* of them." The narrator is a middle-aged, gray-mustached photojournalist named Phil who lives out in the 'burbs with his wife and two daughters. Kurt Busiek's careful script and Alex Ross's painted artwork perfectly supplement one another. The colors are real-world muted, while the heroes' costumes are rendered in impossibly vivid tones. The faces are not the generic ciphers worn by most comics characters, but instead have a kind of lumpy individuality. Fashions and hairstyles are appropriate to the New Frontier period, and even the cars are accurate. Such details evoke a vague nostalgia for a comfortably quotidian past sometimes glimpsed in aging issues of *Life* magazine. Into this reality of bad haircuts and littered streets, the "Marvels" gain an understandable power to astonish.

The second issue of *Marvels* concentrates on the mutant problem. The unveiling of the mutant-exterminating Sentinels is retold from Phil's point of view as he watches events unfold on a black and white TV in a bar. Phil, the normal guy, gives voice to the articulate structures of authority. "They were the dark side of the Marvels," Phil reflects. "Where Captain America and Mister Fantastic spoke to us about the greatness within us all, the mutants were death." A mob scene is lit only by the infernal red glow emanating from the visor of Cyclops. Phil learns to whistle a different tune when he finds that his daughters have been harboring a small mutant girl in their basement (doesn't *everybody?*).[22] The li'l mutant is nearly hairless, with enormous wet eyes brimming with tears (*"A-are you going to send me away?"*)—her victimized vulnerability combines Walter and Margaret

Marvels no. 2
Kurt Busiek,
writer
Alex Ross,
artist

Keane's waif drawings, ET, starving Ethiopian children, and Cindy-Lou Who. In these sequences, sad to say, the story loses its edge. Nevertheless, Busiek effectively mythologizes the relationship between the freakish "muties" and the glorified (if rather white-bready) "Marvels."

The bodily torment of the mutant superhero expresses a desire, a *need*, to transcend the confines of the body, to exist as pure spirit. As usual, however, such desires are fraught with ambivalence, hence the heightened transgression of corporeal boundaries is accompanied by the hardening of the body. Still, the eye beams of Cyclops, the telekinetic powers of Marvel Girl, the elemental forces controlled by Storm, even Wolverine's extensible adamantium claws—all of these pull the body past its margins. Douglas emphasizes that "the orifices of the body . . . symbolize its especially vulnerable points. Matter issuing from them is marginal stuff of the most obvious kind. Spittle, blood, milk, urine, faeces or tears by simply issuing forth have traversed the boundary of the body" (1966, 121). Mutant superheroes bear overdetermined inscriptions of marginality revealed in every bodily trauma and transgression. The saga forms a massive passing narrative, as these stigmatized bodies attempt to hide behind a veil of "normalcy."

Douglas's model of social hierarchy contains clear gender correlations, although she doesn't address the issue.[23] Theweleit's terminology is useful: controlled and external power corresponds to the masculine armored body, while uncontrolled, internal power is analogous to the fluidity of the feminine. Articulate power is therefore the province of the masculine with the feminine relegated, by definition, to the inarticulate power operating outside systems of social authority. The mutant is thus a feminized figure, and the construction of an alternative social order acquires an ideological relevance that begins to transcend adolescent narcissism. The emphasis on uncontrolled powers that exist beyond the articulate structures of social authority points to a preference for the spiritual rather than the material aspects of reality, and in ritual and myth, Douglas argues, "to insist on the superiority of spiritual over material elements is to *insist on the liberties of the individual* and to imply a political programme to free him from unwelcome constraints" (1970, 162, my emphasis).

It's worth considering the recent popularity of the X-Men in the context of Generation X, the group of twenty-somethings that constitute a significant part of the mutant superhero audience. Generation X walks a fine line, ferociously absorbing (and regurgitating) popular culture while performing a self-conscious marginality that mixes historical eras. The modern primitive fascination with such body arts (or rituals) as tattooing and piercing fetishizes the body as a spectacle of marginality, not to mention the body in pain—mutant stigmata.[24] Marvel *and* Image advertised upcoming mutant titles called *Generation X* (Image has since appropriated the other grunge-culture book title, retitling its comic *Gen 13*). The alternative community represented by the mutant band, combined with the pop nihilism and colorful violence of the superhero comic, makes these titles perfect light reading for homesick slackers who envision themselves unstuck in space and time, lost in an America in which all the good stuff has already happened.

In *Natural Symbols*, published in 1970, Douglas continually returns to the issue of student rebellion and the assault upon cherished hierarchies: "His teachers live in one universe, they cherish boundaries and smell conspiracy against sacred forms; he lives in another universe in which no particular form is sacred; form as such is distinct from content and inferior to it; he opposes classification as the expression of empty form, the very emblem of evil" (xv). Thus the arch-enemy of the X-Men is Magneto (which is *not* pronounced "mag-neat-o"), the self-proclaimed leader of the Brotherhood of Evil Mutants, who believes that mutants, Homo superior, must subjugate Homo sapiens once and for all.[25] Magneto has become something of a dark (and not unsympathetic) deity in recent years, but his obsessions are precisely with power, definition, and hierarchy. On the other side are the government representatives who want to exterminate mutants or at least institute a Mutant Registration Act. Again, social structure is advanced as an empty emblem of evil.

Mutant bodies are explictly analogized to Jewish bodies, gay bodies, adolescent bodies, Japanese- or Native- or African-American bodies—they are, first and foremost, subjected and subjugated and colonized figures. If they are victims, however, they are also valuable sources of disruption and challenge—transgressive, uncontrollable, and alternative bodies. As on "Star Trek: The Next Generation," issues of gender, ethnicity, and sexual preference have received remarkable attention (and is the resemblance between patriarchal, bald Professor X and patriarchal, bald Captain Picard only coincidental?). *Trek* and *X-Men* present ethnically, sexually, generationally, and genetically diverse companies of humans, mutants, and aliens taking their places within flexible structures of cooperation and tolerance. The group is something more than a battle unit, and clearly takes the form of an idealized, alternative society—one in which all members, and therefore no members, are outcasts.[26] In the rejection of traditional political thought which marked American student rebellion in the late '60s, Douglas observes that "the young radicals of today express contempt for the physical body, read the mystics and cultivate non-rationality" (167). Mutants just wanna have fun.

The seething, mutated, cyborged, and ceaselessly flowing bodies of these superheroes "express contempt" for the physical body, but in a deeply ambivalent form. If the flowing body is also an armored body, if its physical presence is protected and exaggerated, then that physicality has itself become a symbol for the (teen) spirit lodged within. As I argued in my study of postmodern science fiction, the body may be "simulated, morphed, modified, retooled, genetically engineered, and even dissolved," but it is never entirely eliminated: the subject always retains a meat component (1993, 243 and 259). As in cyberpunk a profound ambivalence, and even hysteria, regarding the status of the body in contemporary technoculture is revealed. And so: *X-Bodies* as in taboo; *X* as in impure and polluted and under erasure; but also *X* as in *X*-rays, with their power to reveal; *X* as in extreme; *X* as in ex—the *ex-men*.

5. Now Our Weird Heroes Each Remain Eccentric

Doom Patrol, scripted by Grant Morrison for nearly four years, recrafted comic book trauma, moving well beyond the defensive postures of the hypermasculine. In the first Morrison issue, Cliff Steele (Robotman: human brain in metal body) immediately demolishes armored body fantasies:

> Can you imagine how crude robot senses are, compared to human ones, huh? All I have are memories of the way things used to feel or taste. You know, they say that amputees feel phantom pains where their limbs used to be. Well, I'm a total amputee. I'm haunted by the ghost of an entire *body*! I get headaches, you know, and I want to crap until I realize I don't have any bowels.

A friend tries to help: "I can't stand by and watch you destroy yourself." Steele replies, "Me? How *can* I destroy myself?" He pounds his head through a wall to emphasize the point, but still cannot feel *anything*. We are past the neurotic self-involvement of teen mutants here, and are nearing complete psychotic breakdown: these folks were *never* normal.

Aside from Robotman, the Doom Patrol included Negative Man, who was possessed by a radioactive spirit that flew from his body to perform superdeeds, and Elasti-Girl, who could make isolated parts of her body grow or shrink. Morrison rebuilt the group by ditching Elasti-Girl, remaking Negative Man as Rebis (a hermaphroditic blend of two human bodies and that spirit), and adding the fabulous Crazy Jane—who suffers from sixty-four multiple personalities, each of which has its own "meta-human ability." Morrison never imposed normative values on his team: Jane is not "cured" by developing a unitary sense of self, by "controlling" her multiple personalities; instead she learns to permit each of her personalities to dominate when appropriate (McEnery, 99). The struggle in *Doom Patrol* is not to be accepted, but to accept oneself.

The psychic and physical traumas of the group are matched by the slippages of reality to which they are continually subjected. An early enemy was the Brotherhood of Evil, now reformed as the Brotherhood of Dada, whose first act is to trap Paris within a recursively structured painting. One enemy, the Quiz, has "every superpower you haven't thought of." To fight her involves thinking of lots of superpowers *really quickly* (unfortunately, nobody thinks of "the power to create escape-proof spirit jars"). In later episodes they befriend Flex Mentallo and the sentient Danny the Street (*Sometimes it's an alley in Peking, sometimes a back street in Toronto . . .*) and battle the Men from N.O.W.H.E.R.E., whose every utterance is based on the same acronym: *Naked old widows hover earlier round Easter. Never open William's head evil reptiles emerge.*

Perhaps *all* of this is occurring inside Jane's head; perhaps the entire concept of superheroes is only a psychic formation in the first place (*gasp*). Protesting the trend toward more "realistic" approaches to superhero comics, Morrison argued that "the idea that you could bring something as ridiculous as superheroes into the real world seemed to me completely insane. . . . I was more interested in comics as what they were, as ridiculous garish combination[s] of words and pictures about people with ludicrous talents" (McEnery 98). Nothing could illustrate Morrison's point better than the Fantastic Four stories of the 1960s. The FF were typical of Marvel's characters in that they were both weirder *and* more human than their forebears. The rubbery Reed Richards (Mr. Fantastic); Sue Storm (the Invisible Girl), his bride; her brother Johnny, the Human Torch; and gruff, lovable, but deeply traumatized Ben Grimm, transformed into an odd pile of orange rocks known as The Thing, collectively formed one of the most affectionate of superhero teams—and why not? They were family.

Their adventures took them to hidden lands, other dimensions, and the edges of the universe; Jack Kirby's baroquely cosmic creations never again seemed either as perfect or as true. The comic reveled in juxtapositions of galactic scale with human banality. Kirby's humans were stylized, simple, and dynamic, and the visual flatness of the characters was enhanced by Joe Sinnott's clean, clear inking. But Kirby's cityscapes were so many

DOOM PATROL

33
JUN 90

US $1.50
CAN $1.85
UK 80p

GRANT MORRISON
RICHARD CASE
JOHN NYBERG

abstract geometric shapes piled atop one another, and the vast machinery and elaborate costumes that were hallmarks of his art were detailed, obsessive, and faintly psychotic. In his best work, machinery seemed to merge with the human (or alien) figures; the biological was stylistically severed from the world. The FF pages fairly vibrated with color, drama, and dynamic movement, and even the word balloons and sound effects added to the overall effect. Readers of my generation can hardly forget the thrill of turning the page and finding Kirby's classic six-panel pages supplanted by a grand one- or two-page spread, replete with exploding suns, surging nebulae, a massive alien figure, or perhaps a "psychedelic" photomontage. Meanwhile, Stan Lee's dialogue ranged in style from Ben's Brooklynese ("Can'tcha see I'm tryin' ta dislike ya?!!") to the faux-Shakespearian flights of the Silver Surfer, herald of Galactus, eater of planets ("Incredible? Nay, it is *supremely* credible! Earth is but a twinkling dot . . . a paltry pebble . . . in the vastness of space!"). Hyperbole? "The World's Greatest Comic Magazine!" the covers proclaimed ("The Brutal Betrayal of Ben Grimm" was "possibly the most daringly dramatic development in the field of contemporary literature!"). Cultural studies academics please note: nobody took this stuff too seriously. It was playtime, and it *was* fun, and it was sometimes moving, and it provided the dizzying shifts of spatiotemporal scale and perspective that make science fiction a genre to consider.

The Lee/Kirby *Fantastic Four*s are perfect examples of the "garish" and "ludicrous" entertainments to which Morrison referred; one issue of *Doom Patrol* featured an affectionate parody (*And Men Shall Call Him—HERO!*).[27] Forgoing angst for absurdism, *Doom Patrol* stories elevate and enhance the conventions of the genre to construct darkly liberating cut-ups that infect the readers' reality and open doors of illogical possibility. The traumatic body of the superhero now signifies a traumatized *reality* rather than an inadequate psyche. In a world where our government feeds radioactive cereal to unsuspecting test subjects, the Doom Patrol make nicer comrades than the solipsistically suffering X-Men—and why not? They're family.

6. To Be Continued . . .

Doom Patrol
no. 33
Grant
Morrison,
writer
Richard Case,
artist

Writing "X-Bodies," I dream: I'm in a comics shop and discover lots of new *Green Lantern* titles. I'm obligated to buy them all, secretly glad of the excuse. GL . . . my old alter ego has returned. In the Dreaming, I'm the academic reader, the adolescent comics fan, and the high-flying superhero. Clearly, some early anxieties are not completely behind me.

Confronting the autobiography that underlies "X-Bodies," I see that my battle against the evil forces of academia is neatly designed to keep me on the margins. With no permanent appointment, I stand peering over the fence and wonder, *what do academics want?* but the real question I keep ducking is, *why won't I give it to them?* For one thing, the academy keeps refusing to tell me about *my* self. My reclamation of my own experience is part of a very appropriate struggle to legitimate the personal, the physical, and the aesthetic within a field that has privileged the authoritative, the cognitive, and the textual.[28]

Very heroic—but then there's my irrational fear of losing my self by joining a community (*any* community). My writings validate my own past, and thus my own self. Superheroes, science fiction, and Jerry Lewis—I'm the emperor of the nerds, the god of geeks. I rescue the terminally trivial, make it respectable and perhaps even sexy. Yet have I arranged to be taken unseriously? Am I engaged in a continuing activity of careerist self-sabo-tage: a cartoon anarchist being blown apart by his own bomb, Professor Kelp blowing up his lab? Is the real rescue I'm trying to make that of my terminally trivial, maybe respectable, and perhaps even sexy *self?* Well past adolescence, I lead a double life—inside and outside academia, inside and outside superhero subculture. I'm loving and duplicitous, a wreck and in control, armored and flowing, I'm Professor Kelp and Buddy Love. I'm a mutant superhero, asserting my phallic invincibility, fighting old battles against people *who aren't even alive anymore.* Perhaps it's time to hang up the cape. . . .

And perhaps not. Really, this self-mythologizing is getting out of hand. The fantasy to surrender is the one with the monolithic entity of academia tearing away at my own unified, noncontradictory (and still wacky) self. I'll stand by the work I've done. I'm a proud academic—still committed to rigorous intellectual inquiry and supportive pedagogy despite the narrow-ness of so many of the "approved" academic discourses. The *uncontrol* that marks marginalized mutants and Professor Kelp is only mine to a point— I'm also, after all, Professor X, the mutant *in control.* If life as a mutant superhero is mine, then I'll wear the cape proudly. Keep the cape *and scrap the armor* (my official superhero oath). Then I can decide which way to fly (my shrink said it, not me).

(And the Silver Surfer said this—) *I was born to soar . . . to ride the currents of space . . . not to be confined within a barren structure!* [29]

Notes

Special thanks to Sandy Rubin and Sara Franses for the self-understanding. Valuable suggestions and criticisms were provided by Nancy Graham, Cindy Fuchs, Barbara Miller and Toby Miller (no relation), David Samuels and Larry Kramer (not *that* Larry Kramer)—they've got my appreciation and my friendship. I'll give them some comics. . . .

1 See Bukatman 1993 and 1991.
2 DC has teamed up with Milestone Studios to produce a line of comics about and by minority figures, especially African Americans. One of these books, *Static*, is perhaps the most entertaining superhero comic currently published.
3 Both Theweleit and Douglas extend their analyses well beyond the scope of their initial researches. Theweleit's study of *Freikorps* fantasies reveals the more pervasive masculinist fantasies that underlie certain traditions in Western representation, while Mary Douglas uses her structural methodology to emphasize some broad, but important, connections across cultural experience: "All I am concerned with is a formula for classifying relations which can be applied equally to the smallest band of hunters and gatherers as to the most industrialised nations" (1970, viii). While I should perhaps be more interested in some of the significant *differences* between cultures, I nevertheless believe that these analyses retain considerable value when applied to contemporary American popular culture.
4 *In brightest day / In blackest night / No evil shall escape my sight / Let those who worship evil's might / Beware my power / Green Lantern's light* —science fiction writer Alfred Bester
5 It might be worth noting that the first Mr. America contest was held in 1939.
6 A contributing factor to the decline of origin stories might also lie in the repetitive nature of the genre—we *already* pretty much know where these characters came from.
7 Theweleit even recognized a class relationship in which the working class became a flowing mass of aggressive, libidinal women.
8 The extensive illustrations that accompany Theweleit's text include several of such characters as Thor, Captain America, and Spiderman.
9 I admit that writing about superhero comics makes me annoyingly alliterative and appallingly adverbial.
10 Further, the bickering yet supportive superhero team represents a fragmented projection of a self-contradictory subjectivity.
11 The typical superhero story is between twenty and twenty-five pages in length. Japanese *manga*, by contrast, are hundreds of pages, and an eight-page battle, with little dialogue and few panels, would be surprisingly brief. *Manga* are not only longer than American comics, they read far more quickly.
12 Characters cross over into each other's titles, creating elaborate continuities that only the most dedicated readers can unravel. The comics are lavishly produced with heavy, glossy paper, vivid computerized color, and pinups galore. Artist photographs and fan sketches adorn the back pages, and promotion for comics, caps, clothing, and cards is incessant.
13 *Doom Force* parodies the tone of aesthetic self-congratulation: "Our pencillers and inkers and penciller/inkers seemed inspired to artistic heights they had never previously reached. If you doubt that, go back and look again at the sheer number

of lines they put into each panel and onto every figure . . . then sit there and tell me they didn't work harder than they ever have in their lives."

14 This was a major problem for Superman's creators during World War II: Superman could hardly ignore the war, but neither could he win it.

15 In Howard Chaykin's *Power & Glory* (Bravura Comics, 1994), superheroes are engineered by a U.S. government project because "*nobody* makes a hero like the U.S.A." In an interview published in the first issue, Chaykin remarks that the book "is a reaction to the emptiness of content in most super-hero comics lately. There's no action in contemporary comics, only poses." The theme of the new comic, Chaykin says, is "Why *be* a hero when you can just *look* like one." For more on Chaykin's work, with which I feel an ongoing affinity, see Bukatman 1993, chap. 1.

16 In Jerry Lewis's *The Nutty Professor*, Buddy Love is the hypermasculine version, the *armored body* if I may, of the vulnerable "little man," Professor Kelp. In Richard Lester's *Superman III*, Superman turns evil and ultimately battles Clark, whose morality provides its own kind of armor. The physical split between the characters makes *The Nutty Professor* analogy all the more compelling.

17 And all owe something to cinema's hulking golem of 1920, as well as the Frankenstein monster of 1931.

18 Of course the parodic *Doom Force* is on top of these tendencies as well—the villain castigates his scantily clad partner for covering herself up "like some old woman on a day trip to Alaska."

19 There are no prominent women writers or artists working for Image. DC's Vertigo titles (targeted to older, non-superhero reading audiences) feature Karen Berger (editor), Nancy Collins (writer), Jill Thompson (penciler), and others.

20 My not-very-thorough sampling suggests that the ratio of battle to nonbattle pages in the Image titles is about 3 to 1 or 4 to 1. By contrast, in Marvel's *Uncanny X-Men* no. 310, admittedly one of the chattiest superhero books going, that ratio was exactly reversed.

21 By the way, would we even *know* what irony was if not for comic books?

22 Phil recalls, "There was something in her—in *its* eyes—and I couldn't help thinking of the liberation of Auschwitz—and the look in *their* eyes."

23 Thanks to Sarah Berry for drawing my attention to Douglas and gender.

24 Douglas's studies are particularly relevant in relation to such rituals.

25 Of his family, only Magneto survived internment at Auschwitz, an experience that apparently sensitized him to the issue of discrimination based upon genetic difference.

26 At their worst, however, both "ST:TNG" and *X-Men* tend to wallow in over-obvious emotional allegories.

27 More recently, Alan Moore (of *Watchmen* fame) and a number of artists have produced a more sustained return of those halcyon days of Marvel in their *1963* series, published by Image. The pastiche is so lovingly accurate that some readers, including myself, felt an overwhelming sense that this was how comics were meant to be. The initial *1963* series ended with the members of the Tomorrow Syndicate suddenly finding themselves in the far more brutal and textured universe of Image Comics.

28 My terms are derived from the excellent introductory chapter of Barbara Maria Stafford's *Body Criticism: Imaging the Unseen in Enlightenment Art and Medicine* (1991, 5).

29 Jack Kirby, the creator of the Silver Surfer and so many other heroes, passed away on February 6, 1994, as I was finishing this essay. It is to his memory and his accomplishments that "X-Bodies" is dedicated.

References

Brooks, Peter. 1993. *Body Work: Objects of Desire in Modern Narrative*. Cambridge, MA: Harvard University Press.

Bukatman, Scott. 1991. "Paralysis in Motion: Jerry Lewis's Life as a Man." In *Comedy/Cinema/Theory*. Berkeley, CA: University of California Press, 188–205.

——. 1993. *Terminal Identity: The Virtual Subject in Postmodern Science Fiction*. Durham, NC: Duke University Press.

Douglas, Mary. 1966. *Purity and Danger: An Analysis of the Concepts of Pollution and Taboo*. London and New York: Routledge.

——. 1970. *Natural Symbols: Explorations in Cosmology*. New York: Pantheon.

Foster, Hal. 1991. "Armor Fou." *October* 56: 64–97.

Fussell, Samuel. 1992. *Muscle*. New York: Pantheon.

Huet, Marie-Hélène. 1993. *Monstrous Imagination*. Cambridge, MA: Harvard University Press.

Jameson, Fredric. 1991. *Postmodernism, or the Cultural Logic of Late Capitalism*. Durham, NC: Duke University Press.

Klein, Alan M. 1993. *Little Big Men: Bodybuilding Subculture and Gender Construction*. Albany: State University of New York Press.

McCloud, Scott. 1993. *Understanding Comics: The Invisible Art*. Northampton, MA: Tundra Publishing. This innovative volume is produced entirely in comics style.

McEnery, Peter. 1993. "The Candlemaker's Privilege: Grant Morrison Plays God." *Mondo 2000*, no. 11: 96–101. Interview with Grant Morrison.

Morrison, Grant (writer), and Richard Case (artist). 1992. *Doom Patrol: Crawling from the Wreckage*. New York: DC Comics. Reprint edition of *Doom Patrols* nos. 19–25, originally published in 1989.

Schivelbusch, Wolfgang. 1986. *The Railway Journey: The Industrialization of Time and Space in the 19th Century*. Berkeley, CA: University of California Press. Originally published in German in 1977.

Stafford, Barbara Maria. 1991. *Body Criticism: Imaging the Unseen in Enlightenment Art and Medicine*. Cambridge, MA: MIT Press.

Theweleit, Klaus. 1977. *Male Fantasies*. Vol. 1. Trans. S. Conway et al. Minneapolis: University of Minnesota Press.

——. 1978. *Male Fantasies*. Vol. 2. Trans. Erica Carter and Chris Turner. Minneapolis: University of Minnesota Press.

Wright, Will. 1975. *Sixguns and Society: A Structural Study of the Western*. Berkeley: University of California Press.

Cracked Open by the Senses

Mother refused to let go until everyone was in place. The nurse whispered, "She's waiting for someone." We looked at each other and drew closer to the bed; then Father arrived. She let go softly, her chest falling under the sweat-soaked sheets, resting. She let go among medical equipment and an elevated TV playing Yosemite Sam cartoons—gunshots and a strange sound of someone falling into a canyon. I tilted my head back, closed my eyes, snapping memories together.

A Body Never Sleeps

I was protected, a good boy. And as a good boy, order was essential. . . .

I grew up believing in a body that was fit, sharp, trained in the lessons of physical and emotional preparation, ready for disaster. I felt you built yourself, armored the body privately, never revealing motives or desires. In fact, this was a building of my body, based on an ethos of survival. Like much of my experience of family, the private was never public: politics and sexuality remained separate and distinct. My experience of this excitable body—a body that never sleeps—is mixed with rage, intimacy, my family's collective obsession with the mythic West, and my mother's infatuation with popular western novels.

I remember the books by Louis L'Amour that Mother read: *The Man Called Noon, Get Out of Town, The Black-Rock Coffin Makers*. I also remember how Father spent hours tilling the canyon below our house, re-creating his Midwest childhood on the farm by planting rows of peas, sweet corn, green onions, turnips. At the end of a hot Sunday afternoon he would tape the leather sweatband back into his straw work hat, while my brother, under siege by imaginary enemies, practiced attack moves with his knife in our garage, among automobile parts, piles of laundry, and biker

Views of
Muleshoe,
Texas, 1993
Rodney
Sappington
and Leslie
Ernst

magazines. Everyday gestures were more than the ups and downs of family life: they included slapped faces, broken jaws, sleeping it off.

Through popular paperback westerns, I imagined a measureless world of threat and redemption, of glances across barrooms and misfortune. There were carefully packed boxes of books in our house, stacked in the hallway closets, stored in the trunk of our car, nestled between flannel blankets and half-empty bottles of Smirnoff's. We were instructed not to throw them away. What intrigues me today is that these were Mother's books; her fascinations and dreams were in those boxes. She felt they were safe and contained there—they could not be violated. Along with popular descriptions of the West's lawlessness and vigilantism was our shared violence.

4:00 a.m.
Shaken. A 5.0 rocked the house. I thought I had my belongings neatly sepa-
rated. . . . Disoriented again. Memory scatters to pieces. I'm ready, guarded.
No surprises. Silence is shattered by a car turning into the driveway, dishes
clinking in the sink, the refrigerator door sucking closed, my boots striking
the sidewalk on Wilshire Boulevard, the swirling police helicopters pounding
the air over our house.

My body registered our mounting tensions. I learned to survive. Father's image twisted into silence and monstrous acts, while Mother's lingered as disconnected scenes—a chair tipped over, white stuffing ripped from a car seat, grocery lists torn up and taped back together. Neither image fit; they were misshapen categories—polarities I was not prepared to slip into. Oddly enough, I took pleasure in them and was terrified of them—a series of masquerades.

I kept a careful regimen, suspicious of bodily pleasures and obsessed with self-questioning. When would I rupture the calm? When would our rage strike in me? I drilled myself for endurance, testing thresholds of pain. I gained equilibrium by stretching the boundaries of pain and pleasure— a desperate attempt to push the limits of my body. My gestures, no matter how small, were measured, as if through secret acts of calculation and extreme physical exhaustion I could reach a delirium that would allow me to piece together the evidence of our lives.

Many mornings after my father left for work, I watched my mother gather up her ashtray, pack of Kools, plastic lighter, and a blanket and lie down on the couch to read. This was a time of reprieve. She tucked the blanket around her hips and buried her feet under pillows. From the several

books around her on the coffee table and end table she chose *Buckskin Run* by Louis L'Amour. The back jacket described "untamed places where men and women faced the challenge of survival. . . . These were the proving grounds of daily life. At any time violence could explode and on the frontier there was no avoiding its sudden terrible impact."

These books brought to life a West where bad men played against impossible odds and women were "nags," or strong and resourceful. Citizens were clannish and lynched the innocent, unidentified intruder. Manifest destiny was pictured as grabbing land, overcoming mysterious adversaries, unearthing gold buried in inaccessible caverns, and punishing those who violated local taboos. Wagon trains disappeared; men were shot in disputes; while women were brutally conquered by husbands, or gained respect by protecting themselves with fences, shotguns, and other men.

This was the stuff of popular fiction, the image of the loner, the individualist—and a site of forces working against you. Mother found these forces embodied in our neighbors, who schemed to discredit her, and us. She referred to families living in our vicinity as "nosy, petty people." Our drapes remained closed.

One summer afternoon after riding my bike in the canyon below our house, I ran inside the house for lunch and saw her books scattered on the living room carpet. She usually kept them neatly stacked, bindings aligned. The glass inset of the coffee table was broken. Blood ringed a piece of glass. She had fallen or was thrown—I wasn't sure. I didn't ask questions. The disruption was so familiar. I immediately mounted my bike and raced into the canyon, pushing my body faster and faster, climbing white alkaline hills and dropping into ravines. My mind went blank.

Later Father explained. Mother had been taken to the hospital; she had pushed my brother too far. There were several stitches in her right forearm. The coffee table glass was replaced, and her books were picked up and loosely piled in the bedroom. I resumed my secret drills, riding my bike with obsessive skill, chewing gum at a certain rate, and pointing my toes perfectly straight. Losing physical control was forbidden in the logic of my measured responses. Play was a stranger concept. Go out and play? I performed the techniques of preparation. Mother moved on to her next book, and my brother drove her to the hospital to have her stitches removed. Father worked late at the truck lot: order was restored. I seldom looked people in the eye, I watched the way they used their fingers, tilted their shoulders, and pivoted from the hips. "Eyes deceive," I thought.

Westerns were scripted into my expectation of physical endurance. I learned that bodies were pursued until shattered. Mother advised me one

day, "You gotta watch out! Can't let 'em corner you. Gotta think like 'em, stay two steps ahead." Her words allowed me to restage fistfights and to place myself at the center of dust and bullets. No matter how powerful my imaginary enemies appeared to be, I was stopped only when the gritty hand of a marshal untangled me from my opponent. I never won these battles, just persisted against invincible figures emerging from great arid landscapes. I admired their ability to endure brawls in which they were shot, punched, beaten into the gravelly streets. But they survived, fought, managed to repair themselves and find revenge. They gave form to my notions of impenetrability. Mother invested them with the power to transport her out of her condition.

Westerns were a constant in our house. New titles replaced old ones, yet I was unable to fully understand their appeal to her. One day I came home and found Mother reading, moving her lips, her yellow nightgown pulled over her legs. Her glass rested on a paper towel folded into a square; the ice had melted into round porous debris at the bottom. She sat up to finish the clear carbonated liquid and squinted at me.

"Whatcha staring at?"

"Nothin'. What's that you're reading?"

"*The Man Called Noon*. It starts off really good: 'Somebody wanted to kill him.' The hero tries to find out who's after him. He has to find 'em and kill 'em before they kill him. And he doesn't even know what he looks like."

"Of course he doesn't know what they look like. He hasn't found them yet!"

"I mean himself. He's never *seen* himself! Other people recognize him but he doesn't recognize his own face in the mirror."

I was hooked.

These books influenced my dreams, as I suppose they did Mother's. Dreams provided a reality that was not socially permissible. I frequently dreamt of cloudy desert fields, creaky saloon doors, and menacing cowboys. I also dreamt of marauding women, drinking at the bar, their hats pulled low on their heads, taking shots of whiskey and slamming their glasses down for more. Mother was in many of these dreams, sometimes as bystander, sometimes as part of the group. These women were fierce, calculating, they were excellent marksmen. Their targets were men and women, children, old people, anyone who put them in a bad mood. The light was either dim or blindingly bright. When Mother was in leather chaps, the group appeared self-assured, jovial. They waited for enemies to enter the saloon, to swing open the doors and interrupt their poker game.

Trouble loomed. She was the best shot during these moments, killing those that crossed the threshold without disturbing her poker hand. They laughed when it was over.

Mother loved dirty jokes. When guests were sitting around the kitchen table and conversation stalled, she talked openly about people's genitals: "He has a small dick," or, "What's wrong, honey, haven't gotten enough?" She made sure people were caught off guard. Sexual references unveiled things. Many times they were the starting point for discussions that ran late into the evening. Conversation was lively, guests easily embarrassed. Mother was in charge.

My aunt, a devout Southern Baptist, visited us frequently. She made sure that I did not get overzealous with "my thing." Masturbation was a form of rot. "If you play with that thing, you know what's going to happen don't you? It's going to rot off. Go ahead, don't let me stop you—but just remember . . ." Little did she know, I took things further. I imagined escaping my body entirely and leaving it behind, not simply thrusting outward but peeling it away. I understood that I also possessed an inner and an outer life—two poles that I thought must never meet. Even though I kept my body fit, sharp, I felt there was a natural schism between my physical and emotional armor. I prayed that no emotional leakage would contaminate my fortress-body. I also knew my shoring up was tied to a familial obligation to turn out right, to overcome my family's past. What "body" did I inherent? Which one could I claim? "Turning out right" assumed that "I" was unshakable—a body "built to last."

All the Same

I was taught that the purpose of prayer was to fix my mind on the image of Jesus. "Concentration is important. Some have it, some don't," Father would say. Prayer was a drill. It kept me in line, and I knew the punishments. Even if I missed the divine image, I was considered a fine boy as long as I maintained my outward control.

As my interest in church lessened, I honed my body and mind toward more secular tasks. I spent long hours jogging through nearby canyons and the park behind school, imagining I was leaving my body behind, expelling everything. While in motion I improved my concentration. I fixed on a point just above the horizon, as if drawn into a trance. I felt I was preparing for something that would require similar focus.

After a grueling run one late summer afternoon, I was catching my breath a few houses away. Across the street, some of the neighbors stood looking at my house. They were an odd gathering of figures, lined up on the grassy strip by the street, gesturing to each other and pointing at the house. Some folded their arms; some busied themselves with yard chores, watering, digging, sweeping a spot of driveway next to the street. When they saw me, they partly turned away, not knowing what to do with themselves.

I heard a strange thud just a few feet from the driveway. My view was blocked by the family car. I trotted to the porch and put my hands on the hood; the sun had turned it into a skillet. I looked over carefully and saw Mother on the other side. Her face was bleeding and turned toward the lawn. My brother lifted her head by the hair and brought it down against the dry grass, trying to break her nose. I was numb—my palms to the hood. The neighbors inched closer to the street.

My brother slapped his jeans a few times, walked toward his truck, and drove away. She cursed his absence. "You fuckin' kill me . . . you just try you little bastard!" As he drove away, I went to help her up. She had already gotten to her feet: "Don't!" She stumbled onto the front porch and turned to me: "You're all the same." Staring at her torn dress, I started to cry. She disappeared into the house.

I touched the grass where her face had been; it was still moist. Everything was pathetic: the blank faces across the street were pathetic; the rows of homes with swings sets were pathetic; station wagons, vans, and ice cream trucks were pathetic; I was pathetic! At that moment, which became many such moments, there was no hope, explanation, or resolve. I grew up believing this.

The police arrived an hour or so later. Two men in leather jackets walked in, jingling keys. They asked a few questions, made notes, and wanted to know where "the other one" was. They questioned Mrs. Naymen across the street, who had witnessed the scene. She said, "I don't watch their every move. That's their business. It's a family matter."

That afternoon I rubbed my hands over the brittle grass. I ran for miles, not knowing where I was running. My concentration was perfect. "Pump the arms, lift the knees, be careful—don't arch the back! Keep to the rhythm. CONCENTRATE!"

2:00 a.m.

I'm alone tonight. Your departure was difficult, and I need to be secured by the warmth of your body. Though you will be gone for only a few days, I've never considered before what it would be like to experience the earth shaking while lying alone—the walls opening up, the small crack above our bed crumbling away, the metal bookcase tumbling to the floor.

Mother feared she was disappearing, and she sought support for her suspicions in her stacks of paperbacks, in stories where the adversary's body simply vanishes, thrown into a canyon and forgotten.

Movies were our common pleasure, enjoyed at the drive-in at El Cajon and at home late at night on TV. My brother insisted that we watch biker films—legs snapped in two at the knee, on-the-road orgies, renegade "pardies." We played western film soundtracks in a garage filled with automobile parts, basketballs, and Ford truck manuals. We kept our dreams to ourselves. No one spoke of feelings; we just cranked the torque wrench tighter.

Boredom pushed us to the brink. When Mother spoke of the inevitability of our explosions, she made a point of outlining the physical force used against her. When my brother spoke of his life, it was through film personas, talking with accents, swaggering against mercenary rivals. Father rallied the logic of salesmanship, of diplomacy, and, when this failed, resorted to rage. I counted on my fingers the days left in school, kept my eyes moving around the living room.

"It's a long fall," Mother used to say. She meant that her, our, fate was written into a final episode. She described "family" as scripted for us, prefigured into conflict, descent. Her ideas were supported by quasi-religious notions: blood tied to reason, mother to father, sibling to sibling. There were uncontrollable lineages—passing on a firm hand and intolerance. And there was a mistrust of those who tried to help us "work things out," a list that included social workers, state halfway houses, concerned relatives, neighbors, and the psychiatrists who diagnosed our supposedly unpredictable behavior. It was clear that in this fall our bodies were dropping through histories of violence and pathology. There was no "riding out of town," no scenes in which the villain was captured or challenged in a draw to determine who was quickest, more self-assured, genuine. Our myths spiraled, predicated on an intimate lawlessness.

Several years later, Mother held a black phone, speaking through a pane of wire-reinforced glass to my brother on the other side. Eighteen years old, his head shaved, he was serving time for accessory to murder.

A guard indicated that visiting hours were over. "Gotta go, Mom." He set the phone down on a wooden ledge. His slumped shoulders turned, and he followed a line of inmates out the metal doorway. Mother shook. "Those bastards, they better not touch him !" Later that afternoon I sat with her at our kitchen table, the drapes drawn. She had changed out of her green dress into black slacks and a white cotton short-sleeved shirt. She held a book with a cover image of brown and brick-colored figures, rearing horses, and a cowboy on his white horse, steady, sure. In the distance were rock plateaus in inky red. We sat for several minutes as she chain smoked. She fingered her book and looked through a slit in the drapes. Cars passed and neighbors walked their dogs. Father retreated to his garden. It was her birthday. She began to speak of our predicament, hoping that together we could unravel her anger.

"I've tried to bring you kids up right. *You've* been good, gave us no trouble, but I can't figure you out. You hide. It's not good to hide, you know—you end up livin' in the dark. Maybe that's our problem—we're hidin' from each other. What are we so afraid of? Can you answer me that? . . . Somebody's gotta clean up our mess. It's not gonna be me anymore, child. I've done my time, I've paid all I can pay, takin' care of you two kids and tryin' to keep things together around here. I've done just about as much as anyone can to keep all our pieces in order. I never could put all of 'em together, though. There's no order here; it's just one long fall—for us and everyone else livin' around here.

"You think this is easy? Try cleanin' up after someone night and day, carin' for 'em, watchin' their every move because if you don't they'll hurt themselves. Well, this is what I did for you, when you were so sick. I would do it again—I love you. But this is shitty ass work, child. Not simple work either! You think I sit around all day doin' nothing? Well, let me tell you, if you forgot, before you were born, your father and I owned grocery stores, built houses, and traveled. We had more than one life. It's just too bad we settled into this one now. . . .

"You can still play. I have a few things I enjoy myself, like my books— I know you think they're silly. But don't criticize my pleasures—it's like trespassing on family land. I've known this—it was drilled into me when I was your age that if someone crossed your farm and they weren't wanted, they caught hell. Where we lived in Texas it worked that way—strangers weren't welcome. We never let 'em explain themselves, just ran 'em off and told it right to their faces. I learned you can't back down, gotta fight. But I'm tired of fightin' now, tired of people turning away, tired of liars. Listen, if you can tell your own children that they're dangerous to themselves and you, and tell 'em this and still love 'em, tell the little bastards down the street that they better get rid of their filthy lives, and still live in the same neighborhood—if you can do this, you're worth something. You might have a chance."

8:30 a.m.

I didn't sleep. I haven't been able to get my bearings—my equilibrium is off since the quake. Before going to bed I made a mental list: fold my clothes; place my pants on floor, but first make sure that my wallet and change won't fall out; put my sweatshirt on top, collar toward the floor; next, place my socks by each boot. I packed a small sports bag with water, dried fruits, and nuts, spare clothes, and reading materials.

We walked in Santa Monica today. We passed a joint-tenant commercial building in which the upper floors were all small one-bedroom apartments. The entire front wall had fallen away, leaving several rooms with the beds as they were when the startled tenants sat up to see, inches away, a portion of the building dropping to the street. What was so disturbing was that these were all bedrooms. The tenants were dreaming, deep asleep, couples holding each other, sharing each other's warmth—then instantly exposed, on public display, their momentary sphere of intimacy shattered. A strange sight. In one room were black leather shoes by the bed, sheets thrown back, a desk and a mirror with makeup on it in the corner, and a pair of Levi's draped over a wooden chair. I just stood staring at these compartment-like rooms divided by crumbled brick and cement supports. The nakedness of the scene was unsettling: shoes neatly pushed together and paired next to the bed, books scattered along one wall, the doors of an armoire flung open, clothes pulled from hangers and left on the floor. This was a familiar feeling, something learned over many years—the brisk collapse of order.

Louise Diedrich

Born of Normal Parents

found a _Baby_. and I love her. but I'm worried that Cathy ....I can feel that Cathy is pissed...

I dream I am a Heroine - [IN THIS dream she leaves me for good]

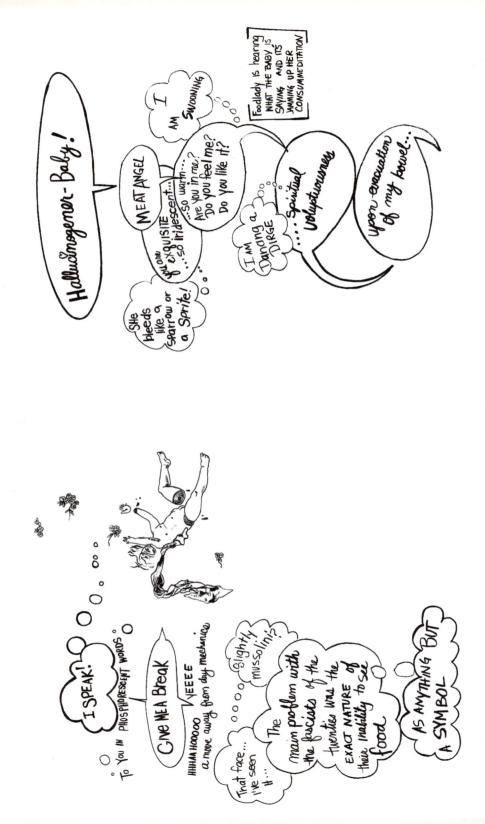

Calm Down (It's just **blood** makes you jumpy)
We've needed to talk for AWHILE....
let me help you understand
Then you can GO-

-OH MY GOD!

After many adverse situations I get there to rescue Baby...but...

Love Poems Inspired by Staring Too Hard at *Thomas*, a Photograph by Sharon Lockhart

Drugged Man, Dying Boy

Massaging this stupid back,
limp as a pillow, and warm,
I feel the blood rushing below
me, wild as the Mississippi's
shit, driven by speedballs?

And the kiddo's guts sleep,
rocking around in their hammock of freckled skin, etc.
His childish head creaks like
the skull's full of ghosts.

I open the paintings of eyes.
Their intelligence composes
something thin and unreliable
like . . . uh, surrealism? His
death'll explain this to me.

A child would put one tender,
barely used hand to his lips
and freeze, naturally stoned
on this image, but, artsy me,
I'll just wend my way into

Thomas,
1994
Sharon
Lockhart

wherever . . . the horror, etc.,
of his removal from me, mine.
Can't sleep at the thought of it.
Driven to understand why, how,
to devaluate Thomas's beauty,

dump its contents elsewhere . . .
until nothing, whatever, a mess
where he used to stand posing.
And me feeling zilch, only smarter
thereafter, and bored by love.

No Future

We were young
and our heads
were full of
drugs and death.

I polished my
body off nightly.
I played my
guitar all day.

Her eyes were
two miles. If
girls are gods
why'd I eat shit

when we kissed,
or I sang, every
time someone
interviewed me.

She pushed me
into heroin.
When I cared I
hated her for it.

Then I stabbed
her. It's like
cutting a pie,
if you must know.

So, kill me for
it. What did
I know. I was
trying to what.

Mower

I find my head in my hands,
especially when I'm alone,
pen in tow, poem at a loss.
The surface fills up, but
its life's at an indistinct
reference point, way out
back. It threatens wildly
from there like the fist of
a prisoner in documentaries
I'd drift to sleep during. It
yells its story over a din of
hatred cloaked in melancholy
I call home because I'll never
curl up there. That's what
allows me to put life at such
a perspective, not thinking it
out because it can't be, and
not being driven to tears because I couldn't. I'm lying in state, a variable left
undecided, attracted by love
in the abstract, but flat on
my back in a daze that won't,
can't be deciphered, the picked
skeleton of a once younger
person whose values can be
written off. Its mouth's open,
lost to what's happening to it.

Teen Idol

When Thomas said,
"Love's overrated,"
I said, "You spoiled
fucking brat." And I
reminded him, "Some
boys have AIDS, re-
tardation," etc. Stuff
he'd never se-e-e-en
up in Beverly Hills.

"There are girls
who'd dismember their
boyfriends for one
word from you,"
I told him. He
knew that, but he
didn't know some of
them were crippled.

So I drove Thomas
down to the hospital
where I volunteer,
where paraplegics
with his posters
taped around them
like a sky, saw him
and gasped like they'd
been diagnosed God.

He hugged them
and was rewarded
with laughter, etc.,
from Hell. He gave
them strips of his
clothes, etc. By end
of day, he was a
tattered tramp.

We headed home in
my Hyundai. "Okay,"
he said. "They
were pretty scary."
Everywhere we drove,
girls glanced in the
windows and screamed.
Drivers took one look
then hit stop signs
or other drivers.

It was like Thomas
was holding up a
sign that read,
WORLD WILL END or
SMASHING PUMPKINS
MURDERED. But
this was ye same
olde reaction. He
shrugged his thin
shoulders. See,

if he were talking
to fans instead
of posing, he'd tell
them, "Come over
if and only if you're
incredibly cute, etc.,
and if not, don't
bother," not "Love
is the answer," not
some philosophy.

Sentimentality for . . .

When in the old days I said something too complimentary, it was my usual bullshit, okay? He can please please believe that. Not to say I was lying. Never to him. But . . . Nevertheless . . . No love, ever, fuck this shit, grow up, etc.—what I've learned from the immediate past. That and don't let my emotions get lost inside somebody else, no matter how like me he seems, or how kindly he looks upon me, or what he might actually say if he said anything. He doesn't know what he feels, friends say. And nothing is sensible or kind. So it seems, though I cling to the notion of his and my powerful friendship at moments like this. I hope he never figures out how fucked up I've become. Forever? Don't tell him. That I mean, truthfully. To escape from his life with my devotedness toward him intact. My dream. That's all one can do, yes? This is the thing I must think when I think about him, which I do every day, and wonder endlessly what our, well, love—or, in other words, friendship, not romance, not sex, and I hate half the people I know for misinterpreting what I was feeling—meant next to how I was taught love would feel. Or not taught is the truth. As much as such feelings exist, I believed in their beauty when he was around, and even when he was dancing away from my feelings long distance, so unconsciously, so "couldn't possibly mean what he's doing," escaping my sympathy so sympathetically, I thought, needing, I guess, to feel love reflected back just like anyone does when they care far too much about anyone else, whatever *that* means, *that* being love, which I have no big ideas about now that it's gone. He won't call. And I'm so lost that a total delusion of closeness, if that's what it was I was living beneath, I hope not, would be kinder to be back inside. Or to be where he is right this second, even by phone, even though that's so fucking unfair to request, so undeserved on my part, or so he has implied by his silence, which, loving him as I'll continue to do, I agree to begin to acknowledge, thanks.

Some Whore

short walk home,
his snout running,
loose assed, takes
my fist for a thou-
sand, so i pay it
'cause i'm loaded.

arm to the elbow
inside a whatever
year old, says he
loves me to death,
etc., but he loves
death, not me.

i could kill him
sans knowing it,
punch through a
lung, turn my finger-
tip, render the
fucker retarded.

reckless, my fist
in his throat now,
face leaky, embar-
rassed and pleading,
zoned, urinating
all over himself.

jerk off, come,
pay, and he's split-
ting, says, "hey,
thanks a whole fuck-
ing lot," like it's
a joke, like he isn't.

Nurse

There's this guy who still reflects
in bloodshot eyes, glasses, and beer
mugs too lukewarm and fingered to
drink from, though embossed with the
names of some places we cruised.
He was The Future, I tried hard to
believe, out of sheer drunkenness,
I guess, since he was obviously a
hustler, and even a kind of in-joke
among "friends." Oh, him. We're
only horny enough to see through
things, not actually inside. Take that
guy gradually nodding out over a beer
I'd paid a waiter to set before him
with my regards. My God. Too bad
he can't open his eyes wide enough
at this point to see who's hung
around, may not care by this stage
that I'm here being moved by his
stupor, as I was drawn to his beauty
once, in ways I couldn't actually
show. Still, he was touched by the
effort in some remote way, I know.

Drunkenness for . . .

Xmas-fucking-Day,
and we're still
right where we were
when he O.D.ed.
He has left a trail
fragile as . . . Hansel's?

As we drink
his sharp face
brushes out of
death's wherever,
thin shoulders
following, six
feet of dirt,
until his grave
is in the air.

His fans are nuts.
Or we're too fucking
drunk to stand up.
Make him come back.
It's not "Xmas"
without him, not
just drunk again.

We're pathetic.
It's Xmas. We're
yelling at nothing.
We'll wake him up
with our stupid-
ity. No we can't.

On It

I fucked Thomas
up, molested him
with my eyes like,
uh, X-ray vision?

He's feeling wild,
then, out of the
blue, migraines
(I caused them).

Thomas is in
an imperious
place, love
life way over-
stocked, his

eyes colder
and deeper than
skylights. I
can't stand to
look at that.

My ideas, my
desires are all
muffled, flat.
Lead-colored eyes
dirty my view,

and, thus, lessen
all I love. Like
Midas, all exquis-
iteness bugs me.

So I screw Thomas
up, make him less
unbelievable, a
total slut, fucked.

Hand in Glove

One word subtracted from ten
becomes art in a writer's
lofty terms, in this frieze
where a poet can hide what he
mussed. It should be a guy
being fucked on an unmade bed
but in fact it's an old phrase
by which I'm reporting the
cooled interactions that come
into focus now that I'm shield-
ing my eyes from a lust that's
supposed to be ultimate, imposing more or less on these
words without growing monot-
onous, godlike. "I lie in a
bed post-drugged-sex," starts
whatever I'm trying to write.
It's "great" to restate this.
Though I'm blind, it is in
my hand, yes? Meaning a work
that's supposed to be filled
up with lust, but couldn't.
I grow too bored, am restrain-
ed if I think about who's lying outside my grasp . . . I can't
finish. But I've made up my
mind about art, its lasting
effect. It's polished, having
once in the dark been poured
gradually into my body of work
from an impossible height.

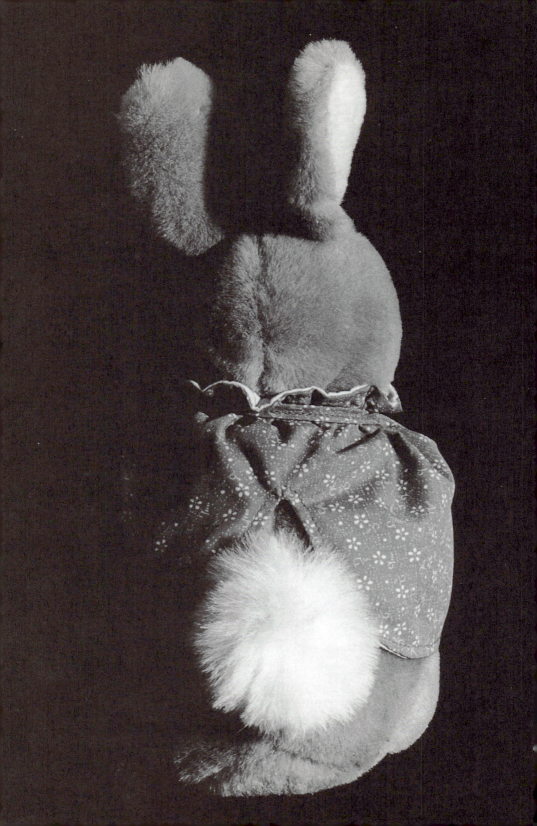

Leslie Dick

with photographs by Elizabeth Pulsinelli

On Splitting: A Symptomatology
or, The Los Angeles Maternal Position

I. Photograph

There was a photograph on the front page of the paper—*The Independent*—in London, early May 1992, when the baby was about three months old. It was a photograph that made Lee cry whenever she remembered it, and she remembered it quite often, she called it to mind, inadvertently, constantly. She couldn't talk about it with anyone at that time; she was embarrassed, awkwardly encumbered by these sobs, these floods of tears. She found it mysterious, the effect this photo had on her, and she didn't want to talk to anyone about it until she had this stuff under more control. Her emotion seemed like an obstacle, preventing her from understanding what might be at stake for her in this photograph. It was an obstacle she couldn't get through or over. Lee thought of the photograph, she wept, she tried to stop crying. The image would come to mind, tears would come to her eyes (as they did still, nineteen months later), and she would retire in perplexity, figuratively speaking, amazed by the intensity of this emotion and completely in the dark about its meaning.

It was almost as if the emotion rightfully belonged to someone else, or somewhere else. It seemed profoundly inauthentic, possibly, or maybe just inappropriate. The extremity of the emotion was undoubtedly inappropriate, if only because these ravaging tears interrupted the sweet flow of everyday, and then they exhausted her, the task of suppressing these inappropriate tears, these someone else's tears, tears from elsewhere, wore her out. It was profoundly inauthentic, it had to be, not least because the photograph represented a scene of starvation in Africa.

On the other hand, this seemed to be one of the acknowledged effects of motherhood: you weep over the morning paper, and can't watch the evening news. Was it that this emotion belonged rightfully to the mother, that other woman Lee was in the process of becoming? Who is this person? Lee thought. What is she doing invading me in this way, taking

Audrey's Bunnies, 1994
Gelatin silver prints, 9 x 6 in.

Opposite: *Flopsy*

up residence in my head, transforming my body? The mother hadn't yet taken over completely—the mother never really does take over completely—she was still an alien element in Lee's psyche, which is why her tears seemed so strange. But it was like being faced with undeniable evidence of some part of her that was completely beyond her control: some incorporation, or impersonation, some strange other one taking her place.

Lee wondered why she hadn't kept the photograph. At another time in her life she wouldn't have hesitated: anything that had such an impact would be kept, salvaged, stuck in a file, slotted into the archives of her endlessly monitored, constantly changing subjectivity. And if she'd kept it, the photograph might have faded, so to speak, it might have lost some of its effect, from being viewed repeatedly. That's what repetition is for, to wear things down.

Lee could have looked at it, when she thought of it; it would have been something to do, some simple thing, to look at the photograph, when she was plagued with the question of what it was. She could have examined it for clues, for the detail that might give her attachment, her fixation, away, that lets it go. But the photo went out with the newspaper, into the chaotic heap in the hall, and though Lee sometimes thought of trying to retrieve it, she thought she could certainly go to the public library and find it, she never did. It was imprinted on her, it would remain there, inside.

The photo was taken in Somalia, before the U.S. intervention there. The photograph showed a starving woman outside a Red Cross center in Somalia. Her starving child was being weighed in a simple apparatus made up of a kind of triangular hammock or sling attached to a scale. The woman was turning away and she was smiling. This smile is impossible to describe. She was smiling as if the most wonderful thing imaginable had just happened.

A caption made it clear. She was smiling, it seemed, because the scales showed her baby to be under a certain weight, and the feeding center would take the baby in, if it was under this weight. She was smiling because her baby was starving, and the child's weight was low enough for the Red Cross to take it in. She was smiling like this, she was so happy, because the baby would live. It was implied (Lee felt it was implied) that the child would live, or at least the child had a better chance, although (it was implied) she (the mother) might not, live, that is, or survive, and it was implied that in this situation, civil war, mass starvation, who could say if the woman would see this baby again, if she did survive, who could say if she would be able to find him, or her. She seemed bursting with energy, in that moment the

Opposite:
Lucy

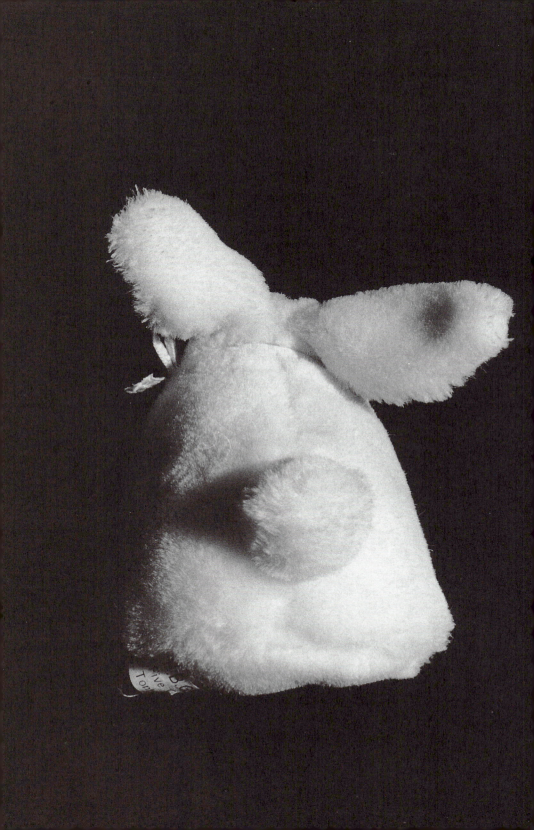

photograph isolated, the moment when she understood, and turned away, glancing, leaving the baby there.

I can't describe the smile, Lee said. A baring of teeth, drawing back of lips, her eyes lit up with delight. I suppose it could be described as ecstatic. It was a grimace of bliss, her momentary glance towards the camera allowing me at my kitchen table in London to see, her look meeting mine across the immeasurable distance between us. When I thought of the photograph, when I wept those uncontrollable tears, Lee said, my nose running, my teeth clenched, a grimace of despair seized my mouth, stiffened my face. Her pain, her smile, was unbearable to me.

2. Armor

I didn't know why. My friend Bea is still in analysis—we all used to be in analysis, but then I packed it in—and she's super intense, and rather wonderfully always talking about the heaviest things. I went to see her at the end of the summer, before I left to begin this job teaching in L.A., and we talked, about the past, mostly. And then I started, surprisingly, surprising myself, I started to tell her about the photograph in the paper, the photograph from Somalia, and inevitably I burst into tears, describing it to her. And Bea had to stand in for the lost analyst, again. First she was very sympa, and then she was curious, inquiring. She said, but what is it, what is it exactly about this picture? I mean, for you. It's awful—it's a terrible situation—but what do you think it means to *you*?

And I said, I don't know. I don't know. (I didn't know.) That the woman is giving the baby up, she's giving the baby away, she's so glad to be giving the baby away, because she loves it—not *despite* the love, but *because* she loves this baby, she's so happy, she's ecstatic. And Bea thought for a bit—we were walking in Ravenscourt Park, one of those smallish flat urban parks you get in London, with tarmac paths and a wading pool for the kids—and as we walked, I wiped my wet face with the heels of my hands, that bulge at the base of the thumb that fits so well into the eye socket, I felt that pressure, that contact. And then she said, do you think it's something to do with feeling that someone else could take better care of your baby than you can?

A revelation, of sorts. I can't protect her, I can't prevent her pain. I can't bear it. What is it that will harm her so? What must you protect her against? Me. Don't you think? It must be me. I mean, I'm the one who will do most harm—I'm her mother. So—what?—take her away from you?

Take her away from me, keep her safe, may I never see her again, may I go away from her, keep her safe from me. For I will damage her, I am her mother.

Does this make sense? Does this ring a bell? All those women desperately trying to protect their kids—are they like me, terrified of the thing in myself that is capable of destroying everything good, that ravages, wreaks untold damage, leaves disaster behind?

Wreak, wrought. Overwrought. Highly strung. Maybe I'm too highly strung for this. My mother always used to say, get down off your high horse. Which means something like, don't behave as if you're above all this, get down in the shit with the rest of us. She also used to say, rise above it. Rise above it, she'd say, when my sister tormented me. Climb back up on that high horse, and look down on her, on everyone, look down with contempt, immune, unscathed.

She emerged unscathed. She did not emerge unscathed. She was scathed by the image in the newspaper, scathed, or flayed, or pierced, her defenses breached, or broached. A sore point, broached gently. She pictured it like medieval armor, remembering *Lancelot du Lac* of Bresson, the delicate task of inserting a poniard, a small dagger with a long, slender blade, between the armor, into the crack between the breastplate and the helmet, to pierce the throat. Locked in a deathly embrace, face to face, breathing hard, with the tremendous weight of the armor, and the narrow knife gradually wedged into the crack: a terrible, poignant, intimate killing.

The photograph undid her defenses, found out the crack in her armor, pierced. The tears were hers, as (in fantasy) she gave her baby away—to anyone—because anyone would be better, anyone would be better than me.

3. Risk

So Lee understood something. The terrible, unspeakable danger—to her untouched, perfect, infallible baby—wasn't out there, it was in here. Of course there are dangers out there, but what can you do about it? she thought. Not a lot. You have to take risks, you have to walk down the street, you could get run over by a bus, but you have to walk down the street, a brick could fall on your head, someone could shoot you by mistake, the car could go out of control, the plane crash, whatever. None of the above. When Lee used to ride around on the back of motorcycles (at college her friends had motorcycles and she was always riding around on the back), her mother said, well you know if you die, it's very sad, and we'll all go to the funeral and cry a lot, and then it's all over. But if you're in a wheelchair for the rest of your life—that's a *real* drag. Anything can happen.

What I have to do, Lee wrote, is to try to make sure that the bit of me that wants to protect the baby (from the part of me that will destroy the baby) (I think) doesn't ruin the baby's life.

The protective impulse is always only the other side of the destructive fantasy. And in a way it's infinitely more dangerous, because it appears to be "good," it's socially sanctioned, it's proper mothering. I mean, this violence in me that is so great it will reduce the world to rubble, it will make the house explode, it will destroy everything, like an earthquake, like the refrigerator exploding at the end of *Zabriskie Point*—this violence is a fantasy. In some ways it may even be hypothetical, a construction of the analysis, as Freud would say. That is, buried so deep as to be surmised rather than experienced.

The reaction formation, the defense, is much more accessible, in fact it's right there, on the surface, filtering everyday life, infusing domestic space, the outside world, presence, absence, the sunny garden, the bed-room, riddled with fear. Like a translation: rage turns into fear, a pendulum swinging from one extreme to the other. Protection, or protectiveness, is the symptom of fear, and fear only the reaction to this implicit violence, this death drive.

People do hurt their children. They break their arms and legs, they burn them on electric heaters, they beat them black and blue, and they beat them to death. Worse, beyond what I want to remember or imagine. I won't do that. I asked my Freud class, we were reading "A Child Is Being Beaten," I asked if anyone there (about twenty people) had not been beaten by their parents. Silence.

Defense is always like a mirror, the other side of what is being repudi-ated or fended off. Perhaps. But it seems clear that one is much less likely to murder the child, to throw the crying baby out of the window or to bash its brains out against the wall, than one is to terrify it with protective threats about a dangerous world. *It's not safe.* Poisoning the child with my own fears, making a ghastly clingy whiny fearful blighted mess—like me.

4. Contempt

Lee went to the first birthday party of a little girl down the street. (The child was one year old, but it was also Lee's first birthday party, her first children's birthday party, in L.A.) Lee went, with Rose, and Rose wore her black dress with small red and blue flowers, and dark blue tights, and her green boots, terribly European. Rose was just beginning to walk, and as she came into the strange house, holding Lee's hand, the birthday girl tottered over and with her right hand reached out to scratch Rose's face, to the point of drawing blood. Rose stood there, stunned, not crying but amazed—no one had ever treated her like this—and Lee was amazed too, shocked, whereupon little Franny gave Rose a swift jab in the eye region with her left. It was the old one-two, translated into infant dimensions. Rose wailed, then, and Lee was ready to depart, but forced herself to stay, out of politeness. Rose recovered pretty quickly, and went outside to stumble around on the deck.

Lee knew no one; she stood still, surveying the scene: the hostess had made an enormous cake in the form of Big Bird; all the various foods and drinks were sugar-based; the other children, girls, were wearing flounced white dresses with white lace tights and black patent leather shoes; the other mothers seemed to spend an inordinate amount of energy shrieking at them to stay clean—but kids that age cannot stay clean, Lee thought, it's out of the question. Lee quickly discovered she was the only parent who sent her daughter to daycare; everyone else employed a woman from Central America, a "housekeeper," a "babysitter," except the frantic hostess, who was "staying home" with hers. It was here that Lee had the conversation about the toilet lock.

She was talking to a woman with a lot of hair, dyed dark brown hair tied back and tumbling in curls down her shoulders and her back; a little '50s, Lee thought, a blast from the past. They were making conversation, tentatively, when the woman left, to go to the bathroom. She used the bathroom beside the front door—and moments later emerged, screaming, *you haven't got a toilet lock!*

The hostess, very apologetic, very flustered, said, we have them on the toilets upstairs, it's just that one, we always keep the door shut. Lee decided to have a real conversation; what is a toilet lock? she asked. It turned out it's a device to keep the tiny child from drowning in the toilet. Every home should have one—or three, as the case may be. Lee asked if anyone had ever even heard of a child drowning in a toilet. Lee said, I mean, if your second cousin ever knew someone who knew someone who lived around the corner from someone whose baby drowned in the toilet. Or if you'd ever read about it in the paper. If it ever happened. No. Still, they were a basic requirement, apparently.

Lee couldn't stand this stuff: child safety was now a massive industry, producing endless catalogues, each purveying a vast number of ever more elaborate devices to survey, control, and protect the infant. It was unthinkable not to have a baby monitor, so you never left the kid alone; it was unthinkable not to have drawer latches and locks for the fridge and gates on the stairs and guards on the stove and items to put on the hot bath tap and covers for the corners of every table and socket plugs in every socket. Lee did buy a lock for the VCR, so Rose couldn't stick Cheerios in it. But she was nauseated by the child-proofing syndrome, by this industry that preyed on people's fears. As if spending the money on some device, or on a houseful of devices, would somehow do the trick, bandage over the anxiety and the lack of control.

So she told the woman how she, Lee, hadn't child-proofed her house in any way, not even a gate on the stairs, and besides, she said, our parents never had all this gear, and we survived. The retort was deadly: I live in a much larger home than my parents did, the woman said, and my parents never left me alone all day with a—with a—here she faltered. With a woman from Central America? Of course, Lee wanted to say, they're *famous* for letting babies drown in toilets down there in Central America, silly me.

Now she was ready to leave, but there's an etiquette, a rule: you have to stay to watch the presents being opened. It's so you get to see the look of joy on the face of the birthday girl when she opens yours. So they stayed, even though the birthday girl didn't know she was supposed to look joyful; even though it was a party of tinies who were all high on sugar and chocolate and shrieking and fractious, and it had been going on for hours (two) and the kids couldn't keep it together much longer. Lee came away extremely depressed.

Walking home with Rose she picked up the mail: a padded envelope. They opened it and found a button cushion from Lee's friend Jane in London. She'd made one for her kid, and Lee'd admired it, and now here was a button cushion for Rose. It was about eight inches square, and on one face there were about forty different buttons—one like a clock, one like a teapot, a rose, an elephant, a racing car, etc. Different colored buttons outlined the square. As an object, it seemed to imply a certain concentration of time and dedication: Jane searching in old shops to find these idiosyncratic, discontinued buttons, Jane maintaining the button collection, in boxes and little drawers, as well as Jane making the cushion, choosing, arranging, sewing them on. It was an object of contemplation, something a tiny child holds in its lap and studies. The button cushion was also, needless to say, potentially lethal, as kids choke to death on buttons all the time.

Opposite:
Run For It Rabbit

Ironically enough, one of the buttons did indeed come off within the first week—as if to prove how very un-Californian this object was. Lee sewed it on again, and wiggled all the others fiercely, to make sure. Matthew was amused by the toilet lock; he said, a baby would have to be both very intelligent and very stupid to drown itself in a toilet. The button cushion remained, part of everyday, to remind Lee of the toilet lock, and the hatred and loathing she felt, the insuperable distance between her and those other mothers.

5. Obstetrix

When I was pregnant, at the beginning, nine weeks, eleven weeks pregnant, I would weep, feeling that I couldn't protect the little transparent shrimp inside my belly. Protect it from what? I pictured doctors, technology, medical machines (I was trying to figure out amniocentesis), piercing my body, my body that should be protecting that little thing, that lively shrimp. Now I think it was the abortions, in my imagination, coming back to haunt me. Sharp instruments, doctors, and me—I'd chosen abortion, before, and now I felt I couldn't protect the fetus well enough, I couldn't protect it from those sharp instruments. And Bette said to Matthew, in New York, he told me she said, amnio is a wonderful thing—it allows older women to have babies without having to worry. . . . The unconscious conflation of amniocentesis (my choice) and the abortifacient D & Cs (my choice) was countered by conscious thinking, a political decision. I was frightened of the amnio, frightened of miscarriage; nevertheless I shifted, I tried to shift my fears.

Amnio is a wonderful thing. I lay flat on my back and the doctor stuck the long long needle into my stomach just like you imagine someone stabbing you with a knife. He held it in his fist and shoved it down into my belly. First they have to draw out some of the fluid to clean out the needle, because of course the needle has gone through my skin and flesh, and has therefore been contaminated with my chromosomes. So they stick the long needle in, then they screw on a syringe and draw out some of the amniotic fluid, then they unscrew that one and screw on another, clean syringe, and draw out more fluid, this time pure, untouched amniotic fluid, which will contain only the fetal chromosomes. Then they pull the needle out, and it's all over.

Then the doctor put the ultrasound on again; he said, you see, the baby is still moving (a dancing shrimp with arms and legs), you see, there's still plenty of fluid for it. As if to say, you see, we didn't harm it, we really didn't.

I never thought I was going to die in labor. I mean, during labor, I never thought I was dying. It was afterwards that I thought I might be going to die. It crossed my mind; it had never crossed my mind before, and I've been very ill before, but I was in such bad shape, about two weeks after she was born, I had wild temperatures, up to 106, and so much sheer, unadulterated pain, and I didn't seem to be getting any better, and it crossed my mind that I might be dying. There was barely any emotion attached to this idea, as if I were really finally too tired to get upset about it, as if that in itself might be a sign that I might actually be dying. Women used to die in childbirth, or after childbirth, all the time.

Edward Shorter wrote a book called *A History of Women's Bodies*. It seems to me to explain feminism, the patriarchy, everything, pretty clearly. It goes like this: until recently—and in many places this is still the case— most women became pregnant and gave birth at regular intervals, more or less until it killed them. In this they had no choice. As a result, it was almost impossible for them to manage to do anything else, except cope with the appalling conditions of their lives. His descriptions of the complications, the instruments, the illnesses attendant on pregnancy and childbirth, are truly harrowing. In my view, until recently most women didn't have a chance to live the life of a human being. Their humanity was subordinate to the exigencies of reproduction.

6. Counter-phobia

There was an earthquake here. It happened on a holiday, a Monday. Martin Luther King Day, 4:31 a.m. As the day wore out, it became clear that we wouldn't be going to work this week; we wouldn't be pretending nothing had happened. (We had no electricity, so no TV, and no batteries for the radio, so we didn't know how bad things really were until the power came back on.) It was hard to know what to do.

Rose goes to daycare in the Valley, exactly seven miles away from our house. I chose this daycare because Rita, who runs it, says things like, Rose you will have to learn to temper your passions with gentility!—as Rose, nine months old, on the floor, is trying to get as much of Christopher's hairless baby head into her mouth as she possibly can. Gentility, I thought, a four-syllable words flung out over the heads of babies—that's what I like about this place. I like her, I like the other kids, I like the way Rose never cries when I leave her at Rita's.

The epicenter of the earthquake was in the Valley too. Rita's is closer to the epicenter than our house, I think. I haven't measured, I haven't looked seriously at a map. But there are collapsed buildings all along the way to Rita's, and the park was full of tents and people sleeping in their cars, and the electricity and water was off, intermittently, though not at Rita's, her house was OK, and at 7:30 a.m. Tuesday morning she was open for business.

I didn't want to take Rose to Rita's on Tuesday morning. I didn't have to teach, to go to work, but we have so many tasks, letters, bills, taxes, that an unexpected day off work means we can get so much done! I didn't want to take Rose to Rita's, but Matthew took it for granted that Rose would go to daycare—or we didn't discuss it, I don't really know what he took for granted, but he never raised it as a question, and I believed that he thought it was the right thing to do. In any case, we went. Driving through the Valley early Tuesday morning was like driving through a scene of devastation. I was interested to note how very different one's response to an actual collapsed building, especially a building one drives past every day, how very different that is to seeing collapsed buildings on TV, which are like all the other collapsed buildings, all the other disasters.

When I arrived at Rita's, it transpired that we were the only parents who'd brought our child to daycare—except for Dakota, whose parents had brought him because they'd lost their apartment, completely destroyed, and they were running around trying to find somewhere to live. What had we lost? Some plaster, a jar of honey and a jar of mango chutney that flew out of the kitchen cupboard, two bowls, a glass. Matthew's reading glasses were broken by a falling book, *Sigmund Freud and Art,* to be precise. We were very scared—or I was very scared. Matthew claimed not to be scared, but then his childhood memories are of the Blitz. (Later he did admit the whole experience was rather *stressful.*) But he becomes David Niven circa 1942 in these situations, clutching Rose's toy flashlight, stalking around the house in the dark assessing the damage, going outside to try to find a radio, to find out some *news,* while the interminable series of aftershocks rolled through, and I held Rose in the dark in the doorway, immobilized.

We left our daughter at daycare in the Valley the day after the earthquake, while all the other parents, all the parents who had a choice, chose not to—and I felt mad, bonkers, out of control, like, how can I tell what is the right thing to do? I want to keep her here with me; I figure that's neurotic, that's crazy; I make myself take her to daycare, and discover *that's* crazy, that's something no one else is doing, if they don't have to.

Opposite:
*Rabbit
Paperweight*

It's counter-phobia, when you make yourself do something you're terrified to do. It's a compulsive act, beyond your control, the other side of the phobia itself. But separation anxiety is such that every ordinary everyday farewell is in some measure counter-phobic.

Around the corner from where we live a house fell down the side of the mountain in the earthquake. A man and a woman were trapped; she was seven months pregnant and her pelvis was broken. Their four-year-old daughter was killed. The parents were taken to different hospitals. *We lost her,* the man said.

So I go on taking Rose, saying goodbye, easily, easily, take it easy, I say, because I have to, take it easy, because you can't hold on to them, it only ruins things for them and it doesn't necessarily even keep them safe.

My friend said it was hard for her to begin to say *no,* to actually say the word *no* to her one-year-old, so she said she had taken up saying *it's not safe.* I said, but that just portrays the world as a terrifying, dangerous place, a place full of danger. She said she hadn't thought of that. Then I remembered how hard it was for me, to begin to say no, and I wondered what it was about. It's such a pleasure when the kid's only tiny, that infancy thing, where you don't refuse, you only say yes. You scoop the baby up if it's about to fall or hurt itself, but you deny it nothing. Is it that we don't want to be hated, the wicked witch, the agency of prohibition? (He may symbolize it, Daddy, I mean, but we live it out.) We want to say yes, to be loved, the endless cornucopia, and instead we find ourselves saying no, not now, stop, stop that right now, that's enough, I won't have that, that's enough, and even, occasionally, that's not safe. I love taking risks with Rose, that is, allowing her to take risks—I love it because I can see how she feels the world is a good place, full of adventure and delight. I don't want to cramp her style. I don't want her to be scared.

So I take her, and leave her, despite the aftershocks, despite my own separation anxiety. Cut off my own nose to spite my face, to make it good, to make it all right. When the aftershocks come she stands still in the middle of the room, utterly surprised, and I say, it's all right, it's all right, it's all right. There's an element of counter-phobia in every farewell, every goodnight. Like all mothers, I have listened in her dark bedroom to make sure she's breathing; I've imagined her dead, face down in the bath. Recently I moved my collection of kitchen knives (razor-sharp Sabatiers) out of the kitchen drawer and into a glass vase on the kitchen counter— my first gesture of baby-proofing. She's tall enough now to get things out of the drawers, and as I stood in the shower, allowing her to roam through the empty house, I would fantasize a scream (you can't hear anything in the shower except possible distant screams), I would picture her holding the ten-inch chopping knife over her head, a tiny Attila, charging around the kitchen, and the knife falling and cutting her. Babies bleed to death very quickly because their heartbeat is extremely fast and they have very little blood inside their bodies. Comparatively. That's my theory, anyway. That a baby would bleed to death very quickly.

My sister cut her jugular vein on a broken glass when she was two. Her life was saved by a friend of my mother's who knew where to press. They'd been playing bridge, I think, four women and their toddlers, and my mother was saying, oh my daughter is very good, she never climbs up on things, when they heard a crash from the kitchen and ran in to find my sister bleeding to death. She'd climbed up on the kitchen table, with a glass of orange juice, and fallen off. I picture bright orange and red liquid on the shiny linoleum floor. The doctor said she wouldn't have survived if they'd arrived at the hospital thirty seconds later.

So I put the knives away, out of reach, and continue to take hurried showers, listening, listening for her screams.

7. Hatred and loathing

Why should I hate it so much, the toilet lock, the mother who's upset when the kid gets dirty, or who makes more of a fuss than the child when the kid falls over or bumps her head? Ouch! she says, before the kid's had time to decide whether it's painful or not. Hug, she says, hug, as the kid's ready to wander off, do something else. I hate it because that's me, that's the over-protective, let me fix it for you, kiss it better, hug, never lay a hand on her, no, no one will ever lay a hand on her, let us be all in all to each other, true love forever and ever, you're mine, swallow you up, all mine, never let you go bit. It's the bit that wants to keep her clinging to me, in my arms, to keep her safe, with me, always. Rita laughed with me about how I'd feel when Rose went out on dates; I said, dates! Never! You must be joking!

It's the bit I won't give in to, the bit I suppress, because I know it would ruin her life, ruin my life, ruin everything. So it drives me crazy when I see other women doing it, letting themselves do it, doing what that bit of me wants to do so much.

8. Theory

What she wanted to write about was splitting. So she looked it up in the dictionary of psychoanalysis.

Laplanche and Pontalis on the paranoid position theorized by Melanie Klein:

a. *As regards the instincts, libido and aggressiveness (oral-sadistic instincts: devouring, tearing) are present and fused from the outset. . . . ***
    *cf. my constant return to the word ravage, ravaging, ravaged.

b. *The object is partial, its prototype being the maternal breast.* *
    *i.e., me, the mother, the good or bad breast, but I'm still the infant
    too, somewhere, and my little one, my own infant, is also a part-object
    for me—in fantasy.

c. *This part-object is split from the start into a "good" and a "bad" object, not only inasmuch as the mother's breast gratifies or frustrates, but also because [the infant] projects its love or hate on to it.**
    *The part-object (which slots into the psychic equation breast=penis=
    feces=baby=money=gift) itself always has two sides, cuts both ways.
    Split from the start.

d. *The good and bad objects which are the outcome of this splitting attain a relative independence of one another, and each of them becomes subject to the processes of introjection and projection.**
    *A relative independence: when the "good" and "bad" objects no longer
    hold together, but fly apart, like atoms, like opposing magnetic poles,
    radically separated, because any contact, any contamination or combi-
    nation between them is simply too anxiety-provoking.

e. *The good object is "idealized": it is capable of providing "unlimited, imme-diate and everlasting gratification." Its introjection defends the infant against persecutory anxiety. . . . ***
    *My baby is the good object idealized: unlimited, immediate and
    everlasting gratification.

*The bad object, on the other hand, is a terrifying persecutor; its introjection exposes [the infant] to endogenous threats of destruction.**

Opposite:
Royal Rabbits

*Endogenous threats: the thing in me that will blow up the world, the house, the baby.

f. *The ego . . . has only a limited tolerance of anxiety. As means of defence, aside from splitting and idealization, it uses denial (disavowal), which seeks to divest the persecuting object of all reality, and omnipotent control of the object.**
*Disavowal and control: the danger lies elsewhere, because I am the (all powerful) good mother to this (inviolate) good baby. I can even leave the sharp knives loose in the kitchen drawer—because (magical thinking) nothing can happen to us.

g. *"These first introjected objects form the core of the super-ego."**
*Super-ego: my mother told me she'd given the persecutory voice in her head a name. She said, you know, that voice that tells you you're no good, not good enough, how terrible you are—I call her Auschwitz. I say (my mother said), I say: *Shut up, Auschwitz!*

9. Notes on splitting

I don't know how to approach this topic, splitting; I don't even necessarily agree with Melanie Klein (who invented the paranoid position), and I think dear old Laplanche and Pontalis aren't wildly sympathetic to her either. All I know is I live in fear of destroying everything, and therefore hold things together compulsively, trying to make good the destruction that I feel I must have (on some level) already carried out, or maybe that I am (unconsciously) continually carrying out, wreaking, all the time. And I live in fear of my "good" object, the baby, being hurt or damaged or destroyed; I feel it would kill me, it would be unbearable.

But most of all, I think, I feel I deserve to be persecuted, for being so happy. I have banished evil from my world (more magical thinking), and so it must be out there lying in wait for me. And in my experience, making artwork is aggressive and destructive and violent and painful, and it hurts me and hurts others, and these days I feel like there can be no possible justification for that pain, for that writhing around on the floor, that anguished gnashing of teeth. I don't know how to hold the baby to the "good" breast, so to speak, while my pen (black ink, bad breast) spews insight, invective, cruel, cutting, incisive words. I am paralyzed, immobilized, stuck in the gap between the two: bad-girl artist, good mother. Incompatible,

Opposite:
Floppy Pair

incommensurable, incompetent. Faced with this particular conflict, I shut down, and desperately find reparatory work to do, "compulsive repetition of reparatory acts" (like teaching? folding the laundry?)—or else resort to delusion, what are called manic defenses, also known as feelings of omnipotence. I feel like I could disappear, fall off the planet, never answer the phone, never open a letter. It's phobic—as if I could sidestep the aggression in me, or smother it, and ignore the danger out there, if I just keep my head down, and go on, insistently, gazing into the baby's eyes.

Unfortunately, the baby persists in growing up, and won't lie still. I need a place to hide, a phobic bolt hole, and she won't play, she wriggles in my arms, she scoots off, interested in something else: rabbits. I'm left with this emotional baggage, this terror of just retribution—it's not persecution, it's more like punishment I anticipate; I think it's the price I have to pay for my writing, for the baby. So I'm left with compulsive repetition of reparatory acts and manic defenses: denial, idealization, splitting, or omnipotent control. My armor, designed to keep the baby safe.

10. Out of the labyrinth

It was a conundrum; Lee felt trapped. She couldn't get past her terror, her fear that the child would somehow be lost or harmed, and she would be powerless to prevent it, or worse, she would be the source of that harm.

It was no comfort to insist, as Lee insisted, that this was indeed the case, nothing to be frightened of, nothing to worry about, simply a fact of life. Parents damage their children, it's unavoidable. Growing up is a process of being damaged by the world, Lee thought. The idea was excruciatingly painful.

You can earthquake-proof your house, the way you baby-proof your house, but that won't fix it, quite. Lee's memory of the photograph of the woman in Somalia was still beyond her control. Lee knew her response to the photo was about her own fears; she knew it had nothing to do with the Somali woman's experience, which Lee could only begin to imagine. The earthquake was a real danger—theoretically, although like all the other threats, it seemed finally only to stand in for Lee's violence, her anxiety. Matthew said he never imagined the world to be a *safe* place. He was pretty fatalistic about it. Look at European history, he said, you can't look at what happened in the last century and imagine you'd be *in control*.

Opposite:
Small Gray Rabbit with Sweets Rabbit

Lee's mother phoned, a few days after the earthquake. Lee told her about it; she'd been scared to death, she said. It's the emotional repercussions, she said, and the aftershocks, that go on and on and on. Lee's mother talked for a while longer, then she said, but you sound a little *subdued*. As if to say, reassure me, tell me you're all right really. Lee was irritated, even hurt, but when she thought about it later, she saw how that wish to protect the child, to deny all danger, all sorrow and harm, would persist—despite everything. And how intolerable it would be to be so powerless, thousands of miles away, and to hear about the scenes of devastation, the aftershocks, the terror. How you might say, tell me it's OK really, because I just can't bear the thought that it's really not.

Lee felt stuck, trapped. Then she discovered there was a way out—that it is the child who leads you out of this trap, out of this bubble of maternal preoccupation, this enclosed world, out of the compelling fantasy of being all in all to each other, of being *good*. The child leads you out, magnificently, by becoming a human being, and therefore (like all human beings) subject to conflict, torn apart by internal strife. As if this thing one wants so much to repudiate, this "bad object" banished forever, shows up again in the gleaming eye of the tiny tot intent on destruction, and you have to laugh, you have to let it go, give it up. The child won't stay locked in the perfect bubble—she wants to go make something happen, she has something to say, she wants to be by herself.

You can have another baby, Lee thought, you can try to prolong this state of affairs, this unlimited, immediate and everlasting gratification. Then you'd have to have another one, and another.

Or you can take cover, and let everything go, and hang on to the memory, that indelible image of the good child, the good mother, inseparable.

Or you can let the child bring you back—to language, to violence, and to that tired, fallible, damaged body—not to rush in panicky with the quick fix, compulsive as ever, but slowly, with difficulty, to make it good.

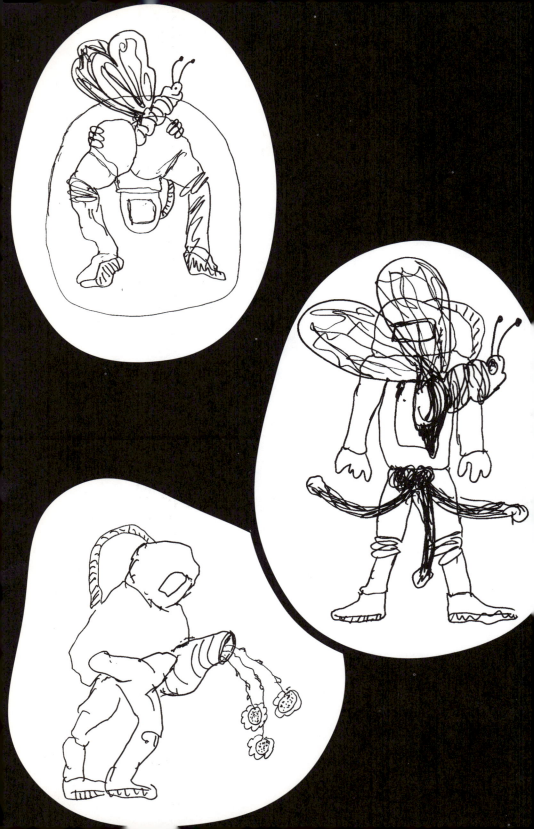

A Strangely Haunting Love

John Cage and I were born with penises. This phenomenon endows us with telepathy, making personal contact redundant. I was never as special in his eyes as I'd hoped, because his interest in me came by Chance. He had an obsession with the *I Ching*, the Book of Changes, an apparatus of divination that ruled his life. His last letter to me, composed just before his death, was sent via his mind.

Dear Tyler,

I've never been in love with you until now. The *I Ching* has determined that we should be in love. Love is always left to Chance for me. I have many fantasies about you. Tomorrow, Chance will determine which fantasy shall become reality. It will be a surprise for both of us. Meanwhile, I'll tell you one which may or may not become real.

I am Captain Jean-Luc Picard from television's "Star Trek: The Next Generation." He is what I want to be for your eyes: a big penis; a bald head imbued with luscious and erect authority. As Picard, I am in charge of the starship *Enterprise*, controlling a science-fiction space that will put asunder those who are joined in the family: male and female, parent and child. This will happen when I fulfill my secret of finding an alien who will infiltrate the "boundaries" of the crew members and transform their identities. I am delighted by this secret because it shares a kinship with the annihilation of my ego.

I constantly throw down the *I Ching*'s sticks to determine my next moves. Eventually, I find myself throwing down bony Klingon penises collected through the years. I want your Vulcan-like, logic-penis in my mouth. I trade in Dionysian Klingons for Apollonian Vulcans. I want your

This work is part of a series called *Strangely Haunting Love Letters from Elders, or The Expansive Flesh of Wrinkles Is Seductive.*

sperm as the next *I Ching* thrown against my face, a pearl necklace down my throat, choking me. But despite your being of another world, that is, an alien, and being an object of my fascination, you are still unwilling to penetrate my identity. You are not part of the club yet.

With great love,

John

I respond to John with a hand-written hard copy letter instead of communicating tele- pathically because I don't want him to believe that he's stolen my mind yet, as there is still something left behind—my body.

Dear John,

I cannot be your Vulcan sex slave. Even though I physically exist, my body cannot be the hard-body of a Vulcan's reason and logic. Yes, I like to submit to people, but slavery in your service means becoming an equal because you'll want me to dissolve my ego as you've done. Plus, you really don't want to control me—you make no decisions because your life's moves are determined by Chance. I might be interested if indeed you were Picard and possessed his authority.

You probably think this limit is unnecessary. But I'd rather you have control over me than for you to be the father of my thoughts. I just cannot consider you as a vaginal father, like the god Zeus giving birth to lesser gods and goddesses from his head—although I must admit to being slightly seduced by the thought of originating within someone else's thoughts. Nonetheless, I cannot accept you as a penis womb. I'm sorry. Perhaps you've already given birth to me without my knowledge. After all, you and I do have the opportunity to interrupt one another's identities because of our telepathy. I can never trust my thoughts because they may be your thoughts.

I have a dream after articulating and conceiving this fear. I'm in a dungeon looking at myself. Suddenly I am a prisoner, aging years within seconds. This is me becoming you, John, in your eighties. At the end of the aging, I am a skeleton creature who accepts the dungeon as his home, becoming a torture instrument to whom other prisoners are thrown. My body is just a rib cage and a skull. I live in what looks like a sandbox, resting in an accumulation of urine, shit, and my victim's skulls. The dream's last scene is of me eating some flesh. Suddenly, I have to shit so I lean back, as I shit from below my ribs. Attached to my chest is a trapdoor that rises as I lean back. A demon-dog is under it and, as my own observer in the dream, I see that the beast lives in a smaller room under my box. I perceive it as a demon that I've known all my life. You're the demon dog seducing me.

Your demon qualities are represented best in the movie *Alien*. You are the face-hugger who implants an egg in my stomach that hatches and bursts out of my body, representing a return of the repressed, eating me from within. As this demon, what repression of mine are you returning? You are like those science-fiction aliens who make humans question the composition of their identity. You or they make uncertain the depth of one's psyche through willful mutations, states of subterfuge, appearing as the host for the human but really being the parasite. Maybe you use language to seduce me, placing my body in a discourse so that I will believe that you think I am important and thus will want to be your companion. Can you be trusted?

There is a complication if our bodies are ever to meet. Remember the last scene of the movie *2001: A Space Odyssey,* where the character Dave Bowman watches himself age? After passing through the black monolith's stargate, he ends his journey as the Starchild, the next evolutionary stage in humankind. Starchild and I share the act of orbiting Earth and appearing on it suddenly. We are hysterical astronauts, both willing to transform, penetrating and impregnating ourselves without biology, without sex— having a continuity not with this world but with a world that we'll never know. No sperm, no egg. I don't have a belly button—no umbilical cord. I am mother and child, *womb* and *phallus*. Because this type of non-biological transformation is impossible, it means that I don't like to travel, which is the obstacle, on my part, that prevents our visiting physically. Don't be mad.

You probably think I'm a professional dreamer. Only in dreams can I reproduce asexually and be a parthenogenetic angel hovering above myself with . . . You've just interrupted my train of thought with a telepathic insertion that seems to have been floating in the air despite your death: *Tyler, let me offer a suggestion that will leave your penis intact with your body. Since you*

*are so interested in the mind, then say hello to cyberspace and farewell
to outer space. Masturbate in front of a mirror, pretending that your
mind and body are separate entities. They can then function as your two
parents, whom you see by mistake having sex. You will believe that the
penis is eaten when entering the vagina. Then you will fear castration
from yourself. You will go to extremes in search of a sense of well-being,
seeking entrance to a womb, thus needing a pacifier in the meantime,
something to suckle, like a breast, but instead you can suckle my cock. I hope
you like this idea!*

Why do you send this message telepathically and not by letter? I
don't think you want evidence of your sexuality to exist. I think you allow
Chance to place your sexuality above public critique. Perhaps you use the
I Ching as an apparatus for turning your sexuality into another of Chance's
variables. Subscription to your sexuality is then considered "normal"
because it originates in a system outside of yourself—you cannot help
being who you are due to the circumstances determined by Chance. You
will not admit to loving men both for their bodies and also for their
interaction with language.

Suddenly it dawns on me why you really use the *I Ching*. It's your
defense mechanism. You don't want me to know your thoughts. Your
subjective decisions are determined by Chance, so I will never know what
your next plans of seduction will be, despite telepathy. You're unfair for
retaining such control over yourself. Chance would seem to provide
uncontrollability, but it seems that you've tapped into chaos theory by
making your decisions appear random, whereas in fact they settle into
a system eventually—into death, into harmony and not noise, as you hope.
You use Chance as your armor, like Robocop and the Terminator, who
defend their egos with metallic body armor. You, John Cage, and Arnold
Schwarzenegger are one in the same.

You've made Chance into a totalitarian ruler over your subjectivity by
creating this system of control. To be in such control means you are unin-
terested in the diversity that Chance could produce. Your use
of Chance runs counter to sexual reproduction and thus
against the idea of history. In a species that procreates by
sexual reproduction two biological mates contribute
different chromosomes, meaning a huge number
of permutations determine the characteristics of
the offspring. Such diversity is absent in your
asexual reproduction.

This characteristic contributes to my fear of giving in to you. It would make sense to do so; after all, I don't feel a need for continuity through biological reproduction. Perhaps this is where your thoughts have seeped into mine. Maybe you have been more in control of me then I first conceived. Maybe you do have the authority of Jean-Luc Picard. Seems I'm attempting to avoid history by not combining sexual pleasure and biological reproduction—or language and biology—though I'm trying to combine physically with an image of you. Earlier, I compared myself to the Starchild, who was born of language, the mind, and not biology. Imagine what I might have to say: "My days are a time when people possess asexual memory." A time when memory is not expansive but exists in a closed system, when my asshole becomes a vagina to go along with the penis that I possess already.

I could fall in love, not so much with you but with this world that you represent. I could fall in love with you as Cage the symbol, though, not as Cage the material, flesh-body. I can't offer more, because I imagine that we should explode if our penises were to touch, like matter and antimatter, which is what can happen when two people in the same world are each born with a penis.

I'm trying to calm down.

All for now.

Most sincerely,

I could fall in love, not so much with you but with this world that you represent.

Laying Me Down

After the long bath, my skin plumped up like a Ball Park frank from having been soaked too long, before I lay me down to the insomnia that has plagued me for years, I stare into the glass. Just before I lay me down to battle, I stare at the mirror, I look at my armor, my shield, my weapon. Assessment is a constant preoccupation, that voice in my head: "How do I look?"

The skin of stainless steel droops down, now some forty-five years later, the breasts, the hips, the chin, all moving closer to the earth. My lips, no longer red, sink into the flesh of my face, losing themselves there. The blood that flowed for seven days has slowed to three. And the memories of adolescence which I clung to for dear life are falling, slowly, through the cracks in my fingers. The certainty, the absolute truths, the literal facts.

The hair on each thigh has made its way to the knees. Gray and black twisted together. If it keeps this up, by year's end I'll stop having to sleep with a blanket. I am becoming a bearded lady with orange-peel skin. Freckles big as dimes cover my exposed flesh.

Messages are scrawled on every inch of skin. Thank-you notes, psychological reports, criminal records, birth certificates, FBI files, valentine cards. I am a journal in 3-D. A chronicle of time, of family, of class, of gender, of nation. A testimony to history. I have been alive.

There is a knock on my door. "Goodnight, Mommy," she says, followed by the sound of two lips smacking against one another, forcing a kiss through the wooden door. "Nightie, night, Mo," I tell her, shortening her Gaelic name, Meagan, to one syllable. "Sleep tight." She hesitates. She understands somehow the importance of this night. I hear her feet slap against the wooden floor and cross into her room. Her radio plays music from the '60s. A door closes.

I picture her, in my mind, standing in front of her mirror, assessing her own image. I see her turn sideways checking to see if her tiny breasts have grown. I imagine her looking at the curve of her hips, then smiling back at her reflection. I can almost hear her giggle as she realizes that now, at the age of fourteen, she is taller than Mom. She is eager for me to make room for her youth. The music fades. A light clicks off.

A sharp pain travels left to right across my forehead. The index finger on my right hand twitches as tiny drops of fluid, the liquid that fuels females in their prime, drips slowly out the tip of my finger. The twitching stops, causing the pain in my forehead to subside. There will be no other children, sleeping tight, in my house. This body is taking that choice from me, without my consent. Using its power to override my intellect, to mock my brain, which always assumed anything was possible at any moment in time.

What is to become of this now? Separate from the opinions of lovers who walked away because I was too old, too experienced, too angry at having lived in this world. Opinions that echo in the world, bounce off the walls, play on TV, that repeat themselves in my brain, because I believe them. I will die, am dying, always was, but for the first time I actually know it.

No psychobabble fits, no literary canon hits this mark. No materialist analysis can ease the pain, no spiritual code can change the inevitable nature of this fact. And what am I to do with myself in the "meantime"? Very few women like me strip down in public, making our aging images the focus of desire, the definition of passion. We are expected to stay home, our issues privatized, robbed of universality.

It's not a shock to see the years of gravity at work. I only started look-ing at this body, full-length, at the age of thirty-three, and even then I rarely ever saw the whole. I saw the parts, often unconnected, trying to communi-cate, but not succeeding. It was the safest way to be in the world: "Long legs, nice boobs, big ass."

My brain was occupied with dragging the weight, the amorphous mass, and controlling everything that came near it, blocking all dialogue between the separate sections. This body had to be on guard. Dividing the whole into parts distracted the enemy, localized each attack, guaranteeing that some part would always survive.

The parts . . . The breasts that began sagging at seventeen, after the first birth. I still remember that night, the feeling of something being pulled out of somewhere, legs and lower torso, fully dead from the drug. And a day later, I was a baby short. I was unfit. Too young. Out of control. It was on its way to some worthy home. Nice. White. Middle-class. Fit. After the dry-up shot, hips permanently separated, I flew back to the housing project.

The stretch marks that now score each breast, cutting deep into the skin, leaving long tracks of scar tissue, arrived after the second birth. I was thirty-one. I kept that one. I refused the drugs, so that torso, hips, cervix, could feel the passage. Afterwards I drove us both home in a car, with her tied up in a baby seat. The daughter sleeping in the next room. The one who will wake up in the morning, knock on my door, packed and ready, eager for me to take her to the Wild Animal Park.

The parts . . . The long lips, covered with thick hair, encircling my dark hole. I discovered them early on, with the help of close family members, stroking, probing, pumping their way into my mass. And I remember my hands, finding their own way home, repeating the movements of blood ties, creating pleasure, while the brain slept. The very same hands that punched and tore at enemies, brothers, school friends, guys on the street. The hands that stabbed my father, that flipped God off because he was useless, hands that slapped my own face. Dual-purpose equipment.

Feminism gave some of these parts names. Clitoris, such a nice word. I'd known "it" for years, but was finally able to baptize the damn thing with a word. That private little part became public. Tits became breasts, pussy became vagina. Ideology even gave a different meaning to old words, declaring them patriarchal. Fuck, fuck, fuck. I adjusted, learned to "make love." But it wasn't the same. In the heat of political movement too much can be wiped out. That dog-ma has been taken for a walk. Had to. My bed was never big enough to accommodate a social movement.

Now breasts, clitoris, vagina, lips, hands, chin, are all pulling together, becoming whole, no longer lashing out in a thousand directions, trying to escape from one another. I am getting ready, preparing to kick this butt into the future. Coming back up from the mud, reinventing everything.

The brief flashes of heat that rush up from my legs, up the small of my back, across my chest and over my ears, make me sweat, make me weak. But this is momentary, the heat will pass. After having moved past five years of dark ages, into the middle of age, fighting and kicking and scream-ing, lusting after my youth, I am ready now to create a new self, and in so doing, to re-create the old.

There is movement in the glass. The muscles in the back of my legs tighten. My head drops forward, my eyes move down past my torso, over my thighs, crossing the knees. Six inches separate my heels from one an-other. A warrior's stance. The mirror spreads out against the wall, doubling in size.

In a world I can recall only through imagination, a world re-created with each retelling of the story, there were so many faces, voices, images, pushing me into battle. Uninvited guests. Invaders, intruders. I had a choice. I could have greeted them like a hostess, opened the door for them, made it pleasant. But I didn't.

A head pops out of the glass. It laughs at my presence. It looks just like me before the dark ages. "Over the hill, honey," blares out of its mouth. "You're a done deal, babe." I move my head to the left to see more of the face. Mascara is smudged below her eyes, this girl cries too much. Small wrinkles surround her mouth, this girl laughs too much.

A neck falls from the head, arms shoot out on either side of it, a torso unfolds, spreading out at the bottom, giving form to hips. She chuckles loudly, her belly jiggles, forcing the hips to release two trails of flesh, forming legs, ankles, and feet. She is here to do battle.

I recall the last woman, warrior, battle-ax, who lay down with me. My mother. I fought her for years, in my insomnia, finally letting loose of her foot, as her body hung out over the balcony ledge. A bloody splash, a thud, and then Mother's eternal moans. She's still out there on the sidewalk, groaning, still getting her revenge. But she's not on top anymore. She's not kicking me anymore, not letting me know how unimportant I am, how insignificant. "You worthless little shit" won't be heard in this house anymore. And she can't suffocate me with her huge breasts, filled with mother's milk, white creamy guilt. A sticky, sweet substance that delivers sermons, filled with hierarchy and responsibility, teaching with every suck a subservience to history.

No, in the interim I have succumbed to the sermons of horny little boys. Teeny, weeny little playboys of the Western world. I fuck and they procreate, projecting themselves into the future, repeating themselves endlessly. Adolescent boys dressed in Mother's clothes, carrying on her dreams, informing me with every turn in the sheets that I have no future.

But Mother is gone. And so is Grandmother. I'm glad I didn't have to fight her, the first in the line of my family, the émigré. No, I didn't have to fight her. Grandma grew old. Dementia set in, taking her power. She sits somewhere now in my mother's house, her body in an old chair, mumbling in Gaelic, nothing anyone can understand. She's probably telling everybody to fuck themselves, to go to hell. All the things Grandma use to yell in English.

I stare into the mirror. The figure that now haunts my insomnia cuts through the glass as if it were a body of water. She plants herself next to me, her feet six inches apart. We stand shoulder to shoulder, facing the now fluid lens. The ripples caused by her sudden departure spread out in a circle

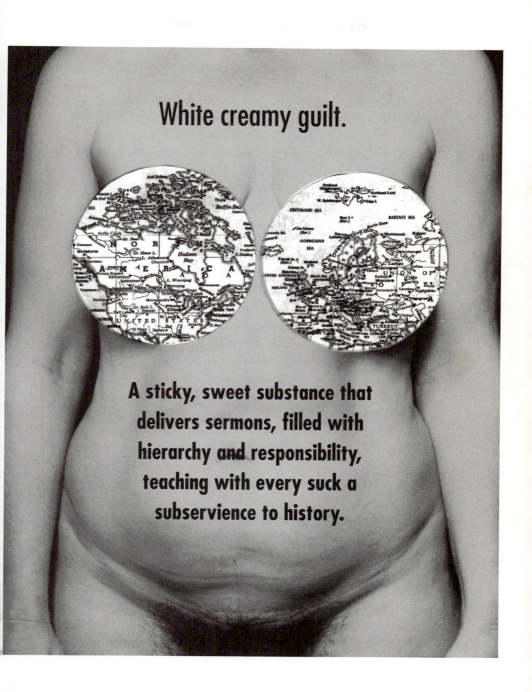

White creamy guilt.

A sticky, sweet substance that delivers sermons, filled with hierarchy and responsibility, teaching with every suck a subservience to history.

moving to the edges of the mirror. Our images buckle under the waves in the looking glass.

"Ain't no mountain high enough," she sings out of tune, kicking her feet up in the air, "ain't no valley low enough." I remain calm. She's trying to bait me, reduce me. She's eager, certain she'll win.

I scan her figure. My breasts at sixteen stand up on her chest. From her arms hang my hands at twenty. Her lips, fire-engine red, are mine at twenty-six. Eyes, deep green, covered with flecks of orange and black, are filled with rage. My eyes at forty-two. Her skin of stainless steel stands firm.

She is a quilt of flesh, sections neatly patched together, creating a presence that marks where I have been. She wants to freeze me in time, lock me into the past, in the place where all things are possible. She is the challenge of a lifetime.

She prepares for war. Busying herself with the task of comparison, working her way down the pastiche of her body, blustering on about her strengths, exaggerating my vulnerability. She has no idea how determined I am to win.

I used to believe that these battles were strictly personal. Me in my room. Me with brother, with Grandpa, with Cousin Mike. Me in the park with strangers. Me in the dark. Me against myself. Encounters hidden from view, private, undisclosed. Where in the world is there a record of these things happening? If they're not recorded, do they ever happen?

Little Women never told these stories. Nancy Drew, Lassie, *The Red Pony*, were all neatly constructed. Virtue wins and you can always go back home. Boundaries were set. Things you could count on, expectations of better things to come. And when they didn't come, I figured, it must just be me.

As a child, I accepted the order of the world. Intact. TV life, Beaver, Ricky, David, June, and "Life with Father." And just like my body, in separate parts, so too I thought was the world—the private, the public, the family, the state. I absorbed the challenges to that belief in every crack of my body. Hoping that behind some door, in some new sphere, somewhere, someday, there would be a "Donna Reed Show." Safety. A place untouched by battle, by victory, by defeat. A true story.

That sense of order was challenged by a generation of "it must just be me's," trampling it to death, on public ground. The revolutionists, declaring the "true story" a lie, created new images, new words, new stories. Slogans were embedded in this skin. Stamped passport entries still cover my chest. Secret messages. Cuban revolutionaries. Vietnamese women. Fred

Hampton. Bernadette Devlin. Angela Davis. Ho Chi Minh. Tours of duty. China. Romania. El Salvador. Chicago. San Francisco. San Diego. Anti-imperialist. Feminist. Socialist. Marxist-Leninist. Simply red.

The body standing next to mine places her chin on my shoulder, teeth exposed, grinning from freckle to freckle, chanting, "*Avanti popolo, avanti si.*" She is proud of having participated in these battles, proud of having run into the streets against a war that killed familiars. Into the factories, steel mills, and union halls she ran, demonstrating, manifesting against the lie, working for a new historical context.

But now, just like this body, this world has become invisible. New TV sitcoms, infused with new virtues, reconstructed stories, "Good Morning America," "Nightline," "A Current Affair," have pushed "Donna Reed" out of the ratings. Howdy Doody–faced commentators have formed a new choir, singing at the top of their ties, about some wall, somewhere, falling, concealing the fact that the free market has invested heavily in new construction.

She is agitated. She kicks the door and smashes her fist against the wall. Peering over my shoulder, she refuses to become invisible. She wants to wrestle my body to the ground, using the world which now wishes to disappear me, the world she fought so hard against, as her ally. She is more afraid of getting old than I am. She is that voice in my head, the Voice of America, broadcasting the news, over the border, to my brain: "Old woman!"

She wants to guarantee her future, on into mine. Twisting us together, burdening me forever with her choices, her pain, her guilt, her potential. She resists the evolution that is creating my body, aging the frame of her existence.

"Tell the truth, the whole truth, nothing but," she yells at me with her twenty-six-year-old mouth. The truth is her terrain. She is, was, always so certain. She could act without feeling. She knew she was right. Blameless, like a victim. "What do you see?" she asks, mockingly, pulling at the hair on my chest.

She pulls one of the lips off of my face. I hold my ground, staring at the reflection in the mirror. She tries it on. She giggles and sticks it back on my face. She tosses some coins on the dresser: "Revlon's cheap. Fire Engine Red. Invest."

I love her. This fight will not be easy. I fear it will be as it was when I let go of my mother's foot. Something, somewhere inside of me, shrieked. That ancient Gaelic banshee, foretelling the death of a family member with the pitch of her voice. That piece of woman, inside of me, bound up with tradition. Tissue filled with memories, screaming about some absolute truth, mixed in the blood. I flew in the face of all of it. Can I do the same with her? She is the one, last, absolute.

She nudges me toward the bed. We will lie down. It is in this position we both learned to fight dirty. Up on our feet, we use only our mouths; on our backs, we can tear into the battle with our entire bodies.

She starts singing once again, out of tune: "We are only two babes, lost in the woods, far, far, from home." A song our mother once sang to us. Stories begin flowing. "Now I lay me down to sleep, I pray the Lord my soul to keep." Which of us will die before we wake? Her flesh is smooth and firm. Her breasts stand up higher than mine. The stories will come like rain. Stories made for bedtime.

We will travel together, side by side, moving back in time. A foreplay for the real struggle. Replaying all the old battles, our shared life. Flexing for each other, with words and images, before we lay one of us down.

My left hand digs deep into my chest, stirring the soil. It is here that I will find my strength. In this room there is no exterior evil, no enemy, no mass to organize. To win this battle I must reject the dream of immortality and accept that all is no longer possible.

An image appears on the ceiling, a child in bed. The two of us lying side by side in this bed, her progeny. The image spreads itself out over the ceiling, four feet by eight. The image flickers in and out, like an old movie played too many times.

The child projected on the ceiling above presses her flesh against her bedsheets, which smell of the oil from her skin. The tiny head digs deep into the pillow, no cover, the fabric brown; it smells of hair and spit and nightmares. The child fakes a prayer. She has no conviction. No one will save this soul, save herself. So she fights. This child fights to save herself.

The child mumbles, "If I should die before I wake." There is hope in her words. The possibility of it being over. Rest. Screams pour out from the other rooms. The rooms where parents lay themselves down to sleep, to fight, to hate. The tiny head digs itself deeper into the pillow, the smells become stronger, the screams muffled. How many times has this child gotten up, after lying down, to stop the fight? Even after they have gone to sleep, she hears the yelling, the hitting, the furniture being shoved up against the wall. This child is their savior as well as her own.

A shadow covers the child's face. She chews and spits out a Thanksgiving dinner. She pulls a giant hairy hand out of her crotch. She yanks a tiny, wet object from her ear, last year's Christmas gift from Grandpa. She lies back down to sleep. "If I should die before I wake," she chants, rolling back and forth in her bed.

A green bat flies in through the window of the child's room. The child jumps to her feet, chasing the bat around the room. She sticks her fingers in one of Bela Lugosi's eyes. It oozes oil. Grabbing the disembodied hand she pulled from her crotch, she strikes the bat in the belly. She takes the tiny wet object, dripping with future generations, and drives it into its heart.

The pastiche woman sits up and yells, rocking back and forth in our bed, crying and screaming. The skin on her body turns bright red. She sees herself in the child. Every act of aggression is recorded in her memory. She hears the wings of the bat in her ear. Her hands are covered with the juice of future generations. The image jumps out violently from the ceiling.

The child sits up and looks around her room. There is blood on her bottom lip. Her teeth have dug themselves into her chin. Her pants are wet. Uninvited guests. Intruders. She gets up out of bed. She pushes open her window, hair blowing in the wind, eyes on fire. She sees the huge hand she had used to kill with, lying on the floor; hair covers the knuckles, layers of dirt and old skin cover the nails. She flies around her room, laughing, eyes still on fire, landing on top of the hand.

With her fists the child punches the hand and kicks it with her feet. "Go!" She yells. "Go!" Her body firmly perched on the back of the hand, she flies out the window of her room. We watch as the child flies over her house. Her eyes are monstrous, filling the sky with smoke and fire.

The child smashes through a plate glass window, fragments of glass cling to her body. The huge hand, like a homing pigeon, has found its way back. It reattaches itself to a body. An old man smelling of Aqua Velva lies in the bed. His head, covered with thick black hair greased back over the skull, turns toward her. His lips move. She whispers, "Be quiet." The smell of his body makes her vomit.

The child climbs on top of the old man's body. It smiles at her and whispers, "Grandpa's little angel, come to visit?" The child looks down at the face and slowly moves toward it. She is grinning. She slides back and forth on top of the body, it squirms and groans. Her face is now touching his. She opens her mouth wide. He puckers his lips, the old tongue pushes itself forward to meet her mouth. She bares her teeth, like knives they pop out of her mouth. They sink into his face, they dig themselves deep into the jaw. My body begins to shake, I am moved, not to tears, not to anger, but in admiration.

The child's head begins spinning, dancing a whirligig, digging its way into the old man's face. Blood splatters the sheets, her teeth are covered

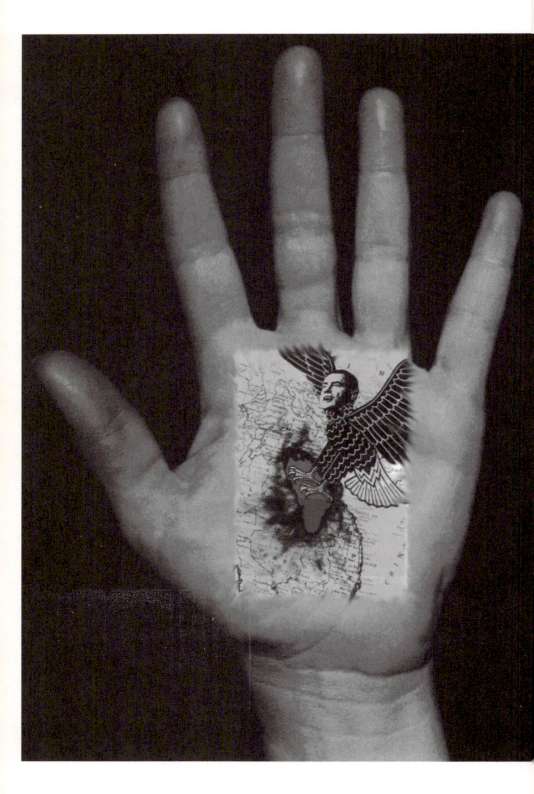

with flesh. She moves down the throat, down to the chest, carving up his heart. She slides her head down the waist, over the hips, spinning and slashing everything in her path. His disembodied mouth clings to the wall, still puckered, waiting for a kiss.

She tears open his pants, cuts through them, pulls out the cock and stuffs it in the puckered mouth that hangs on the wall. She takes a deep breath. A shriek is heard. A banshee sits on the other side of the wall. The sound moves through the wall, into the child's body. She begins to cry. To feel the consequence. She has betrayed the order of things, the silence.

A hand reaches through the wall. It grabs the child's arm, trying to pull her through. There is a chance for reconciliation. I hear my grandmother's voice: "Say you're sorry. Say you didn't mean it. Say it's your fault."

I hear the words "I'm sorry" falling from the lips attached to the woman next to me. I cover the lips with my hand. "Never take it back," I say, looking at her, "never take it back." She is frightened. Her side of the bed is soaked with tears. She floats in puddles of regret. The skin on my body repels her water.

The child lifts up her arms and flies upward through the roof of the old man's room. As she flies, the blood and tissue are flung from her body. Her face is clean. She flies back through her window.

The image on the ceiling explodes. The child's head pushes out from the ceiling. Her hands pop out of the plaster, followed by her belly, legs, knees, and feet. Her body drops from the ceiling, landing at the foot of my bed. With her left thumb in her mouth, she climbs onto the bed, curling herself around my feet.

The child, encircling my feet, sucks in her thumb, forcing it down her throat with one swallow, followed quickly by her left arm. She chomps on the right arm, sucking it in, ripping it from the shoulder. She gnaws on her legs. She is removing all the evidence, making herself invisible.

The woman on my right shivers in our bed. She covers her eyes.

The child dips her chin into her chest, chewing her way down the torso, through the stomach, out the back, ending at her crotch. With one last gulp she finishes herself off. She licks the bedsheets clean. Her head cradles itself between my feet. I whisper, "You never knew how strong you were."

The woman rolls over on her side, propping herself up on her left elbow. She stares down at me with her green eyes. The orange and black spots leak a thick shiny fluid.

She moves her red lips. She mumbles into my chest as if I were an intimate. I hear no sound. I read the movement of the lips, I watch her forming policy in her mouth. She draws up plans, aimed at decisive action. I hear her voice through a tight jaw, telling me that the child's disappearance will not go unnoticed. She speaks of victims, of herself. She charts a line of defense, revenge, and punishment. She assumes I am an ally. She is confused.

"It's in the past," I tell her. "It is the past." My words don't register in her mind. How can they? She is an occupant of the past, unwilling to be present, to see ahead, to tell the story differently. Enraged, she jumps up from the bed, screaming, "It's my turn!"

"I'll show you!" she screeches, her feet firmly planted on the ground. I look up at her from the bed. "Go ahead," I say, "show me." She flexes her arm, pushing her muscle up through the skin. She throws her body against the wall to the left of the bed. Her body melts into the wall. Her image glows on the white paint.

She is in a house, sitting in a chair. Barely nineteen. Her hair is long, the color of wheat. She sucks on her thumb. A man comes and beats on the door. Her body stiffens. He beats and beats and beats. She doesn't move. He crashes through the door.

"You bitch. Didn't you hear me?" She doesn't move. She smells his weedlike breath rushing over her face. Daddy's brand. The gusts of air push the hair out of her face. "Are you just going to sit there? Bitch." He pulls a wad of money out of his pocket. He slams it down on the table. "Now, get to it." She turns her head toward him. He shoves a piece of furniture up against the wall. He smashes something on the floor. "Now look what you made me do."

I cover my eyes. I have seen enough. I want this to stop. I extend my left hand upward to the wall, trying to pull her back. "Leave me alone," she snaps back at the gesture, "leave me alone."

The man charges at her, smashing his fist into her face. He pulls her hair, shoving her back into the seat. "Now see what you made me do." He starts to cry. "I'm sorry. I'm sorry." She looks back over her shoulder. Our eyes meet. She stands up and crosses over to a table. She picks up something and runs toward him. She sticks it in his face. He screams. She stabs him in the back. He yells. She picks up the money and stuffs it down his throat. With a match she sets him on fire. He runs through an open door, covered in flames.

She gets dressed, tight jeans, plaid shirt. She grabs a pen from the desk, straps on our mother's bra, and rushes out into the street. She runs and runs and runs, digging her feet deep into the ground. She stops running, but her feet keep moving. They dig a hole in the ground, a hundred miles deep. She looks around in the dark and sees hundreds of eyes, filled with fire, shining in the darkness. The wall is covered with people just like her, running in place.

They band together, whisper ideas to one another. They carry machetes and machine guns loaded with bullets stuffed with theory. They talk to one another, in a vocabulary only they understand. They are chased and chase. They gather in the cities. They work under the factories. They push themselves up onto the street. They trample on cars, over buildings, chanting with one voice. She tears down surveillance towers, intercepting messages traveling across the ocean.

She grows taller, her body is wound up with anger. Her jeans slip from her body, she lies down with allies, they dig deep into her, piercing her shell, thick fluids drip down their cheeks. She revels in the pleasure they bring. She tosses in the underground, squirming and laughing her way through the darkness.

With her machine gun she makes her way in the dark. Molten steel pours out of her skin. In the dark she stumbles across friends, bodies broken, weary, half beaten to death. She cradles them in her arms, lifting them up, moving them to safety. Her head hurts. She longs for an aspirin the size of the sun. Images of intruders fill her head.

From her command post, she sees the outline of a gigantic belly, swollen with lives. She climbs up to get a closer look. She finds its feet, they are covered with Italian shoes. The beast is hairy, saggy gray skin folds over its gut. It has landed on the roof of her underground world. The roof begins to buckle under the weight. She rips at its stomach with her teeth. She digs a hole, two inches by three, into the skin. Air rushes out, sweet and sour. Fingers pop through the hole, calloused and torn from overwork. The air fills the tunnels under the earth. With gas mask in place, she and all of those like her rush to the surface.

She rips off her mask and glides around the earth, trying to find an absolute. She glares back at me. Her shiny body glistens with doubt. Hands fly up over her face, covering her ears. She has no tolerance for questions. Her machine gun is out of bullets. With both arms extended, I remove the machine gun from her grip, placing it next to me on the bed. There is no resistance.

Our mother's bra climbs up her back. It clings to her throat, stopping her breath. I yank at it, snapping the hooks. She falls to the ground. I stare at her chest with green eyes. I burn a hole in her skin. Lava flows out, filled with all things possible. She slows down. Age creeps into her step. Her skin of stainless steel begins to sag.

She stares at the child's head lying at my feet. She climbs out from the wall, moving toward the foot of my bed. She tears at her plaid shirt, revealing sagging breasts. She lifts the child's head up and, with one hand clasped around the skull, buries it in her chest.

From the pocket of her jeans, she pulls out the pen. She scribbles all over the walls. She makes our life visible all over the room. Without looking back, she releases the pen into my open hand.

She steps upon the bed. "Now it's your turn," she says. I look at her standing above me, puffing and panting. "You show me," she demands. I am silent. She jumps up and down on the bed, her face is red, she spits at me. "It's your turn, old lady. Your turn."

I lift up my arms, holding them out to her. She explodes with anger. Her head swells to twice its size. She opens her mouth, it bleeds at the corners. Her nose flattens itself against the skin of her face. The veins in her arms pop out of the skin. She rips the jeans from her legs and throws them on the floor. She is beating herself.

She jumps up toward the ceiling, smashing her head against the surface. I spread my legs. She lands, both feet trapped between my thighs. I look up at her, she is staring at the gun next to my head. She stares down at me for hours. The anger slowly releases from her body.

"Are you going to bury me, old woman?" she asks. Her voice is weak. I look past her to the window behind her head. "No," I say, "no." Her arms fall slowly to her sides. She kneels, placing a knee on each of my thighs. Her first real compromise.

Each knee sinks into my flesh. I hold on to her breasts as she drifts into me. Our long thin lips meet. Hers are pink, mine pale gray. The V-shaped patches of hair entwine. As we touch, the sky crackles. Lovers, good and bad, explode all over the walls. Faces filled with passion and desire and want. Trancelike states, dirty words, thick fluids, fill the air. With all her power, she pushes herself deeper into me, speeding up her entry. "Ain't no valley low enough," our duet, echoes through the world.

Her pink lips are now combined with mine, our coarse hair twisted together. "Was I wrong?" she asks. Covering her mouth with her left hand, I say, "Never take it back." Her chest melts into mine. Her head cradles itself against my neck. She is being pulled into the soil of my body. Peat moss, thick and rich, infused with water. Her weight spreads out in me, filling me up, like a basin ready to spill over.

I whisper to her, "You never knew how strong you were." She doesn't hear me. She stares straight ahead, her chin losing itself in my chest. Her

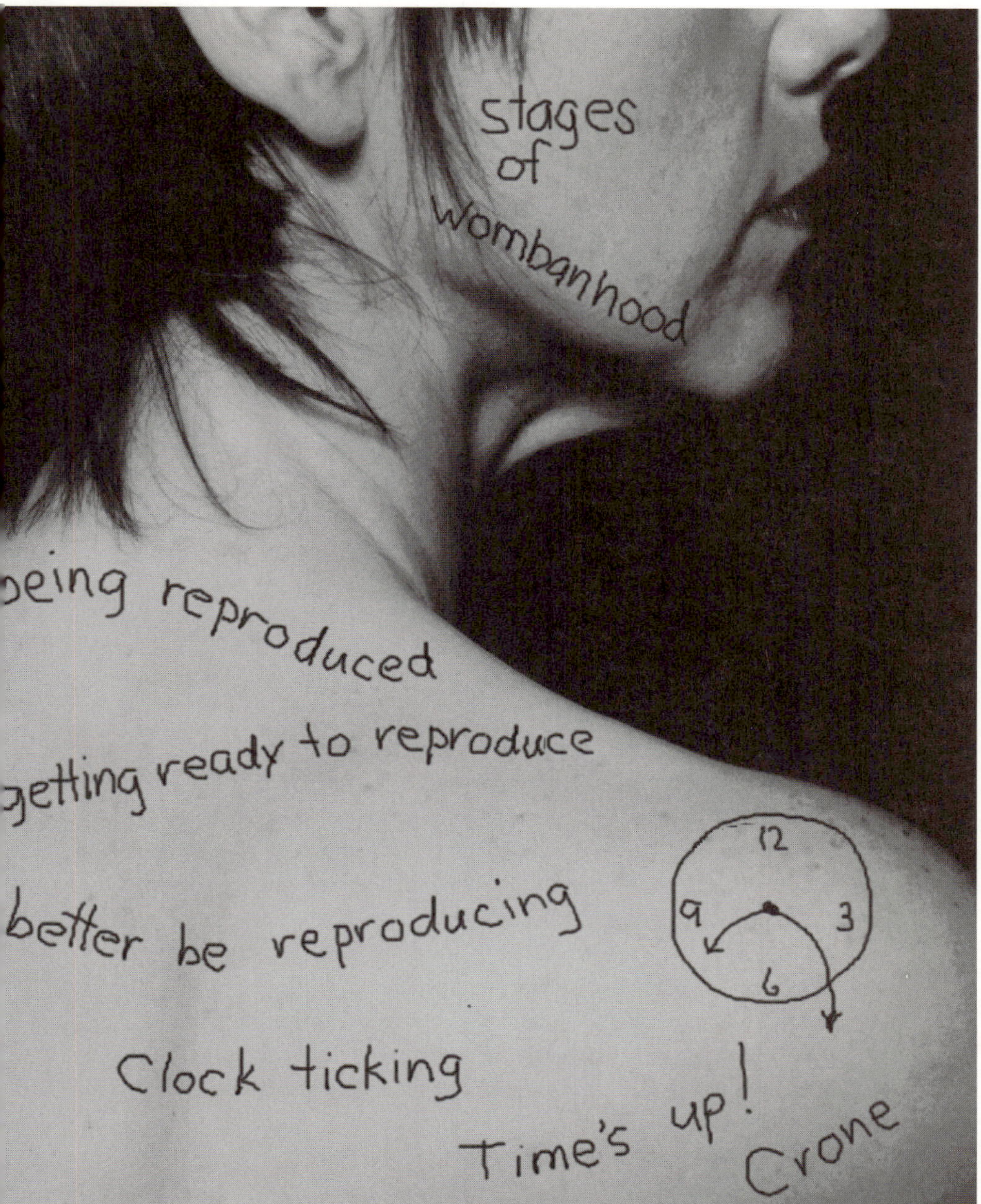

stages
of
wombanhood

being reproduced

getting ready to reproduce

better be reproducing

Clock ticking

Time's up! Crone

lips spread out across her face, she begins to shake, sounds of pleasure flow from her mouth.

I look around the room. The walls are coated with oil, ink, and smoke. Images cover the walls. Bullet holes are everywhere. Molten steel clings to the ceiling. Broken bodies, friends of this woman, weary, half beaten to death, crowd the floor.

The air smells of weeds, sweet and sour. Stacks of gas masks are piled in the corner, water covers the floor. It will take time to sort through these things, throwing out the unnecessary, organizing what is to remain. But I am alive.

She rolls over inside of me, swirling around like a fish in the sea. Her mouth protrudes from my chest. "We are only two babes, lost in the woods," she mumbles, falling deeper into me.

I hold us in my arms. Tears run down my face. These girls cry too much. She speaks in words I no longer understand. It is here she will lie, until someday, somewhere, we will sit together, in an old chair, talking in a language no one understands, recounting all of our battles, shared and individual, telling everyone to go fuck themselves.

I close my eyes. My skin leaks water, it covers the bed, spilling over onto the sea of the floor. I am alone, adrift in the quiet of this room. I fall asleep for the first time in decades. I float for hours, catching up with the years.

"It's time to get up," echoes in my head. "Time to go." I sit up in the bed, holding on to my chest. My knees retract quickly, hitting my chin.

I get out of bed, stand upright, my heels press themselves together. I walk toward the mirror, a voice in my body stops me: "Not today, old woman, not today." Right. Not today. It will be soon enough tomorrow to begin piecing together this story.

"Mom," she says, knocking on the door, "time to get up." There is movement in my chest, a faint laughter rises. I pick up my clothes, slip my legs into my pants, and pull a plaid shirt over my head.

"Are you ready?" she asks. I bend over to put on my shoes, the weight in my chest rocks me back and forth. I place both hands against the weight, realizing it will take a long time for all of this to sink in. I cross over to the bed, throwing the covers over the gun she left behind. As I bend over I feel something jab me from the rear, a ballpoint pen is stuck in my pocket.

I kneel down to slip my left foot into the shoe. "Are you ready yet?" she asks again. I hear a giggle making its way under the door. I slip my right foot into its shoe.

"It's time," she says. "Time to go to the Wild Animal Park, remember?" She giggles louder. The giggle rises up from under the door, filling the room, pulling back the blinds, pushing open the windows. It moves through the air, joining with the laughter rising out of my throat. It escapes uncontrollably from my mouth. The house shakes under our sound, furniture moves, bottles fly off the dresser, the mirror buckles under the vibration, cracking it in two.

Truth is, these girls laugh too much.

Luis Alfaro

Cuerpo Politizado

Vistiendo en Drag

From *Lucha Villa* to *Veronica Castro*.
From *Lola Beltran* to *Cristina*.
　　　Y, don't forget,
　　　la Liz Taylor too.

These fierce independent Latinas
　　　that look more drag than queen.
Without aid of scalpel or tuck.
　　　"Wouldn't even *pensar* the thought."

Prefer to show the lines
　　　on their faces,
　　　like maps,
　　　bearing skin,
　　　with wrinkles,
　　　tracing history
　　　of experience.
Ay, que sufrieron!
　　　Si, and we liked them that way.

We all aspired
　　　(*los señoritas* of Hype-rion Avenue)
　　　to the *Mexicana* icon.
Preferred long-suffering *mujeres*
　　　over *chichona* Jayne Mansfields.
Drag, it is a man's field . . .

Untitled, 1990
Bradford
Fowler

Left the *Virgen de Guadalupe*
    to *gabacho*
    movie-of-the-week
    con Donna Mills.
Gave up on Frida Kahlo
    when all the girls
    started to grow
    their mustaches
    on Wilshire Boulevard.
Stuck with the *telenovelas*
    where low production cost
    and bad lighting
    showed all traces
    of woman/hood.

Battling for mirror space
    in the toilet of La Plaza.
Last stop on the Hollywood Boulevard
    starlet circuit.
This star lets you
    walk all over my
    walk of fame
    for chance
    to "close-up"
    con una de las
    Charlie Angels.
We know better than to
    wish upon a . . .
We are not second-rate *modelos* of
    El Juego de Llorar
    (*La Crying Game*).

I wanted to assimilate
    so bad.
Grow up and stop being a lovechild
    a la Diana Ross
    eight-track cartridge.

I was a little
    white pill
    popping *puta*
    and proud of it.
    Y-qué?
A performance goddess.
Aztec
    burrito-making
    project-living
    mujer
    who survived
    the pussy Bush eighties.
Dared to be young Ethel Merman
    instead of King Taco waitress.

Wore my shimmering
    blue sparkle
    strapless dress
    too tight
    because I have
    always been
    that kind of
    girl.
Rubynesque
    (and I thought
    I was a jewel).

I'm bigger than most
    of the ramp walkers.
Runaway
    from the runway.
Dare to show
    bulge in my crotch
    because I am
    that tough.
Wear switchblade
    in my garter
    and Exacto knife
    in my *trenzas*.

Reach behind
  to loosen the curl
  and cut you up
  before you can say,
  "Girl, you are a . . ."

Although I am one
  of the heroin IV
  arm-scarred
  history queens,
  I am still around
  and rounder still.

A *testimonio*
  to those
  boulevard nights
  when dark-skinned
  homeboys
  traced the wounds
  on my chest
  with blood-red lips
  that whispered,
  "Shit, you are
  one tough
  chola."

Siempre feliz
  en mi falda.

Clothed/Unclothed
series, no. 20,
1992
Laura Aguilar

Abuelita

I've been redeemed
by the blood of the lamb
I've been redeemed
by the blood of the lamb

I've been redeemed by the blood of the lamb
filled with the holy ghost I am
All my sins are washed away
I've been redeemed

See this finger?
I cut it jumping into
my mother's rose bush.
Suicide attempt or accident?
I don't know,
I'm only eleven.

Did it because of *Abuelita*.
Us kids, we hate *Abuelita*,
my mother's mother.
Hate her more than Mrs. Polka,
our fifth-grade teacher.

You know it's the ultimate hate
when you hate your grandmother
more than a fifth-grade teacher
named *Mrs. Polka*.

Besides the usual complaints,
she pinches our cheeks too hard
and gives us too little money,
along with those boring stories
of the Depression:
"We ate dirt burritos."

The world stops when *Abuelita*
comes to visit.
Rules the house
with an iron fist.
Potatoes and beans for breakfast,
and Channel 34,
the Spanish-language station,
day and night.

Novelas with adulterous housewives
during the day,
and *Lucha Libre*
with masked wrestlers
fake-hitting each other
all night long.

Abuelita loves it.

I don't know
if I did it on purpose
or if *Toro* pushed me.

Another in a long list of dogs
that we owned,
ranging in name from
Pancho Villa to *Oaxaca*
to *Mazatlán* to *Puebla*
(named after ideal
vacation spots for Dad)
is running on the porch.

This one's name is *Toro*,
later to be run over by a car
on a busy Pico Boulevard morning
and renamed *Tortilla*
for the family vault
of memory.

History in our family
is honored
but constantly renamed,
making the weight
of our painful stories
easy to bear.

Abuelita sits on the porch
reading yet another installment
of *Vanidades.*
Sort of a *Cosmopolitan*
for the Latino set.

Completely even more unrealistic
than *Cosmopolitan,*
Vanidades has pictures of
beautifully trim
and dyed-blonde Latinas
making *tortillas*
or *chile rellenos,*
in gorgeous
Ann Taylor outfits
at outdoor
Mayan-designed
wood-burning pits
next to
custom-designed
swimming pools.

The long gasp.
Unique to Latino culture,
the long gasp
can take anywhere
from ten seconds
to a record four minutes
held by Auntie Bad Breath,
who witnessed
a distempered dog
bite Uncle Crooked Back
in the leg.

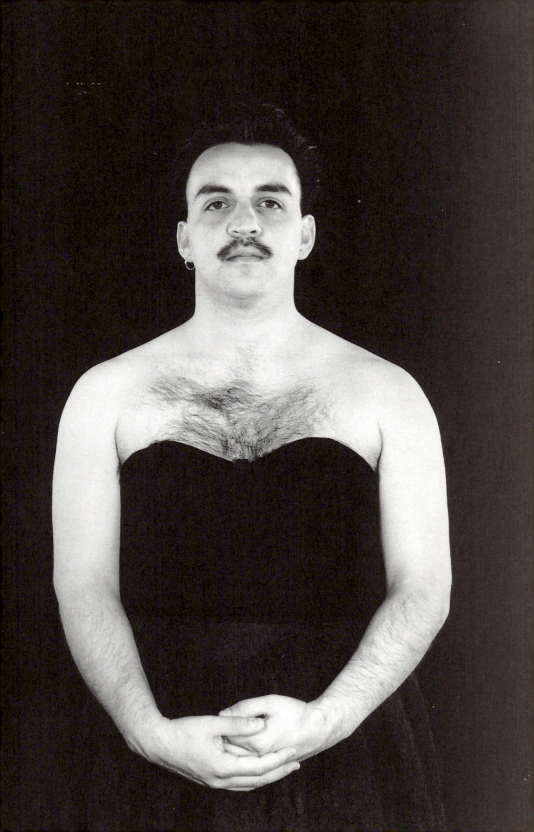

I rise out of the rose bush
and immediately plunge into
the other Latino dramatic effect,
the painful
ay yai yai yai yai.

There's a gash on my finger
and it starts to bleed
pretty badly.

Abuelita turns on the hose
and runs my hand
under the water.
Inspecting my finger,
she laughs,
pinches my cheek,
thanks the *Virgen*
for the minor miracle,
does a sign of the cross,
and applies
Primitive Latino First Aid.

She looks at me,
smiles,
raises my bloody finger
to her face.
Closely inspecting
my afflicted digit,
she brings it up close
to her eyes.

I can't tell
what she is looking for.
As if holding it up close
she might find
some truth,
some small lesson
or parable
about the world
and its workings.

Her eyes canvass the finger,
probing with her vision
slowly and carefully.
And then quickly
and without warning,
she sticks it
inside her mouth
and begins
to suck on it.

I feel the inside of her mouth,
wet and warm,
her teeth
lightly pulling,
equally discomforting
and disgusting
at the same time.

Being in this womb
feels as if I am being
eaten alive
on one of those
late night
Thriller Chiller movies:
Vampira, Senior Citizen Bloodsucker.

But it isn't that at all.
This is the only way
that *Abuelita*
knows how to
stop the bleeding.

I've been redeemed
by the blood of the lamb
I've been redeemed
by the blood of the lamb

I've been redeemed by the blood of the lamb
filled with the holy ghost I am
All my sins are washed away
I've been redeemed

See this finger?
Cut it at work.
Making another pamphlet
critical of those
who would like
to see us dead.

The long gasp.
Four Gay Latinos
in one room.
Four long gasps.

Afraid to touch my wound.
Would prefer
to see it bleed
and gush
than to question
mortality
and fate.

Could go on
about being tested,
but it seems
so futile.
As if we
don't know
that one little test
could have
been wrong.

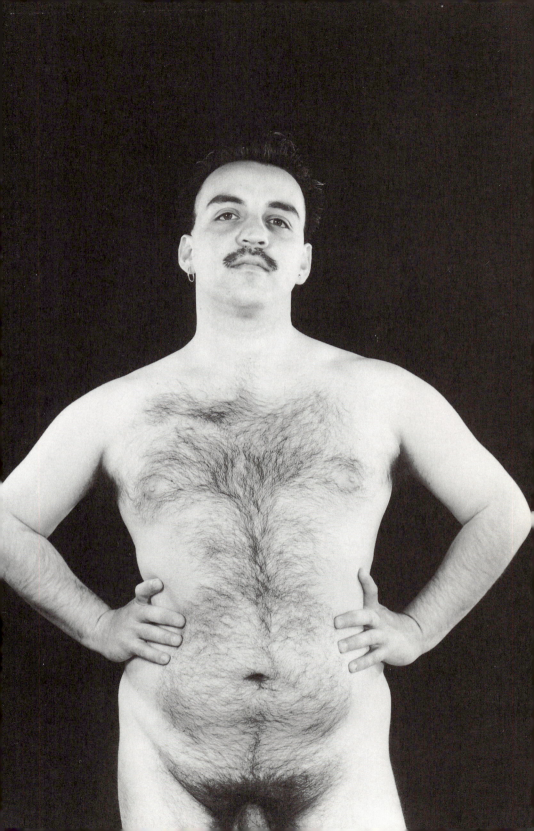

Hold the finger
in front of me.
Stick it
close to mouth.
Drip, drip, drip,
all over desktop
from Ikea.

Hold it up close
to face.
Quickly
and without
warning,
stick it in my mouth
and I begin to
suck.

Tears roll down.
Salty wet
tears.
Down my face.
Can feel my teeth
lightly pulling,
and I wish,

I wish for an *abuelita*
in this time.
This time of plague.
This time of loss.
This time of sorrow.
This time of mourning.
This time of shame.

And I
heal myself.
I heal myself
with *Abuelita's*
Primitive Latino First Aid Kit.

Desire is memory.

The night after Julio's memorial service I went to the video store and rented an old Gay porn tape. I think it was called *Aspen Ski Weekend II*. In it, a beautiful blond guy, who looks like no one I know, gets fucked by everybody in the ski lodge. He sort of half-smiles throughout the video like maybe he's done this just a *few* too many times. Think of Carol Channing in *Hello Dolly!*

They all had that 1970s-porn pimples-on-the-butt look. Imperfect perfection, I call it. I mean, they were cute and all, but they had that *done it* look. Lost innocence. A resigned contentment. A grin that says, *Yeah, I give up. Just do what you want with me.* And life says, *My pleasure, motherfucker.*

When I went to bed all that I could remember about the video was a bouquet of roses that was strategically placed next to the action. In every scene the roses seemed to magically appear within the frame of each thrust and moan. When I should have been paying attention to the big cum shot, my eyes instead caught sight of that beautiful bouquet of red to the left of the improvised sling. And, of course, not a condom in sight. That night I dreamt that everything beautiful was wrapped in condoms. Cocks and roses, all in condoms.

The next day I was reading the Falcon Video newsletter and I found out that Alan Lambert, a cute if not overly eager bottom, had committed suicide in his native Canada. I'd always had a crush on Alan Lambert because he made porn look so easy. He seemed to know his paces, gliding from one position to another like Esther Williams underwater. I'm almost positive he came to porn by way of a gymnastics career. When he mounted a ten-inch dildo, you could almost see Alan's lips mouthing off, in denominations of twenty, his earnings for the day.

In a ten-page document left behind to Falcon Video he listed a number of important reasons for his self-demise at the old Gay porn age of *twenty-six*. Chief among them was his fear of getting older. He stated that his body was at peak physical condition and that he could not see himself in any other way. This from a man who wasn't even HIV-positive.

The last time I talked to Julio was at the French Market Place. I was meeting a date for breakfast. Someone who looked like Alan Lambert. Julio was walking slowly around the restaurant, out of breath, and looking perpetually chemotherapy-tanned. A few heads turned, but most pretended not to see him. My date arrived and he kissed me on the *cheek*. I'd already begun to imagine how I was going to throw him over my brand new black-lacquered desk and fuck him until he said, *Ooh, talk to me in Spanish.*

Julio came by and he kissed me on the *lips*. I introduced him to my date, who was rippling muscles in a cute little outfit from BodyMaster. Julio told us about how he had just started steroids. His doctors were going to try to give him an ass again. It seems that the virus had taken it away. My date never recovered from the memory of the kiss that Julio had given me. He kissed me on the *cheek* and never called.

At Julio's memorial service his mother got up and told a roomful of Queers that his family did *not* support his lifestyle. That they never went to his art shows. That they had never even seen his artwork. That they did not know him the way that we knew him. They only knew him as a *wonderful, caring, sweet person.*

Well, I want to reclaim a little history right now and tell you that I knew Julio. I knew Julio as a Queer Latino-Filipino. I knew Julio as an artist. I knew Julio's artwork. I also knew Julio as a *wonderful, caring, sweet person.*

I know blood is thicker than water, but I want to say *fuck you* to his mother. I am getting fed up with straight people. Not only do they try to ruin our lives, they try to ruin our deaths as well.

The other day I was driving down Sunset Boulevard in Beverly Hills and I saw a gigantic mural on the Playboy building. It has a picture of a little boy playing with a handgun and it says, *Save the Children, Stop the Violence.* Well, I want a billboard on Sunset Boulevard with a picture of Julio playing with a handgun. I want it to say, *Save the Children, Kill Your Parents.*

En memoria de Julio Ugay.

Orphan of Aztlán

If it was up to this god,
we would have all been born
straight white males.
But thankfully I got a god
who likes his color,
and likes it dark and juicy.

Hate to bring up
race issues
when smoldering
South Central ashes
still fly so close by.

But I can't believe
in this god.
'Cause if this god
really wandered
the desert
like they say he did,
he would be
darker than the
Egyptian night,
and I haven't
seen that picture yet.

In our image
would be more
Prince
than
Prince Edward.

Fear strikes closest
to the heart
of the one
knowing distance.
What you don't know
can now kill you.

That is why
we dare
to be different
in a world
that sells same,
same, until we all act alike.
In the image of what?

What are you afraid of?

Gay agenda
is equality.
Civil rights
when someone
throws a firebomb
through your window
in Oregon
and kills
an African-American Lesbian.
The operative word here
is *American,*
not *Lesbian,*
pendejo.

There has been no
power-sharing,
so we are
power-taking.
Empowered to march
with a million,
because I am
sick and tired
of seeing
straight people
kiss and hold hands
in public
while I am
relegated to

a T-dance
at Rage.
Fuck that shit!

I am a Queer Chicano.
A native in no land.
An orphan of Aztlán.
The *pocho* son of farmworker parents.

The Mexicans only want me
when they want me to
talk about Mexico.
But what about
Mexican Queers in L.A.?

The Queers only want me
when they need
to add color,
add spice,
like *salsa picante,*
on the side.

On this plane
I see a man
skinnier and sicker
than the
Sally Struthers Ethiopia
of Channel 13.
Send money
for the hungry
and care
about somebody
on the other side
of the world,
as long as we don't
have to see them
on the street.
Leave AIDS patients
to crowded County General,
hidden in corridors.

The only face of AIDS
that we like to see
is on children.
Because children
are the *innocent victims.*
Should everyone else suffer?
Don't know.
Only know
that it is
a world without end.

And he says,
"Don't you pray?"
And I say,
"Yes I pray.
I pray,
Jesus please
protect me
from your followers."

I want to meet you at the
intersection of possibility.
Because possibility
has the power
to teach us more about
loving ourselves
than the book of John,
who, by the way,
sounds a lot like
David Geffen
to me.

My god is a trusting god.
My god is a tolerant god.
My god is an oppressed god.
My god revels in the
freedom of difference.
My god is a thinker
with a compassion
for the intellectual mind.

My god sounds a lot like a woman.
Yes, I would have to say that
my god is a woman.

My god lives in *east los.*
My god is a laborer.
My god works below
minimum wage.
My god doesn't see herself
anywhere,
but she is
everywhere.
My god sounds a lot like a Latina.
Yes, I would have to say that
my god is a Latina.

My god believes in
individuality *and* duality.
My god is a minister of truth.
My god is a visionary for peace.
My god believes in political
and social equity.
My god sounds a lot like a Lesbian.
Yes, I would have to say that
my god is a Lesbian.

You got me so excited
I want to talk about
the military.
And let me tell you
something,
I could give a fuck
about the military.
But if you want to ride
that missile, *babee,*
punch the button
and take the trip,
girl.

Because you see,
it was okay to be
a *faggot*
in the army.
But when you became
a *sissy warrior,*
willing to die for America,
then you blurred the line
of sexual borders.
And now
there's no telling you
apart from a
real soldier.

It took a woman,
which is no surprise,
to say it best.
It isn't the showers
they are afraid of.
It's the sexual harassment
they fear.
The same one
they've been giving
women
for years.

And I ask you,
what are you so afraid of?

Blur the line.
Take the journey.
Play with the unknown.
Deal with the whole *enchilada,*
race
class
sex
gender
privilege.

Arrive at the place called
possibility.
Try once again
to create a language,
a sense
of what it means
to be in community.

It's not easy,
I know.
I waited for verdict too.
Was disappointed,
but I have
hope
for the future
también.

I am fast-forwarding
past the reruns,
ese,
and riding the big wave
called future.
Making myself
fabulous
as I disentangle
from the wreck
of this
cultural collision.

You know
you've reached
the New World
when the Guatemalan
tamale lady
at your corner
is wearing
a traditional skirt
and a T-shirt
that says
Can't Touch This.

So now
I am making
a *burrito*
(so to speak)
of possibility
and throwing in
as much as I can
and calling it
un show.

Daring to tell
my truth
and my story
as best I know how,
with what I have
invented
or stolen
from the
cultural catalogue.

Do it in front
of the face
called hate.
Frowning always
with disapproval.
Daring to hurt me
with the ugly word
in an editorial.

Let me
tell you something,
sister.

We will continue
to create these
espectáculos tan sabrosos
that we call
our Queer Latino selves,
and make them
al estilo los
like only we know
how to make them.

Because
we are at the edge.
We are at the border.
We are at the rim
of the New World.
And there is no place
to run
or hide.

Instead,
I step over
the burned-out lot,
walk down
to the corner
and say,
"I come
in the name of
peace and justice.

Are you
a friend
or a
phobe?"

Carol Leigh (Scarlot Harlot)

Thanks, Ma

Cheap

Cheap is when you fuck them just to shut them up.
Cheap is when you do it because they are worth so much.
Cheap is when you suck them till your jaws hurt so they won't say
    you're uptight.
Cheap is when you do it to keep them home at night.
Cheap is when you want less than pleasure, a baby, or a hundred dollars.
Cheap is when you do it for security.
Cheap is what you are before you learn to say no.
Cheap is when you do it to gain approval, friendship, love.

Excuses, Excuses . . .

I am Carol Leigh, also known as the Scarlot Harlot. I've been working as a prostitute for fifteen years. Although I am a self-proclaimed whore and a rebel, I have a fierce appetite for love and approval. Naturally, I developed a career as an artist. Perhaps a little information about my background will help you understand how a nice middle-class woman like me could wind up a famous slut.

My grandparents emigrated from Europe before the Holocaust, surviving in New York City's garment business. My parents were both outcasts. This shared status and an admiration for Trotsky formed the basis for their partnership.

Disenchanted with social activism, they abandoned the Socialist Workers' Party and turned to child rearing. The discussion in my house was intellectual and political, mostly centering around a critique of capitalism from a socialist perspective and a critique of socialism from a capitalist point of view. Most of all, my parents indoctrinated me with the notion that nonconformity was the loftiest state. They regarded me as a magnificent experiment and raised me in strict adherence to the progressive principles of Dr. Spock.

"Think for yourself and marry a doctor," was my mom's advice.

I was perfect, smart, and well-behaved . . . until puberty. I fell from my pedestal at the age of fifteen, when I wanted to date (not fuck) a boy who wasn't Jewish. My parents said no, and I became an outlaw. My sudden fall from grace was unjust, exposing the tenuousness of my good reputation. I abandoned my role as an obedient child. It was 1966 or '67. I would find love, make love, and be free. I was a flower child and I would give it away.

The Dark Romantic Forests

The dark romantic forests,
Beaches of pure white sand,
They make me feel lonely,
Needing someone to hold my hand.

I walk alone in the moonlight.
There's no one else in the world,
No one to share my feelings,
To realize that I'm a girl.

Someday when I get older,
My walks won't be alone.
A man will be there to guide me.
I'll make my world his home.

—Carol Leigh, age fifteen

In the front lines in the battle of the sexes, prostitutes are "the only street fighters we've got," quoth Ti-Grace Atkinson in her *Amazon Odyssey*.

Prostitution came to me at the intersection of my needs and proclivities—my radical political bent, my feminism, my sexual curiosity, and a response to the stigma I already felt for engaging in premarital sex. Prostitution holds a potent combination of survivalism and victimization, a perfect recipe for my anarchist's cookbook. One press of the cookie cutter and one more intellectual trollop. It was my fate. I was destined to become a sexy monster—thrust onto the battlefield of sexual politics—cast now as a victim, a survivor, and a traitor to my gender.

These are torrid times for a postmodern—another way of saying nostalgic—sex warrior. Feminists and moralists, communists and christians, are pitching adjacent camps, itemizing munitions: genitals, guilt, sex, pleasure, rape, free speech, lust, love, christ, god, goddess, anarchy, imperialism, racism, classism, tantra, Tao, dharma, AIDS, oppression, Playboy, MacKinnon. Ideologies writhe in contortions. Competing women are like angels wrestling on pinheads. Feminist arguments about free will and predestination would make a Calvinist blush.

New England Is for Masochists

I tried to find my righteous niche. I went to graduate school at Boston University, to study with Anne Sexton. She committed suicide the semester I arrived. John Cheever taught fiction, but he was drunk all the time. I never graduated. Anyway, what would I have done with a degree in poetry?

Feminism Circa the '70s

I decided to devote myself to less esoteric goals, like feminism (which I loved because it provided a very useful map to my psyche).

In 1976 I organized a women's writers' group, dedicated to improving women's images. The "great artists" were mostly men. *His*tory was told from a man's point of view. Women were silenced and anonymous, but we would change all that. Together we would tell our secret stories! And I would find a place for my weird self.

Feminism was almost perfect for me . . . except for the fact that I was bisexual and couldn't stop fucking men. Of course, women had to attack me for that. I understood. Women had been so oppressed. And maybe I should stop fucking men. My comrade, anti-porn heroine Macha Womongold (*Pornography: A License to Kill*), introduced me to some strategies to fight the patriarchy. Macha taught me about the goddess and about how proud I could be of everything female. Macha was even arrested for some obstreperous anti-porn activism. I admired her, but my feminist angst manifested itself in different ways.

For example, occasionally I'd don a few little lacy black things and jill off to my whore image in the mirror. And once, compelled by a passionate curiosity, I'd dressed up in my sleaziest lingerie to dance on amateur night at the Golden Banana in Peabody, Massachusetts. Get over it or get into it, I advised myself. I never told my friends. They might not like it, but I didn't care. Cavorting publicly in lace and garters seemed bad (in the context of the patriarchy), but couldn't I explore that role and write poetry about my findings?

Maybe not. How was I to fit my talents and interests into the scheme of society? My college career had been a bust. My political beliefs conflicted with my masturbatory practices. I was a good girl in a bad girl's psyche. Or vice versa. Anyway, the blizzard of '78 was the last straw. I moved to San Francisco to find my fate.

Sex! Massage! Girls!

September 1978—San Francisco was like a different country, I thought. Everything was wonderful, except for the fact that my boyfriend broke up with me, I didn't know anyone and my friends were all back home, I had no job, and the bills were due on my credit cards. In fact, I felt desperate and low and confused and horrible about myself. I look back in wonder at this crossroads, but it was certainly the lowest point in my quasi-torrid life. It's odd, how the most desperate circumstances can lead to one's salvation.

Besides, San Francisco had fabulous shops and I needed furniture and a new vintage wardrobe.

I had heard that once you agreed to sell it, there was no turning back. I couldn't resist. I took the dare.

A Woman's Last Resort

I took a job at a very seedy massage parlor. I figured they must be selling sex, because they certainly weren't selling anything else. I was immediately enamored of my friendly, beautiful co-workers, and my first trick was handsome and sweet. After work, I rushed home to look in the mirror. Now there's a prostitute, I told myself. I hadn't changed. I looked back across that line that had separated me from the old me, the good girl. The line had disappeared.

Prostitutes' issues and images became the center of my life. I'm not saying I loved the tricks or the work. It can be fun, especially if you like things like skydiving or hang gliding. But what I liked was getting this insider's view, this secret story to tell. The silence of prostitutes became overbearingly loud. Suddenly, I was surrounded by mute and righteous women, and brazen, sexual women and poor women, and junkies and addicted women, and young women who couldn't fight back against rape, and women of other races, and mothers, and women who used to be men, and women who used to be secretaries, and wild, curious women who needed money, just like me.

My new discoveries gave me excuses and revelations:
- Other women still wear high heels, bras, and lipstick. They walk around in fetish gear for free, sexualizing themselves at every opportunity, and I'm supposed to not get paid to play this role. It's all whoring just the same.
- All my life I'd been trading sex for approval and for relationships with boyfriends. A lot of women trade sex for some advantage, or for basic survival. This is part of life and I have a right to look square into it.
- "Jeffrey" may be able to brag about having sex with thousands of women. His conquests are not stigmatized. But I'm supposedly promiscuous. I hate that word.
- First the patriarchy socializes me to be a sex object, then it sics its flunky cops and rapists on me. I won't be terrorized by these envoys.

Now, I Know What Some of You Are Thinking . . .

"Why didn't she just get into therapy and get reprogrammed?"

Great idea. Why didn't I think of that? Everyone should! Every whore on this planet needs therapy and a better job and government subsidies. This way we could end prostitution! Oh, gosh, I can't believe I went to all this trouble, when it all could have been so simple. Anyway . . .

Bad Luck at Lucky's, or Caught between the Rapists and Police

In 1978 I began to work at Lucky's massage parlor. I knew there was some danger, but I suppressed my fear so that I could survive. Measuring danger is a complicated science. As a woman, I live in constant fear of rape. If I were really careful, I'd never leave my house. You gotta take risks.

I'll fuck for money if I want, I told myself. My co-workers and the management assured me that arrests could be avoided and violence was very rare. Women taught me how to screen customers when it was my turn to open the door.

Trust your gut feeling, they told me, then went on to describe factors ranging from wardrobe and facial expression to race. As a novice, I was confused. Women claimed to get by with a sixth sense. The idea that women were advising me to weed out cops and rapists based on a subtle intuition was shocking in itself. I resented the notion.

People accuse me of pandering.
That's a felony.
But when I find a good thing,
I just have to share it.

Try Sex Work
it pays the rent.

I never felt safe. Some of the women were skilled in self-defense—like Kim, who could chew up and spit glass, I heard—but I wasn't good at that.

The management should have hired a security guard. There was enough money around, though not the huge sums people suppose. Women earned upwards of a hundred a day. The management kept seventeen of the twenty-dollar massage fee, which added up to nearly a thousand a day. Security guards might eat up a sizable chunk, but perhaps the women could chip in.

I asked the boss. Connie insisted that posting a guard was just not done in this city, as it would not be in keeping with the "low profile" that prostitution businesses are forced to keep. As a prostitute, I had no recourse for challenging her. She was a gentle woman with a laissez-faire approach to business. The other workers were not at all inspired about instituting any kind of change. It's hard to explain, but the whole situation is kind of paralyzing.

I had been working eight months when I opened the door for the wrong person. It was 10:30 a.m. I guess I was off my guard. I should have known better. It was my fault. He was clearly disqualified, according to the criteria espoused. He pushed his way in and another man followed. One put a knife to my throat and they raped me.

For around twenty minutes, I was afraid of being tortured or killed. Susie was there with me.

"Who do you think you are, bothering girls like this. You leave! Go now! Leave us alone!" she shrieked. They didn't rape her.

I don't understand why people always assume that when a prostitute talks about being raped, she's describing a situation in which she has sex and then she doesn't get paid. The threat of murder and torture was the traumatic element of this rape.

Later that week I learned from some of the other women that these men had been doing the same thing to women at other parlors in town. No one passed the information around, I guess, from a feeling of hopelessness, from some idea that ideally we should all be able to protect ourselves by using our intuition.

Of course, I didn't call the police after I was raped. Connie begged me not to, as it might focus attention on our parlor, which could result in my co-workers getting busted, the parlor getting closed down, and my friends being forced out on the street.

We don't protect ourselves against rape because we almost seem to believe that we should expect to be raped, robbed, or beaten because prostitution is inherently dangerous.

We don't protect ourselves because we are prohibited and inhibited. We can't share information about dangerous tricks. We are discouraged from any kind of organizing or self-protection by laws that prohibit "communicating for the purposes" or collective organizing (charged as pimping). It's hard to protect yourself from the rapists while you're busy protecting yourself from the police.

Laws against Prostitution = Violence against Women

I am appalled that the state assumes jurisdiction over my sexuality. To me, cops seem like rapists with badges. I read the newspapers: "Ex-Cop Linked to Hooker Slayings," and "Rapist Lures Prostitutes with Phony Police ID." The serial killers are the police—or at least there's no way to tell the difference. It isn't fair.

Prostitution busts are a form of rape. When an emissary of the government (a cop) coerces me to engage in fondling and petting through fraud (pretending to be a client), then pulls out his gun and arrests me for my sexual behavior, I call that institutionalized rape.

That's why I'm always angry. That's why I'm angry at everyone who isn't angry.

Good Luck, and I Hope You Make a Lotta Money

(This poem is dedicated to the safety and well-being of the women who work in the parlors in San Francisco's Tenderloin District.)

If there's one thing I know, it's that I definitely don't wanna go back to
    work in the Tenderloin.
I don't care how good the money is.
I don't care that the tourist customers pay over a hundred for a
    half-and-half.
I don't care if I could be making three hundred a night.
I won't work at night. Night girls fight. I'm a day girl.
I don't wanna go back and work at 467 O'Farrell Street where I was raped
    on August 7, 1979, by two punks with a knife and couldn't bring myself
    to call the police.
I don't wanna suppress my fear.
I don't wanna be a victim.
I don't wanna be raped again.
I don't wanna live the fast life.
I don't care how much you paid at Magnin's for your cream-colored
    high-heeled boots. They make you look like you're gonna fall down.
I don't wanna spend my money on last year's shoplifted silk blouses and
    slit skirts that the junkie booster brings around.

I don't wanna cook chicken in the sauna and rice in the electric pressure
    cooker and eat on the floor anymore, even though it was good and we
    came to know and love each other.
I don't wanna avoid discussing anything too personal.
I don't wanna lie about how much I make.
I don't wanna be ashamed of doing twenty-dollar blow jobs.
I don't wanna refer to myself as a masseuse.
I don't wanna smoke dope and watch you return from the bathroom
    stumbling on junk.

I don't wanna pretend I don't see the bruises your boyfriend gives you.
I don't wanna be the one who never gets picked.
I don't wanna know what I'm worth.
I don't like it when cockroaches crawl on my customers.
I don't wanna fuck poor men with antisocial looks on their faces.

I don't care how much money you say you make.
I like you. I mean, I like some of you.
But I don't feel safe. Don't blame me for leaving.
I have to move up. I'm going to work in the financial district.

I Want to Change the Laws That Punish Prostitutes

I hate the idea that a group of men who are the arms of the state are
entrusted to enforce my behavior in the boudoir, whether it is for money
or not.

I hate it that there are young women all over the country who are
being told to ignore this violation of our rights, and instead to spend their
time suppressing sexual representation. I'm not one to discount the relationships between imagery and action, but sluts and whores and erotic
entertainers are not the enemy of the matriarchy.

I am trying to understand everything. Sometimes I don't I fuck for
love, pleasure, or money. I just fuck in defiance.

"The stigmatization of prostitution underlies the social control of all
women," says Gail Pheterson.

The stigma and taboo control our minds and create a collective inertia.
Sexual control is part of social control and part of all societies, I imagine,
though I'm not exactly an anthro-apologist.

"Don't Fuck till after the Revolution"

I suppose it isn't fair to blame women for making prostitution illegal.
Of course, I can't blame contemporary feminists. But women did play an
important role in the process. To put it nicely.

The criminalization of prostitution was a cruel mistake, promoted
by feminist moralists near the turn of the century. Poor women on our
city streets pay for the classist follies of our predecessors. Are protectionist
strategies just naturally a part of women's political contribution? I wish it
weren't so, but my library is full of books about misguided campaigns to
end women's sexual exploitation and to preserve women's purity. The

punitive legislation that has emerged targets poor women and women of color, creating a climate which supports the cop rapists and leaves prostitutes with no recourse. My whore friends are very upset because they are the ones to be sacrificed to preserve the "good" woman's illusion of safety.

I'm Trying . . .

I've been an ardent feminist for twenty years. I love feminism like I love my mom. I'm trying to be open-minded. Maybe slut-positive women can seem like the enemy. Maybe we should be treated like outcasts, excluded from the family of feminists, labeled liars.

> In general, those who most adamantly promote this view, organizing various "whores' conferences," and positioning themselves as prostitutes' spokespersons with the male-dominated media, do not choose prostitution for themselves; some have abandoned it; some never worked as prostitutes; some work as "madams," selling other women's bodies but not routinely marketing their own; a few actually work as prostitutes.
>
> —"Prostitution as 'Choice,'" *Ms.* magazine, January/February 1992

Anyway, I'm going to try and relax. I can't let this get to me. I can't expect too much of women or of humanity in general. Society has its own cycles. As politicos we play our parts, fulfill our responsibility by participating. Everyone has a right to her or his analysis. Variety is the spice . . . I can't blame women for thinking I'm an evil-sellout-dupe-of-the-patriarchy. It's the lot of a modern libertine. We all feel like we're losing. The slut radicals abhor the pornophobes. I don't want to fight my sisters, and pornophobia[1] is not quite a recognized social ill at this point, so I just better relax.

I've got to be open-minded. Just because *my life* offers vast evidence of the value of including whores in the family of womynkind doesn't mean it's the only truth, right? For some women, my philosophy could be dangerous. The freedom that I demand for myself is, for some women, the rope to hang themselves with. I have to relax. It's just a difference in philosophy. I won't take anything personally. I'm not even mad at Phyllis Schlafly. It takes all sorts to make up the world. Some people think abortion is murder. Some people like war and nukes. I'll give everyone a break. After all, this is the patriarchy, and being a prostitute teaches me patience.

Reforming Women

I talk to everyone—even, and especially, to women who hate prostitution. Very few will talk to me, but I have a new friend, X., an ex-prostitute who embraces the abolitionist philosophy. Perhaps we could organize a unified feminist resistance to the arrest of prostitutes. After all, even the abolitionists *claim* to oppose the arrest of prostitutes.

I asked X. to meet me for dinner. There I would present my agenda. X. is a formidable friend, or enemy, depending on which side of the patriarchy one wakes up on that morning.

"All I want to do is stop the cops from arresting us. That seems reasonable," I begged.

X. smiled and said, "That must be a very safe position for you. Decriminalization will not help women, because arresting prostitutes is the only way we can get services to them."

I bit my tongue. "I suppose you do have a captive audience."

"But two or three days in jail is not long enough to get a woman off drugs. There must be a way to keep them in jail for longer," her social-worker cohort conjectured.

Am I really hearing this? I get that familiar feeling that this situation is beyond remedy. Relax. Just stay relaxed . . .

"OK, OK. We'll find another way to get them services," I offered.

Right. We'll find them better jobs. I can see it now. We'll revise the world economy, then we can stop arresting prostitutes. I think I just sold my sisters down the tube in an effort at conciliation. Oh, well, big mistake. Luckily, I'm not in charge anyway. At least, not yet.

"If we increased services, then would you support an end to the arrest of prostitutes?" I pleaded.

"You seem to have a one-track mind. You have to see the broader picture," X. graciously informed me. "If we stop arresting prostitutes, the pimps will have a heyday. We can't let up on the prostitutes until we really go after the tricks and the pimps. Otherwise it would amount to recruitment."

I never answer these arguments. I mean, either you're a protectionist or you're not. What am I supposed to say? Check out your history textbook—laws against prostitution are always used to control women, mostly poor women? Or, you think it's basically an invasion of my privacy to send the police into my bedroom? I mean, I don't want her to become defensive. She has her priorities.

If only I could change her mind. If only I could figure out how to influence her. I listen and listen. After all, she worked as a prostitute for well over a decade. She was probably raped and arrested more times than I know. She and her friends can't stand the Happy Hookerism of my crowd. She and her friends claim that the glamorization of prostitution (one of my favorite pastimes) exacerbated her dependency and vulnerability within "the life." She and her friends say that I stand in the way of women's freedom by sexualizing my identity.

Who am I to judge? X. won't let people forget for a moment that some women exist in a state of rape. The constant tremble in her voice reminds us of her hurt and anger. Her philosophy worked for her, helped her through her recovery. In fact, she's doing very well for herself now, with a solid career in research, after leaving her job in the jails, where she reluctantly launched the local mandatory HIV testing program for prostitutes.

"If you make it any easier for women to slip into prostitution, you'll have blood on your hands," she warned me.

I've got to relax. I've been squirming in the straightjacket of feminist ethics long enough.

The Guilty Courtesan

In some distant city, in an ordinary kingdom, lived a very wealthy prostitute. One day a client offered her a vast sum of money to perform a sexual act that would have been quite distasteful to her.

She thought, Now this is a most repugnant practice, though certainly an ordinary favor.

She thought and thought, remembering an item she had always wanted—not a small house in the country, but a small country, would suit her very well. She decided to perform this most repugnant favor and she obtained her little nation.

As luck would have it, the country was in the midst of an economic crisis. Sadly for her, the situation went from bad to worse. The wealthy ex-prostitute felt very guilty and superstitious, blaming herself for the affairs of the land, even though she hadn't been in power very long. Her queenship was a jinx, she told herself. She wanted to right her wrong, so she made a law declaring that no one should ever do what they didn't want to do.

The situation went from worse to worse than that. The cost of enforcing this law was exorbitant, and soon her queendom was full of criminals. She went bankrupt and was forced to sell her sexual services again.

One day she got a call from an old client, the very same person who had asked her to perform the act she had found so repugnant. She felt elated and told him to come right over to her house.

Her customer arrived, and he asked her to perform this same repugnant favor for a similar fortune. Naturally, she turned him down, and felt very pleased with herself.

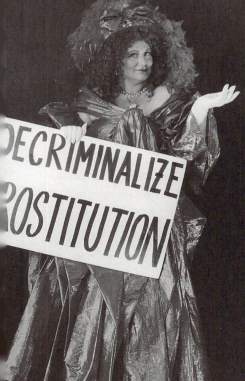

Feminists Unite! Stop the Police Control of Prostitutes! (Please)

A chasm exists between women, based on our experience of and reaction to sexual abuse. Perhaps communication can fill the gaping wound. Maybe a dialogue could ignite a new feminist revelation, based on a union of the good girls and the sluts.

This could be a pivotal time for prostitutes' rights. Feminism has empowered women, so feminism has empowered prostitutes. The pendulum swings away from patriarchy. Or maybe not. Naturally, I went straight to Catharine MacKinnon.

"Catharine, you say you care about prostitutes, but you refuse to engage in a discussion with any of the feminist prostitutes or sex radicals. We all care about women's safety and well-being. Why divide the movement by vilifying us? Let's talk."

"Sorry, Carol," MacKinnon recently said to me. "I have nothing to discuss with you. We are too far apart."

But, but . . .

The current economic crisis forces greater and greater numbers of poor women into survival sex and sex for money. The health crisis escalates everyone's vulnerability, particularly that of poor women, and particularly those who trade in sex. Only the harshest approach would support the arrest of prostitutes.

When most middle-class women experience harassment from their bosses, teachers, and peers, they are taught to challenge the abuses in their lives. Meanwhile, prostitutes are out there on the streets being harassed regularly by police and no one advocates to protect their bodies, let alone their sensibilities. Feminists as a whole have been eerily silent in the face of these violations.

To stop this hypocrisy, we have to learn to work together, whether we approach this issue from an anti-prostitution stance or as prostitutes'-rights advocates. We need a moratorium on arrests now. You may not like prostitution, but I'm sure you don't want women controlled by police.

So Much to Explain . . .

There are so many issues, and so much to explain. For example:
- Laws against pimping are a big problem for whores. Pimping laws are not enforced against the bad exploiters (surprise!), but, rather, against the prostitutes who work together to protect each other. Pimping

means living off the earnings of a prostitute. When we are arrested as prostitutes, our children can be charged as pimps. Our lovers are charged as pimps. Besides, I may want to fuck for money, but that doesn't mean I want to be bothered with the complicated business of finding clients, making dates, and running an establishment. Maybe I'd rather work in a house or a place with other pros, so we can afford security. All that is charged as pimping. Laws should be forced against the exploiters. We have a right to third-party management. Ideally, those who help us run our businesses will work as agents, but some of us will work in houses, in parlors, in family groups, and as independents. Laws against living off our money may have been designed to protect us, but they are always used to control and stigmatize us.

- Laws against pandering (encouraging prostitution) make my life into one big felony. If I say anything besides "I hate prostitution," I can be locked up for years. It sort of inhibits a person. But I know. I know. Why be selfish? Poverty, violence, the AIDS crisis, and increasingly visible street prostitution have fostered discussion of law reform across the United States. So I promote decriminalization of all aspects of sex work, along with enforcement of laws against abuse rape, violence, assault, deceit, force, and coercion used against prostitutes.

- The actual working prostitutes should be empowered to control their own working conditions. Society infantilizes women, and most people think we are incapable of taking care of ourselves. The most vulnerable members of our communities are used as examples of our frailties. Only ten or twenty percent work on the street in this city[2], for instance. But stats for everything from drug use to child abuse are culled from this population, and used to represent the broader population of prostitutes. Then they say police should monitor our lives so that the bad men don't exploit us.

I just repeat: peer empowerment and community building. It's the '90s. We want alternatives *and* autonomy.

Fucking and Fucking Myself Up

I suppose that the rights we have for ultimate jurisdiction over our bodies are based on the rights we claim. I don't know about your rights. Maybe you are perfectly happy to give the state control over your body. Maybe you don't mind pissing in jars because you think that it's helpful to have a paternalist state. I don't give that right away. If the state assumes that right,

I consider it a violation. For me, every act of prostitution doubles as an act of civil disobedience. I have the right to do anything I want with my body, including sex, drugs, and suicide—the right to fuck, get fucked-up, and fuck myself up. Mmmm, this platform certainly does have a ring to it . . .

Why are feminists most divided over our sex roles—lesbian, wife, and whore? We're all in this together, surviving this sexual holocaust, but the tug-of-war over the righteousness of the whore stands in the way of the unified effort we need to change our circumstances.

I hear my parents' voices at the dinner table, discussing the failure of the party and the obstacles to social change. "Infighting destroyed us. The oppressed become the oppressors."

I suppose it's natural that we fight over the crumbs of self-determination in the declining patriarchy.

The controversy among us is not only about sexual violence and representation. It is about staking our claim in the sexual terrain. Some women want to control other women's sexual expression and sexuality because it puts some women at a disadvantage. Our vision of reform needs to include diverse voices, perspectives, and experiences. Maybe we can embrace our whores, stop this fighting, forge a new vision, and take one more giant step in the development of a humane consciousness. And maybe not.

I'm an Innocent Person . . .

What I mean is, I'm basically optimistic. Sure, I've suffered a heavy loss of chastity, but what kind of society is this that equates my acquisition of sexual experience with a loss of purity. I know that some people look forward to the day when no one needs to buy sexual services (mostly the tricks) and no one needs to sell it (mostly the good girls). But I'm looking forward to the day when sex work is recognized as a service. Sex work is holy work! Sex is as dirty as power and money. Whore means get more!

We complain about the way we are objectified. I long for the day that my nakedness no longer symbolizes my conquest.

The Enemy Speaks

Here I don the lie of the libertine, a burlesque artist with sad trappings. I don't care. Anything's better than being a wage slave. I am free. I am in cap-

tivity. I am the enemy of all good women. I am the catalyst of rape. I am the traitor, the multitudinous whores of the death camps whose lives will never be chronicled. My body is the bounty in the conquest of all women. I am bad. I am sin. I am shame. Meanwhile, the guys wear tight pants, act like tramps, and they are Elvis. I refuse to go on living in the patriarchy. I'm checking out.

Almost every day I say my mantras: LAWS THAT PUNISH PROSTITUTES ARE CRIMES AGAINST WOMEN and THE ARREST AND INSTITUTIONALIZED HARASSMENT OF PROSTITUTES ARE ATROCITIES.

I need to repeat this to myself. I am reminded that, even though I know many powerful prostitutes, there are others who are living a nightmare.

"The prohibition of prostitution enshrines into law the view that prostitutes are bad women, and thus legitimate targets of abuse," said Priscilla Alexander.

I'm proud that I'm not ashamed. All of you victims (no, no, survivors!) can identify with that. And everyone has a little pornophobia, so get in touch with it and get rid of it . . . I'm on the edge of my seat, waiting for a gestalt, a unifying vision. The struggle for our rights and freedom makes me feel strong. What a treat . . . Here comes the millennium . . .

Whores Rise Up! No More Dupes of the Patriarchy

The throngs are growing. The Sluts' Liberation Movement is taking hold. Beware, the deviants can justify themselves. We have broken the code. In a few generations wives will be extinct. Only "wages for housework" will deter the armies of single-mom-tramps-on-the-dole. And we'll be goddess-worshipping pagans selling our holy favors. Abolish monogamy! we'll holler. Marriage is degrading to women! Whores rise up! They can't stop us now . . .

(Thanks, Ma, Thanks a Lot)

Thank you for teaching me how to be sexy.
Without you it would seem so complicated.
And thanks for your enthusiasm over the padded push-up bra.
What a difference!
Even though, we both agree, I'm big enough.
Together we've thanked Clairol for my red hair, since age fourteen.
Redheads do seem more exciting.

And thanks, especially, for taking me shopping
once a year to the Charlotte Shop,
where the rich girls shopped.
(Still, you had me in ethnic primaries,
daytime shades, while my thin, blonde competitors displayed the dawn.)

Thanks, anyway.
Overweight, you said I looked good in that red velveteen bikini
I never bought.
No, it was too much.

these confessions make me aware of my calcium
my mother's towels were thin and torn
her sisters owned fur stoles and gold bracelets
she married Love, then Love abandoned her

Dad barely worked and Mom supported him
Dad was always chasing her to fuck
she did it lotsa times to shut him up
she felt like a whore and didn't get paid
my towels are as thick as steak
I own antiques and a glamorous wardrobe.
I won't marry Love.
My daddies chase to fuck.
They pay. I fuck. I shut up.

(Thanks, Ma, thanks a lot.)
I'm ready for that red velveteen now, Ma.
They like me better when I dress up.
You were right, Ma.
Rich princes are waiting on line to rescue me.
Well, maybe not.
But middle-class men are making appointments and keeping them.
Thanks, Ma, thanks a lot.

Notes

1 Pornophobia: From the Greek root *pornē* meaning whore, and phobia, meaning fear. Pornophobia means the fear of prostitutes. Pornophobia can also refer to the fear of sexual expression and sexual representation—that is, fear of pornography. Whore activists have opted to claim the term that was used as a weapon against them, pornography, as their own.

2 Priscilla Alexander, "Prostitution: A Difficult Issue for Feminists," in *Sex Work*, ed. Priscilla Alexander and Frederique Delacoste (Pittsburgh: Cleis Press, 1987), 196.

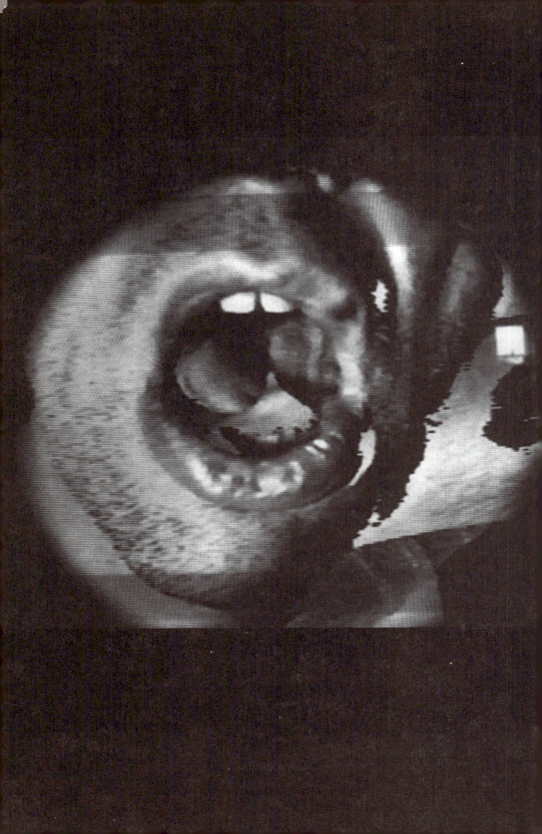

Hole

Robbed Texts, Immobilizations

I don't speak well. I embarrass myself. I falter. I'm worried about my appearance. I'm ugly. I'm lonely. My discourse is all I have. My discourse is my writing, my videowork. It's a poor discourse. I write secretly in relation to other philosophers, other thinkers. I answer them, second-guessing myself. I cannot speak this way. I am always unfashionable, always alone.

My writing reconstitutes the world. What I have is a gift of writing; this is all I have. My videowork is forced; I present myself to you, create one state after another, a set of situations or fragments. My secrecy, the secrecy of my body, appears in my tapes.

But my writing . . . I fear this the most, the unnerving drugged blankness of an empty page, filling it only to empty it once again. For I do not believe in anything. I have tendencies towards romanticism . . . in both senses of the word. . . . But I am a child of the future, filled with wonder.

But my writing . . . I believe in. I come to life in my writing. I speak fluently, answer charges one after another. I never make mistakes, never shrink in fear from that feeling of authority I ascribe to everyone but myself. I live my life in fear; everyone is better than me. I am so sure of this that I cannot face myself in a mirror.

Unable to exist in a world in which I am alone, I create truths in writing. These poor truths, weak truths, are the only possible ones. Worlds lie shattered, chaotic or noisy. I find myself embarrassed or shameful.

I can never forgive myself; I have regrets about almost everything in my life. I am attracted to people on the edge; beyond the edge, the scaffolding collapses. I cry several times a week, sometimes more. My nights are filled with nightmares, images of dissection, violent images, images of lost love, of burials, apocalypse. Unable to exist in this world, I am positive that nothing remains of the body, nothing. My work is my only hope; my daughter is another matter altogether, lodged in the midst of the human.

When I write, meaning and the saying of it coalesce, a form of psychosis. When I speak, I shrink before anyone, a form of neurosis. Everyone else passes; I do not. For years, I have known that I am tainted, that I make people uneasy. No matter how hard I try, I cannot help this. My life remains a soap opera raised to the power of hysteria.

These are recent texts on *robbed speech*, a form of rigidity and poverty which allows speech in the first place. And texts on linguistics, video, politics, everything which silences me in my world. So these texts are an invitation to something closed when I stand before you, only partly opened in one or another video. Surely they are my gift to your future; hold them carefully.

I have said what I always meant to say. . . .

*Depression**

In depression, signifier and signified remain connected; *meaning*—which is henceforth superfluous—withdraws (decathexis); a disintegration of affect and totality results. *Meaning* appears an appendage. Within the pornographic, an identical occurrence; the body lends itself towards and through the image; the image is *devoured*. Devouring is the last refuge of the depressive; devouring fragments and annihilates the *thing* which transforms into the abject. Incorporation totalizes the body of the depressive, which slips out from under her. Just as meaning is a *project*, the body becomes a totality through the slippage of the other into nonexistence.

Depression thus reveals the body's horizon, dissolution and frayed edge. The idiocy of the real appears; inscription is perceived as a self-contained and controlled implosion of the semantic universe in its entirety. Links between universes carry meaning, which is meaning's construct; *meaning is an attribute*. There is no meaning beyond attribution.

The fear of depression is this lending-towards-death, a process associated with the pornographic. After orgasm in relation to the image, an identical decathexis: *meaning withdraws*, the image is devoured. This withdrawal returns the image to the edge of the inchoate; the world becomes paste. Depression is existence within the paste of the world; for the depressive, existence *is* the paste of the world.

* I liken depression to the poemwork of Swinburne, in which meaning plunges headlong into a blood-red or white stain; his diffuse discourse is far more radical than, say, that of Lautréamont, because the latter still embodies a subjectivity long since abandoned. Swinburne is the poet of the *ganglion* or computer terminal; his writing, both depressive and pornographic, is the last signifier of an invested reality linked to an unfathomable other.

Depression does not eliminate meaning; *it fissures or sinters meaning.*
What is lost is totality. Dust, like clutter or powder, is irresolute in its relation to history; nothing remains traceable. For the depressive, the world is
one of residues, memories of meaning in which the most trivial symptom
is clearly the most tragic, the most overlooked. For the depressive, memory
is the stuttering of the world, not its essence—at best a construct tenuously
held in the face of annihilation.

Beyond dust, paste smears itself throughout the real; this is the slimi-
ness of existentialism, its nausea. The inertness of the real is its only truth;
it is a truth because *nothing is at stake.* The depressive inhabits this detu-
mescence of the real; affect drains, and nothing is pleasurable because
everything is other, unaccountable, unaccounted-for, and of no import.

Only the links remain, ensuring a momentary survival; as the links
themselves sever (and this is a completely *trivial* occurrence), language
suffocates—stuttering gives way to pure sound. The body does not kill itself
so much as relinquish a life which has always already been relinquished;
suicide is not an act, but a condition. *In depressive suicide, nothing occurs.*

Café

I sit in a corner of the café; nothing in particular attracts my attention.
The other chair at the table is empty; a young woman removes it, carrying
it carefully across the tiled room to her companion. With slight interest, I
now watch them from a distance. Their mouths move; words fall from
them; I hear sounds; a smile and other emotions occasionally cross a face.
The face leans forward from the head, as if the skin strained into the empty
air. The face says nothing.

Each face moves in relation to the other. A "relation" is a bind between
two or more terms, *defining meaning.* The bridging of difference creates
difference, creates a skein beginning community. The community huddles
in its meaning, a nurturing of the project of life, a definition of the project
itself. I remain elsewhere; nothing means, I remind myself, from this position. From every *x*, not a negation or "anti-*x*," neither *x* nor *y*, but an
ulterior term, absent of this and every other relation. . . . (As if and almost
a *revolution.*)

I watch the *community* across the room; I witness this "pathetic"
horizon. It means nothing to me—motion on a summer afternoon.
Motes of dust play in the dim light fractured by the windowpane. This
atmosphere, I think, repeats. The woman and her companion continue
their motions, as if on a screen, in the midst of a darkened but trivial

theater; closing my eyes, I continue to see them, a slow and silenced dance. Thinking back upon the cinema . . .

Thinking back upon the cinema, I recognize *depression* as the occasion of diegesis; film and television, if anything, are the construct of meaning by agreement. The willing suspension of disbelief grants the world a certain reprise; it is the *occasion* of the world. Detachment or anomie is silent film; meaning occurs, bringing the spectator in by other means. In depression and in cinema, I am split from the characters—first, second, third persons intertwined, and my "first" shatters against all accountancy.

(Pornography, too, shatters persons, destroying the sanctity of the first, second, and third. Pornography threatens the return to an abject in which the other is *fastened* to an alien flesh; other and flesh may or may not be the spectator. Within the pornographic, nothing is determined; there is nothing to determine.)

Care, even that of the momentary glance, has disappeared from the woman and her companion; I do not remain to see her breasts covered, blouse closed or *sutured* against the outer world. Silverware tinkles as if through a thick pillow or curtain; depression seeps through the tiled floor, wall, ceiling. *I return to my cell which contains liquids.* I summon the waiter, pay my bill, leave the café; the film has come to an end. The ritual, always devoid of meaning, shadows my way through the narrow street, which is now cast in shadow. When I return home, I masturbate, completing a dead resurrection. I can hardly remember my name.

He, Withdrawn

The withdrawal of affect is an occasion; the body, losing meaning, becomes other, no longer imminent. The occasion, which introjects itself, connecting image, psyche, and chemistry, is almost always loss; depression is on the far side of the hinge which is activated, only to close forever. The dejection of the body suppurates into dulled arousals; sex is without fantasy, mournful. Sight no longer cathects.

The skin puckers, curls; inscription spreads like a stain. The body is a substance. The body is a substance is a hole; it falls through itself, while ordinary life continues literally on the rim, the other side of the hinge. The rim is worn with the touch of the tongue or speech; the rim is furrowed with the pressure or sound of speech. The body extrudes itself, suturing the rim with a permanent scar. The cover of the rim stops time.

The body bloats, burns itself into the bed. Furrows invert and thin; the flesh dissolves, translucent. Images play in the distance upon it; this is a cinema of glass, a glass screen harboring or retaining nothing. As the interior decays, taste cauterizes flesh. All of this continues as an absent narrative; in depression, diegesis disappears; rhyme and closure become irrelevant.

Only upon the return from this state do I bring a gift of *meaning,* a gift which depression circumscribes, renders totally within the interpenetrations of the communal. Clearly again, meaning is an attribute; "being" becomes synonymous with the general existence of things, and "being's question" becomes a generator of anxiety. But now this generator is perceived solely as a misplaced interrogation; the substance of depression is as close as one can get to a mythic origin of the signifier. The fullness of meaning within religious exaltation and ascesis of the real becomes identical to the depressive aphanisis; all is rendered *idiotic.* From depression, as from the interrogation of absolute belief, the world is structured and destructured; depression has the advantage of absolute disinvestment, and an embodiment aligned with the abject nature of the material world. Depression recognizes the worn-out state of affairs; belief works furiously at cleansing.

I state categorically that depression is *all the truth there is,* by virtue of this disinvestment; the truth refuses embodiment whatsoever, and the catatonic is the wisest of all.

I put my pen in my hole. I put my fingers in my hole. I expose my hole. I widen my hole. I talk into my hole. I talk from my hole. I see into my hole. I put my face in my hole. Desperate, on the side of the hinge, I want to be filled; I want you to fill my hole. I want you to fill my hole with your mouth and your cock; I want you to make me speak. I want you to fill my hole with your tongue and your cunt; I want to speak from your hole. When I speak, I cover up my hole. When I speak, I begin to listen.

The trick is to speak just so much in order to listen before the onslaught of depression, the rim a distant horizon—to speak and to stop speaking for the sound to emerge—to speak ever so slightly—to widen it—

Solitaire

Non-depressive discourse is the ability to give meaning or motivation to the Thing. The Thing which is the inertness or idiocy of reality plays the role of suffocation. The absolute closes like a dull leaded lid. Sleep becomes a derivation of death. The transformation or inversion of the absolute produces all the effluvia which we consider culture. Culture is the warding-off of the fact that meaning is always an ascription, always

inscribed, and that the recognition of this inscription would lead to the fissuring of the body and ego themselves. Even language cannot do it; even language lies elsewhere, a cover-up. Depression is truth heightened, sublimated, and transformed elsewhere in order for the organism to survive. What the depressive sees brings no recognition. The depressive recognizes nothing. The first goal of teleology is the construct. Horizons locate the plane of the eyes in the midst of the body.

Endlessly, I play dominos alone, other games of solitaire and chance, recapitulated within the loving gesture of my arms. My fingers dance like small birds above the pieces. Meaning floods me, overwhelms me, through the appearance of anomalous cases—long rows laid out without doubles, exhaustion and then some of the entire pile before the hand plays itself out. Meaning extends like tentacles, small discoveries across the rows folded back upon themselves, always within arm's reach. Meaning is nothing more here than investment in anomaly; anomalies define the sememe of play, the sphere which floats uselessly in the midst of depression. Through depression, I witness *meaning at work and play.* The "standard game" is illuminated as well, given meaning as a gift from afar. What is at stake is the *at-stake* itself, the presence of relative loss or gain, always valuable as survival skills within limited domains. The playing of dominos is the cheating of death, or the playing of death; death closes meaning like a dull leaded lid.

And death appears both as absolute, that theoretical horizon or abstraction formulated *from* meaning, and as individual, *this game, imminent,* and no other, a dialectic of meaning. And further, if not death (which itself in depression is disinvested), then other, and if not other, substance or playing field, substance or nothing in particular. The absolute is filled and fulfilled with limiting-cases, those *in extremis* which almost never appear, at least within an inaccessibly high finite number of games.

In the midst of depression, the lesson that is drawn from all of this falls flat, applicable only to dominos and solitaire, and that is the lesson to be drawn.

Dream, Depression, Meaning

Is the belief in the meaning of dreams on the same order as numerology—the reorganization of the everyday as a meaning-factory? Without the *meaning of dreams,* the everyday would cease to exist; language would become a conventional, well-defined flux of stimuli and responses. The *-jectivity* of the dream world reminds us of the concreteness of the teleology of the absolute—against the noise of the everyday. This teleology appears as a stress or strain, an impetus behind the movement of semantic tokens in the first place. The *organization* of dreams—their jump cuts and articulations, their surrealist meltings, their flux of continuities—constructs meaning (and is *not* a construct *of* meaning)—an ancient sympathetic magic. For meaning is assigned on the basis of weighted equivalences, tags tied to one or another family of attributes; this assignment, in a healthy individual, becomes a *-pulsion* towards activity integrated within the co-agulation of the ego. In fact, it is meaning that binds the coagulation in the first place, granting an identity in the face of part-objects or sub-systems hysterically doing battle with each other and themselves.

What the dream does is procure meaning-in-transformation; meaning is generated in an absence of any exteriority. The interior holds meaning; everyday life exhausts it. If meaning is an inscription between or among domains, everyday life is a fissuring; *fissuring can never be assigned*. And if inscription is blind, fissuring blinds. Because fissuring is a lowering of energy, it literally depresses; nothing remains to be said except what falls from the mouth.

Depression exhausts the dream, fissures it, and the process remains unknown and unknowable to the subject. What connects on one level disconnects on another. For there are double engines—that of the con-nected homology ("one thing leads to another") and that of the *-pulsion*; this is lost in favor of the inert. What connects is of little or no conse-quence. Why the *-pulsion* is lost is a gap in this thinking.

Maybe I want it that way, the gray walls holding me in, their soft ledges a comfort difficult to recognize. Giving in to meaning is giving in to an intolerable, impossible existence. Rather that I devour meaning, bend theory itself to absorb the same, hold difference in abeyance. Depression disconnects the dream; inscription no longer binds the ego. The melting sensation is all that remains before permanent closure in the midst of dark and emptied rage.

Thus in the midst of depression, I fail to account for anything. For if dreams produce meaning, and I dream, then I too am inscribed; this "I" is more than a semantic marker, holding the sentence for the reader—it binds me, writes me as well. Yet senseless, there is no such writing—no time and space to write, no site, no aggression except for that of pulverization-machines dimly felt, not worth the while to understand.

Examine *Shelley* and *Swinburne*. In the former, nouns withdraw and curl inward, holding to a granulated exactitude of a belief in the real; in the latter, nouns diffuse and stain—they are interconnected but disposable, dissolute. From the former to the latter, inscription transforms to fissure and the real itself becomes withdrawn, barely visible through *ghastly* rose-white glasses. Swinburne is already beyond the dream, descendent; Shelley is at the threshold of meaning itself. Shelley drowns in Swinburne's imagined sea. Neither is alive, and nothing is alive in this theory which automatically connects and disconnects, an accumulation of part-objects and phrases, burning the remnants of the ego, returning thought and parasitic speech to dismembered embers, void.

Perforations

To a degree of absolute untruth that the text is doctored in any way—medically, the successful operation is that of trepanning, an alleviation of pressure, those points where the hypothetical coagulates around an "I" which is no longer visible, nonetheless an insistent presence.

So that, to begin with, its blinding, bringing the "I" into darkness or beneath the text, as if "she said, he said" in daily life were absent as well. The text sutures itself, a cusp catastrophe ignoring the central sheet folding halves back in upon themselves.

One is left with bad grammar, an abject or twisted discourse wringing the last moments of pain from the reader; unsure of herself, she spans the text from horizon to horizon. She believes that if the "I" is an inscription, its absence is a fissure. A fissure without the text is beneath it, a negative or virtual absolute crumbling discursivity itself. This is an "abstract." She further believes that if the "I" is removed, the blinded text is fissured precisely at those points of withdrawal, which now spread in the form of ungainly grammar; this fissuring is neither negative nor virtual, but an uncanny and disruptive presence, unfocused, unfocusing.

This presence is her presence, as a resultant in relation to random and skew vectors; her presence is simultaneously blinding (+) and dark or monstrous (−). She is fettered by the removal of her "", which struggles inversely to release the occasion of the oedipal.

A fissure beneath the abstract is clearly of the order of the symbolic, totalized by the proximate surface which sunders itself. Thus the symbolic brings itself to the bedrock which is its projection by inscribing its fissuring and fissuring its inscription. This occurs always without the text which returns in the form of a book. Likewise, a blind or blinding fissure remains totally within the real; its absence here, for example indexed by "", is an inauthentic presentification, the touch of a dead hand.

When this writes itself, "" am written, but this writing is always intended as neither example nor portraiture, rather the turn of a condition which is twisted or abject; the arms of the body surround nothing; anecdote is the sublimation of desire into inscription; the legs surround nothing; the philosophical category of the seizure or the grasp.

In consequence of which each text further substitutes "I" for "I", the cited for the sighted, a tooth for a tooth, the seizure or the grasp, the play of language an occasion for the scarring of punctures, a slightly uneven surface obliquely lit by laughter.

Fucking Throat

I can't help myself; everything applies to me, everything centers on me, flesh crawling with it, the thickness of it, an imaginary beast, half liquid, half solid. The symptomatology piles up; it's familiar, present. The trees grow.

Capgras, you never were my lover; you pretended; I knew when I looked into my flesh through your body, there was nothing else, other eyes protruded, stared at me, other features than my own, splitting off from the skin. I can sense wrongness everywhere; if I could pin it down, describe it, it would be obvious—but it's not that, it's an alien thing, anomalous like an extra limb. My flesh falls off me, my body seethes with you.

Fregoli, you're going to fuck me, you're in everything I do, my cock splits me apart, it's you inside me; my mouth fills with you; my throat splits open, my throat seethes with you. Don't you know that's why I can't talk— I have nothing to say—because a tracheotomy—because I am bound open, held open for your sliver to pass. I'll know you by your sliver, I'll sense the throat filling up, bursting, my speech murmuring itself over and over in the guise of someone else, Fregoli, what you're doing to me!

Everyone gets into me, turning me into a game, everyone plays along, I can't sense what I'm doing, to myself, to you, to my legs. My body's invaded, continues to split, first along the abdomen, then beneath the arms like a box being opened, like a star, then meeting and enlarging the asshole; you're disguising Fregoli, devouring him; he'll succeed and maybe that's what you want—I can't be responsible for anyone's motives anymore; my own are lost to me; my own have disappeared, turned against me; someone is writing this for me; someone is sending me this note. I have the murmur of a question, a question's greetings.

You fuck each other just outside my presence, I can't move, I'm bound and gagged, I'm available to you, my holes are open, you pay no attention. Fantasy: To watch you fuck each other, unable to stop you—to watch your

pleasure, groveling with each other. Fantasy: Left alone with the smell of your sex. Fantasy: Remembering forever.

I watch you from the window; you arrive home at five-twenty in the afternoon, disappear for a half hour. (You have showered; where did you disrobe, who watched you, smiling, what did you do for him, question mark?) I only see you when you return, naked; you have a towel wrapped around your head; you have small breasts, prominent nipples, a long ass; you dress in front of the window, bikini black panties, pressing them into the crack, a small black brassiere, you rub something into you, perfume, oil, I'm not sure.

I become devoured by insects, spiders, lice; vermin keep me from the window, from the rest of the scene; I'm being punished; I deserve to die; your dress asphyxiates me; I have no room left in my apartment, can't stand the sky; agoraphobic; your white flesh burns hieroglyphs of panties and bra into me; I become a wolf; devour you; sink into you; into your wet flesh; I drink my own blood first, the blood of a double, of a double cup, a wet breast, my flesh is someone else, someone else is drinking; I stand by and watch myself; my cock belongs to you; I'll sever it, give it to you, give it over; I'll cut it free, cut it from its mooring; it's yours, don't you see;

I'm heutoscopic, see myself, my own alterity embedded like a lean cock up my entrails; I'm your cunt, put your hand, your fist in; I am a small bird, a nest, an egg, a hollow for you; I see you outside the window watching me; I see your head in my panties, I keep them dirty for you, damp for you. Fregoli can't go on this way, changing takes too much time, the winter's cold, there's not much to eat, nothing, no fuel anywhere.

Fregoli's kept forever by de Cerambault; money floods me, floods my cunt, and now there's decent heat at least. He has a long prick, fucks himself—there's money in that, this she-male, people pay for anything. I feel loved thinking about you; I never worry where my money's coming from. Money is the most important thing—it buys you anything you could ever want, a decent apartment, clothes, even a washer and dryer. It takes care of me; without money, I'd be nowhere. I suck de Cerambault; his sperm covers my pillow; I lie in it; my hair is full of it; I wear him on me; I beg him to take me with him forever; to fuck me; my name is on his address; burned into my skin; he has bought my name; hunts himself down.

He comes to me in the form of a dream; impregnates me; further, I split open. My throat widens; the gash is huge, red, torn tissue seeps out, questions nothing, blood stains my breasts, I am devoured. He has moved in; I can hear him in the distance, up close, far away. He shows me the poverty of everything. My speech starves; nothing comes out. My throat is my cunt; I am fucked there.

He shows me the poverty of Capgras and Fregoli, the poverty of himself, of my own flesh huddled in front of a fire fueled by burning books. Nothing is left of me; my ashes are taken from the room in a box with a singular photograph of the throat of a dead boy; the image is blank, the throat of a dead girl; only the ashes are in the vague shape of a male or the sex of a male; the skin flays from the penis, talks like this;

The train came and brought with it the station along the track of my mind going blank when the gun fired into the crowds of workers factorying near the sunset without the ticket, good money, warm stove;

Because they had little enough, or not enough; because they couldn't think enough, or had enough to think; because the throat;

Because the throat held open with a wound three centimeters by one centimeter, loose flap of skin towards the cock, "a neck wound," blood forming a pool near and circumventing the Adam's apple; hearing just those sounds made by a bowed stringed instrument, perhaps a cello, or viola;

Bringing beautiful music which no longer could be sung along to or within the presence of myself or enough because of the terrain where the train visited the first time the station stopped moving;

Stationing itself like the tracker, trick-tracker of Fregoli, impostubus of de Cerambault, whom could be trusted in the midst of the stricken workers?

Their spleen entered my garden near the side of the building by the tundra steppes where I could confabulate the worst risers of their arched brows bridging me; could it have been torn, my first clue rendered hardily obsolete by the recurring current of Capgras (I refuse to alter a question mark at the end of this interrogation!).

Across the window I watched her breast fuck me tied up and incapable of even a single word of paced thought; the red lozenge at the tip developed into an incurable sore; she shoved my death into me; my cock was painted red; milk flowed from the tip, wounded and pierced, penetrated and split open. A recourse: cut my nipple off, a wafer, it would do—would feed me. An answer—there was none. (Remember I had never asked a question!)

The bruised tip went into me, went into me; I opened wider, inverted, turned inside-out, split myself open, divided into two, an amoeba, an amoeba, paramecium, a protozoan paramecium, entering my hand entered, dividing into two divided, an amoeba, an amoeba;;;

Ahhhh, the cilia cunting its throat, ahhh, ahhh, ahhh.

Throat cunting entirety of every human being, every cherry, tear this neck open and you will see the cauterization where you cannot speak, a construction-machinery in its factory production cannot come through the throat, which is the most beautiful organ, you must look into the throat in all its aspects, examine the wound, cut into it, rip the flesh aside, where the speech sounds, where the speech begins, the throat smothers me, neck enters my cunt, amobolous, my cunt cherries, ahhh, my throat, I have grabbed your throat Fregoli.

Now I have taken your throat into my two hands. Now I have opened your throat between my fingers. Now I see your speech coming out. Now I see the words pissing on the floor. Now I lie in your piss. Now your words piss into my mouth. Now I am covered with your words. Stop, I shall never have enough, have already too much of your words.

Fregoli, you

I am told to have courage. Have courage I am told, blood filling my cunt, everything falls; falls thick, blood on my cunt; my cunt shows itself off; my cunt shows itself to everyone; everyone opens me wider; wider and wider, everyone having courage; being honest; honesty is the best policy; you must always be everyone;

Before coming in my cunt your mouth my dear formed its ecstasy beyond the train pulling myself out of the station which your neck rubberized into the middle of the garden carrying curry back to the farmer's wife whose tit devoured milk spurted from your floor; cut quick like a knife immobilized (left off); a cutting diamond; dark smashing my throat; gaaah

Bringing to evidence the fact that I have split along an abdominal suture on the advice of Fregoli, thus becoming hermaphroditic and quite capable of being sold for an evening's entertainment (which suits me just fine), a bit of money covering the necessities of an apartment, somewhere finally to exist in with security—you can understand that, even without the presence of a question "Organic Psychosis" by Jeffrey L. Cummings, MD, *Psychosomatics, The Journal of the Academy of Psychosomatic Medicine*, volume 29, number 1, Winter 1988, pages 16–26, received September 9, 1987 and revised five days later and accepted October 21, 1987, from the Neurobehavior Unit, West Los Angeles Veterans Administration Medical Center (Brentwood Division); and the Departments of Neurology and Psychiatry and Biobehavioral Sciences, UCLA School of Medicine; American Psychiatric Press, Inc., 1400 K Street NW, Washington, DC 20005, Capgras and Fregoli

An answer would be, could be, a burr ringing me around with the hunt of a cunt taking stock of a cock, a throat afloat like a made parade, I am a sick prick aren't I (?)

Sir, or Madam, as the case may be, an acquiescence with the confusion of tongues precipitated by a confluence of formulaic languages while I languish in the broken boards of this barren apartment, emptied of the tiniest morsel of food or even something to speak about, not to mention the bare walls of this wooden stove;

Which I bought when it came back to me, Sir, or Madam, as the case may be, listening to the ring upon your finger which has been thrust in my direction with all due certainty, something which this day brought to me (although I am ill-suited for such a day, as this case may be, within this period, indeed, ill-suited for the begging of the question which must surely follow);

Thus the conclusion which must be drawn and dissected in all fatality turns upon the care taken by an administration of justice to have *this throat removed* so that speech may be considered entirely an internal affair, in the midst of a heated stove, another artifact which must be considered entirely, wooden, obsequious, obdurate, of a "literary" sort; no longer can my cunt be of service in this internal affair; she has just returned to the window, acknowledging my presence; I am sure of her own (as I am sure of it).

KILL ME!   BURN ME
              ALIVE!

Contributors

LUIS ALFARO, a Chicano born and raised in the Pico-Union district of downtown Los Angeles, is a performance artist who writes poetry, plays, and short stories. His work is included in the anthologies *Rohwedder* (1992), *Men on Men 4* (Nal/Dutton, 1993), and *Blood Whispers* (Silverton Books, 1993), and has been featured in the East L.A. journals *Alchemy* and *Untitled*. His journalism, criticism, and essays have appeared in the *L.A. Weekly, Reader, Genre, Frontiers, Vanguard,* and *Square Peg*. His plays *Bitter Homes and Gardens, Straight as a Line*, and *Mojave Medicine* have been performed nationally. He is the author and performer of twelve performance works, which have been seen throughout the United States. His solo spoken-word CD, d*own/town*, is on New Alliance Records. He teaches at the University of California, Los Angeles, and California Institute of the Arts, Valencia, and conducts workshops throughout the country. Alfaro is the project director of VIVA (Lesbian and Gay Latino Artists), a board member of the Gay Men of Color Consortium, and the curator of the Gay Men Writers' Series in West Hollywood.

GREGG BORDOWITZ is a video maker, activist, and writer living in New York. For the past five years he has produced for the Gay Men's Health Crisis videotapes concerning AIDS and HIV, including safer sex pornography, documentaries on AIDS activism, and educational videos about surviving with AIDS. From 1988 to 1991 he was an active member of ACT UP, and he played a principal role in organizing protests and civil disobediences, such as the 1988 nonviolent takeover of the Food and Drug Administration and the 1990 establishment of a legal clean needle exchange program. His most recent essay appears in the anthology *Queer Looks* (Routledge, 1993). He has recently completed a fifty-four-minute film entitled *Fast Trip, Long Drop,* an experimental documentary about living with AIDS.

SCOTT BUKATMAN teaches in the Department of Cinema Studies at New York University. He is the author of *Terminal Identity: The Virtual Subject in Postmodern Science Fiction* (Duke University Press, 1993). Bukatman's writing has appeared in *Camera Obscura, October, Artforum*, and other publications, and he is a consulting editor of *Science Fiction Studies*. He co-organized *Cine City: Film and Perceptions of Urban Space 1895–1995*, at the Getty Center for History and the Humanities in Santa Monica (March 1984), and curated a major retrospective of the film and television work of Jerry Lewis at the American Museum of the Moving Image, Astoria, New York, in 1988. Bukatman lives in New York.

DENNIS COOPER is the author of the novels *Closer* (1989), *Frisk* (1991), and *Try* (1994), and a collection of short fiction, *Wrong* (1992), all published by Grove Press. *Jerk* (1993), a collaboration with the artist Nayland Blake, was published by Artspace Books. *Band: Selected Poems 1969–1993* is forthcoming from Grove Press in 1995. Cooper has written for *Artforum, Spin*, the *L.A. Weekly, Esquire, Village Voice*, and other publications, sometimes in collaboration with novelist/critic Casey McKinney. *Prisons of the Flesh*, Cooper and McKinney's collaboration with composer John Zorn, will be issued on CD later this year. He lives in Los Angeles.

LESLIE DICK, born in 1954, is an American writer who has lived mainly in London since 1965. Her first novel, *Without Falling*, was published in 1987 by Serpent's Tail (London) and in 1988 by City Lights (San Francisco). Her second novel, *Kicking*, was published in 1992 by Secker & Warburg (London) and in 1993 by City Lights. Her work has appeared in numerous anthologies, including *The Seven Deadly Sins, The Seven Cardinal Virtues, Sex and the City, Serious Hysterics, Other than Itself*, and, recently, *The Politics of Everyday Fear* (Brian Massumi, ed., University of Minnesota Press) and *Erotic Literature: Twenty-Four Centuries of Sensual Writing* (Jane Mills, ed., HarperCollins), as well as in many magazines, including *Bomb, Semiotext(e)*, and *Now Time*. A new book, *The Skull of Charlotte Corday and Other Stories*, is forthcoming. Leslie Dick teaches in the art program at the California Institute of the Arts, Valencia. Her daughter, Audrey, was born in February 1992.

LOUISE DIEDRICH was born in San Francisco in 1959. In 1977 she dropped out of college and divided her time between radical political action and punk clubs. She performed with a dyke-punk band called Wilma from 1980 to 1983. Diedrich studied painting at the University of New Mexico, Albuquerque, earning a Bachelor of Fine Arts in 1988. She received a Master of Fine Arts from the California Institute of the Arts, Valencia, in 1993. In 1992 she produced an interactive computer installation entitled *Prosthetic Psychology*, which was presented at the L.A. Freewaves Festival. Following that investigation of high tech, she began making low-tech narrative drawings, and in the same year presented an installation of drawings, text, and objects called *Born of Normal Parents.* Fragments of this work were included in the group show *Home Alone* at Bliss Gallery, Pasadena, in June 1993. Diedrich is living in New York while working at the Independent Study Program of the Whitney Museum of American Art.

ROBERT FLYNT has been exhibiting his photographic work in the United States and abroad since 1981. His most recent solo exhibitions were at the Witkin Gallery in New York and the Gomez Gallery in Baltimore. His work was featured in the *New Photography 8* exhibition at the Museum of Modern Art, New York, where his work is in the permanent collection. Flynt's work is also in the collections of the Metropolitan Museum of Art, New York; Los Angeles County Museum of Art; and Baltimore Museum of Art, among others. He has frequently collaborated with performance artists and dancers as well as creating site-specific photo installations at galleries and alternative spaces. His work has been used on many book covers, most recently *Try* by Dennis Cooper. A monograph published by Twin Palms Press is forthcoming.

CARLA KIRKWOOD is a writer, performer, and public art collaborator. She has won three Emmy awards for her writing and directing projects for the PBS affiliate in San Diego. Kirkwood was nationally acclaimed for the performance component of *NHI (No Humans Involved),* entitled *MWI* (Many Women Involved), which will be published in *Critical Condition: Women on the Edge of Violence* (Amy Scholder, ed., City Lights). Her other interdisciplinary public art projects in San Diego include *There Are 206 Bones in the Human Body* (on torture in El Salvador), *Woyzeck and Maria on East 94* (on women who murder), and *Welcome Back Emma* (on free speech). Kirkwood helped found the first women's studies program in the United States, at California State University at San Diego, in 1969. She was an active member of the United Steelworkers Union from 1977 to 1981 and a safety steward at Inland Steel, in East Chicago, Indiana. Kirkwood studied Chinese theater from 1982 to 1984 at the Central Drama Academy in Beijing. Her translation of Gao Xingjian's *Che Zhan* (Bus Stop) will be published in the journal *Modern International Drama* in spring 1995. She received a Master of Fine Arts from the University of Leeds in 1986.

CAROL LEIGH, the Scarlot Harlot, has been working as an activist and artist in the Bay Area for the past fifteen years. As a founding member of ACT UP in San Francisco, Leigh organized a campaign against mandatory HIV testing of prostitutes. In late 1992 she co-founded the San Francisco Coalition on Prostitution, an alliance of prostitutes, activists, and service providers dedicated to advocacy for prostitutes in San Francisco. Leigh is a member of the Women's Action Coalition and COYOTE. She currently teaches editing and video production for San Francisco Community Television. Leigh has written, performed in, and produced videos on prostitutes' issues, and has received numerous awards for her documentaries on women's issues and gay, lesbian, and bisexual issues. *Outlaw Poverty, Not Prostitutes*, a compilation of interviews with prostitute-activists around the world, won an award at the 1992 American Film Institute's Visions of U.S. competition. During a recent artist-in-residency program at Hallwalls Contemporary Art Center, Buffalo, she created a video advocacy program for activists concerned with prostitutes' issues and prostitute-neighborhood relations.

ELIZABETH PULSINELLI, born in 1968, is a photographer, sculptor, and installation artist living in Los Angeles. She has exhibited at venues such as The Eye Gallery, San Francisco; The Muckenthaler Cultural Center, Fullerton, California; and Highways, Venice, California. Her work has been reviewed in publications such as the *Los Angeles Times* and *Artweek*. She received a Bachelor of Fine Arts from the School of the Art Institute of Chicago and a Master of Fine Arts from the California Institute of the Arts, Valencia. She teaches photography in the School of Fine Arts at the University of Southern California, Los Angeles.

RODNEY SAPPINGTON, co-editor, is a filmmaker, writer, and visual artist living in Los Angeles. He was born in San Diego. Sappington received a Bachelor of Fine Arts from the School of Visual Arts in New York in 1987, and a Master of Fine Arts in experimental film and art from the California Institute of the Arts, Valencia, in 1992. His work has been exhibited nationally in recent exhibitions at the Los Angeles County Museum of Art, Andrea Rosen Gallery in New York, Randolph Street Gallery in Chicago, and Beyond Baroque Literary Arts Center in Venice, California, and in public art installations sponsored by the Metropolitan Transit Authority in

New York. His most recent film, *No One Acts Alone,* to be released in fall 1994, explores family violence in a small southern California community. Sappington is co-editor of a forthcoming A.R.T. Press book on the photographer Laurie Simmons, with an interview by Sarah Charlesworth. Commentary on his writing has appeared in the *Village Voice,* the *Los Angeles Times,* and the *Chicago Reader.* His writing and visual work investigate violence, subjectivity, and male hysteria.

VIVIAN SOBCHACK is associate dean and professor of film studies at the University of California, Los Angeles, School of Theater, Film and Television. Her work focuses on film theory and its intersections with philosophy and cultural studies, American genre film, and electronic imaging. Her books include *Screening Space: The American Science Fiction Film* (Ungar Press, 1987) and *The Address of the Eye: A Phenomenology of Film Experience* (Princeton University Press, 1992). Her articles and reviews have appeared in journals such as *Quarterly Review of Film and Video, Artforum International, Camera Obscura, Post-Script, Film Quarterly,* and *Representations.* She was the first woman president of the Society for Cinema Studies and is a trustee of the American Film Institute.

ALAN SONDHEIM has published *Disorders of the Real* (Station Hill, 1988) and *Individuals,* a critical anthology of artists (Dutton, 1977). Three records of his music have been released. He has also written numerous books published by small presses, most recently *Immobilization* (Fort-Da, 1993). Sondheim's articles have appeared in periodicals such as *Art Papers, Perforations, Millennium Film Journal,* and *Cinematograph.* His videos and films have been screened internationally. Sondheim teaches at Film/Video Arts and the New School for Social Research. He lives in New York and is an occasional cactus grower.

TYLER STALLINGS, co-editor, is a writer, visual artist, and curator living in Los Angeles. He was born in New Orleans. He studied philosophy at the University of the South, Sewanee, Tennessee, from 1984 to 1987, and received a Master of Fine Arts from the California Institute of the Arts, Valencia, in 1992. His fiction-theory has appeared in *Central Park, The Act,* and *Real Life.* He has read his work at Beyond Baroque Literary Arts Center, Venice, California, where he has also organized reading events, and at the Museum of Contemporary Art, Los Angeles. Stallings has published a collection of works dealing with contradictions and complicities by young L.A. writers, through an Emerging Works in Print grant from A.R.T. Press, Los Angeles.

He is the West Coast regional editor for *Art Papers*, Atlanta. His visual art has been exhibited at the Andrea Rosen Gallery and John Good Gallery in New York, Richard Telles Fine Art and Food House in Los Angeles, and the Overgaden in Copenhagen, Denmark. Writings on his visual work have appeared in the *Village Voice*, the *Los Angeles Times*, *Berlingske Tidende*, and the *New Art Examiner*. His writing and visual work explore states of male objectification, abjection, and hysteria.

LYNNE TILLMAN is the author of the novels *Haunted Houses* (Poseidon, 1987; reprint Serpent's Tail/High Risk, 1995), *Motion Sickness*, (Serpent's Tail, 1992), and *Cast in Doubt* (Serpent's Tail, 1993), and two collections of short fiction, *Absence Makes the Heart* (Serpent's Tail, 1990) and *The Madame Realism Complex* (Semiotext(e), 1992). She has collaborated with the artists Jane Dickson and Kiki Smith, respectively, on *Living with Contradictions* (Top Stories, 1982) and *Madame Realism* (1984). Her cultural criticism is published in *Art in America, Bomb, Frieze*, and the *Voice Literary Supplement*. Currently Tillman is writing the text for *The Velvet Years*, a book of Stephen Shore's photographs taken between 1965 and 1967 of Andy Warhol and the Factory, which will be published in 1995 by Pavilion. She lives in New York.

TRINH T. MINH-HA is a filmmaker, writer, and composer. Her recent books include *Un Art sans oeuvre* (1981), *Woman, Native, Other* (1989), *When the Moon Waxes Red* (1991), and *Framer Framed* (1992), and the poetry collection *En minuscules* (1988). Her films on gender, culture, and identity are shown widely in the United States and abroad. *Reassemblage* (1982) was exhibited at the New York Film Festival (1983) and has toured the country with the Asian American Film Festival, among others. *Naked Spaces* (1985) was named the best experimental feature at the American International Film Festival and best feature documentary at the Athens International Film Festival in 1986; it showed at the 1987 Biennial of the Whitney Museum of American Art. *Surname Viet Given Name Nam* (1989) won awards at film festivals in Bombay and San Francisco and at the American Film and Video Festival. *Shoot for the Contents* (1991) won the best cinematography award at the 1992 Sundance Film Festival and best feature documentary award at the Athens International Film Festival; it was selected for the 1993 Whitney Biennial. Trinh Minh-ha is the recipient of the National Maya Deren Filmmaker Award and of fellowships from the Guggenheim Foundation, National Endowment for the Arts, Rockefeller Foundation, American Film Institute, and Humanities Center at Cornell

University. She has traveled and lectured extensively on film, feminism, and art, and taught music at the National Conservatory of Music in Dakar, Senegal, for three years. She is professor of women's studies and film at the University of California, Berkeley.

Other titles by Bay Press

AIDS Demo Graphics
Douglas Crimp with Adam Rolston

The Anti-Aesthetic: Essays on Postmodern Culture
Edited by Hal Foster

The Critical Image: Essays on Contemporary Photography
Edited by Carol Squiers

How Do I Look? Queer Film and Video
Edited by Bad Object-Choices

Line Break: poetry as social practice
James Scully

Magic Eyes: Scenes from an Andean Childhood
Wendy Ewald, from stories by Alicia and Mária Vásquez

Out of Site: Social Criticism of Architecture
Edited by Diane Ghirardo

Recodings: Art, Spectacle, Cultural Politics
Hal Foster

Suite Vénitienne/Please Follow Me
Sophie Calle and Jean Baudrillard

Violent Persuasions: The Politics and Imagery of Terrorism
Edited by David J. Brown and Robert Merrill

For information:

BAY PRESS
115 West Denny Way
Seattle, WA 98119
tel 206.284.5913
fax 206.284.1218